Aristotle's Political Terminology

Aristotle's Political Terminology

J. J. MULHERN

Published by State University of New York Press, Albany

EU GPSR Authorised Representative:
Logos Europe, 9 rue Nicolas Poussin, 17000, La Rochelle, France
contact@logoseurope.eu

For information, contact State University of New York Press, Albany, NY
www.sunypress.edu

Library of Congress Cataloging-in-Publication Data

Name: Mulhern, J. J., 1940– author.
Title: Aristotle's political terminology / J. J. Mulhern.
Description: Albany : State University of New York Press, [2025] | Series:
   SUNY series in ancient Greek philosophy | Includes bibliographical
   references and index.
Identifiers: LCCN 2025003554 | ISBN 9798855803723 (hardcover : alk. paper) |
   ISBN 9798855803747 (ebook) | ISBN 9798855803730 (pbk. : alk. paper)
Subjects: LCSH: Aristotle. Politics—Criticism, Textual. | Philosophy—Terminology. |
   Political science—Terminology.
Classification: LCC JC71.A7 M835 2025 | DDC 320.101—dc23/eng/20250305
LC record available at https://lccn.loc.gov/2025003554

Contents

Preface

The author of a book such as this one owes many acknowledgements. The suggestion that the work on Aristotle's terminology already done be drawn together, and that doing so would contribute to presenting an Aristotle different from the established one, was made some years ago by Daniela Cammack, now at Berkeley. Drawing it together made it clear that some important pieces were yet to be written. The additional pieces were previewed at the University of Pennsylvania Classical Studies Colloquium and at conferences of the Society for Ancient Greek Philosophy, the New England Political Science Association, and the Northeastern Political Science Association. An invitation from Athanasios Samaras to contribute to the volume on the *Politics* in the Cambridge Critical Guide series provided the impetus for completing a study of *politeia* in the *Politics*, which has been expanded to include the *Politeia of the Athenians* and the *Nicomachean Ethics* for the present volume. My honors students at the University of Pennsylvania prompted me to be clear about the language of all the authors we read together in my classes, which were given to me to teach by my Classical Studies chairs—Ralph Rosen, Bridget Murnaghan, Jeremy McInerney, and Peter Struck—and by my sometime dean Rogers Smith. The assistance of David Gilman Romano of the University Museum, now at the University of Arizona, with inscriptions, among other things, was invaluable. Professional library support has been needed throughout, and it has been made possible in recent years by the staff of the University of Pennsylvania library, especially Classical Studies librarian Rebecca Stuhr, who coached my students and me in using electronic resources and was helpful in many other ways. Edith Mulhern made helpful suggestions at various stages. As the manuscript matured, Anthony Preus was kind enough to suggest that it might find a home in the SUNY series in Ancient

Greek Philosophy. This volume is dedicated to Mary Mulhern, who has been my most severe and helpful critic in the years since our marriage. To those who have contributed to the development of my approach but are not mentioned because their thoughts have become indistinguishable from my own, my thanks. The imperfections which remain are solely mine.

Introduction

This book presents some of the results of a half-century of studying Aristotle's political terminology. But why study Aristotle's political terminology instead of going directly to what is supposed to be his political thought, as others have done? Much of the language that political writers use today goes back to Aristotle or is thought to go back to him. But during the millennia since Aristotle's political writings appeared, from his Peripatetic successors forward to the latest revival, his language has been interpreted in different and sometimes incompatible ways. Understanding his political thought, and so the history of political thought, thus involves coming to terms with his use of language. A thorough study of his terminology, of a sort now made possible by the Thesaurus Linguae Graecae, may offer the best prospect of recovering what Aristotle actually had in mind. Each of the chapters in this volume addresses a single expression or a group of related expressions which figured importantly in Aristotle's political terminology. As will be seen, one expression sometimes sheds light on others—an indication that the ones discussed here are especially important. In the end, Aristotle's political terminology, when viewed as described in these chapters, suggests that Aristotle had a way of thinking which differs from some currently established views of it.

As Locke wrote in one of his letters in a discussion of "true Politics," "Aristotle may be best to begin with, and then afterwards if he [the pupil] pleases he may descend to more modern writers of Government, as to the foundations and forms of political societies, or the art of ruling them."[1] A

---

1. In a letter of 1697 quoted in J. S. Maloy, "The Aristotelianism of Locke's Politics," *Journal of the History of Ideas* 70 (2009): 251, from *John Locke: Selected Correspondence,* ed. M. Goldie (Oxford: Oxford University Press, 2002), 253.

reading of Aristotle, however, may not carry the student very far along. English-speaking university students who approach Aristotle's *Politics* by way of a translation or a history of political thought, as many do, will find much that seems familiar to them. They will find, for example, what seems to be a discussion of property in Book 2 and of constitutions in Book 3 and elsewhere. Then they will see phrases that combine 'property' with other words to yield phrases such as 'property qualification' and combine 'constitution' with other words to yield phrases such as 'ideal constitution'. Once a few basic translation decisions have been made, a systematic view of the work is built up around them. The situation is not so different for students who speak other languages. And so it is easy to suppose that Aristotle's political terminology and that of later political writers should be understood in the same familiar way as our own even where Aristotle's meaning ultimately will turn out to be quite different and therefore newly informative.

Translators and interpreters may be pulled toward accommodating Aristotle's language to their own in order to make Aristotle seem more accessible or more in tune with the times. One author, for example, professedly studies ancient political writers to seek "resources in these past thinkers for contemporary democratic theory and practice."[2] On this approach the late P. J. Rhodes offered useful advice in saying "the ways in which Athens fostered and employed the skills of a large citizen body . . . are indeed worth studying and may prompt us to think about how things might be done better in our own world. But, as always, history is more likely to be useful to us in our own world if we do not study it with too much attention to our own world and thereby risk finding what we want to find rather than what is there."[3] Sometimes what one wants to find will result in a partial and impressionistic reading which may be quite distorted, especially if what one wants to find affects the selection of occurrences of a word to be brought in as evidence.

Students who approach the *Politics* directly in the Greek will face related challenges. While in some cases what Aristotle has to say is perfectly clear, in others it will not be. Both the vocabulary and the syntax may be challenging, and the challenges they present may be compounded by one another. For these reasons, students who use a Greek text, even one with notes, may be only marginally better off than their Greekless counterparts.

---

2. https://societyhumanities.as.cornell.edu/jill-frank

3. P. J. Rhodes, Review of J. Ober, *Democracy and Knowledge: Innovation and Learning in Classical Athens* (Princeton: Princeton University Press, 2008), *Polis* 26 (2009): 167.

In his landmark translation of Books 3 and 4 of the *Politics*, published in 1962, Richard Robinson reflected: "The ideal translation would make exactly the same impression on its readers as the original made on the original readers, both in thought and feeling and in emotion." He added, "The ideal translation is impossible."[4] He then went on to comment mainly on Aristotle's style and the challenges that it presents. Great challenges are presented by emotion especially because some of the words which translators use have acquired emotive meanings which are not present in Aristotle's Greek, as in the case of 'slave' and *doulos*, and so can distract from one's understanding of Aristotle's thought.[5] All the same, scholars sometimes have succeeded in overcoming the usual obstacles and have added in important ways to understanding Aristotle's political terminology and so the *Politics* as a whole.

In 1973, for example, Robert Develin took issue with using the single expression 'good' as a translation of both *agathos* and *spoudaios* in *Politics* 3.4. This practice goes back at least as far as the third edition of Gillies in 1813,[6] though William of Moerbeke, the thirteenth-century translator, was careful to use both *vir bonus* and *civis studiosus*.[7] In an article in *Phronesis*, Develin pointed out that this translation has allowed people to attribute incorrectly to Aristotle an argument about whether the good man and the good citizen are the same.[8] Jowett, for example, in his note on 3.4.9 (1277a20–23), says that the good citizen is a good man only if he is "the citizen of a perfect state,"[9] whatever a perfect state would be; Jowett does not say. And Robinson, who also uses 'good' for both *agathos* and *spoudaios*, says, "We often worry whether the State's orders conflict with our conscience."[10] Neither scholar needed to be concerned that Aristotle was discussing whether a good citizen could be a good man only in the

---

4. R. Robinson, *Aristotle's Politics: Books III and IV* (Oxford: Clarendon Press, 1962), xxvii.

5. Emotive meanings in the sense of Ivor Richards and especially Charles Leslie Stevenson.

6. J. Gillies, *Aristotle's Ethics and Politics*, 3rd ed. (London: Cadell and Davies, 1813).

7. See the text of Moerbeke in R. M. Spiazzi, *Sancti Thomae Aquinatis In Octo Libros Politicorum Aristotelis Expositio* (Turin: Marietti, 1966), 128.

8. R. Develin, "The Good Man and the Good Citizen in Aristotle's 'Politics,'" *Phronesis* 18 (1973): 71–79.

9. B. Jowett, *The Politics of Aristotle* (Oxford: Clarendon Press, 1885), 2: 115.

10. Robinson, *Aristotle's Politics: Books III and IV*, 14.

perfect state. Aristotle neither affirms nor denies that the good citizen is a good man or that the good man is a good citizen here; he is not using the language that way.[11] He is talking about something else here—that the city is made up of (is from) unlike people, as he says in 1277a5, which has a parallel in 1 Corinthians 12 on the diversity of gifts and the parts of the body, where we read, in v. 21: "And the eye cannot say unto the hand, I have no need of thee; nor again the head to the feet, I have no need of you." To interpret: The hand is a very poor eye, but it is required all the same, and the feet are a poor head, but they are helpful to the body anyway. A city needs a range of citizens just as the body needs a range of organs. Develin suggested that using two different words, such as 'good' and 'effective', would give a better result. Some would minimize the issue here by observing that *spoudaios* often is a favorable term, which it is; but that fact does not begin to explain why Aristotle chose to use *spoudaios* here instead of *agathos*, which latter expression lacks any association with *spoudē* (haste). Many words in Greek as in English are favorable and are used to commend; they do not all have the same sense or associations.

In 1995, Fred Miller published *Nature, Justice, and Rights in Aristotle's Politics*, which attempted to rehabilitate the view which enjoyed some favor in the midcentury that Aristotle had a theory of rights comparable to what one finds in modern political writers on natural rights. In 1996, Malcolm Schofield argued convincingly, in a special issue of the *Review of Metaphysics* devoted to Miller's book, against using 'right' in translating Aristotle's *dikaion*.[12] Aristotle, he showed, was talking about citizen participation, honor, and so on, not rights, and certainly not natural rights in the modern sense.

In 2000, Martin Ostwald argued against the practice of using 'rich' and 'poor' both where Aristotle uses *plousios* for the rich man and *penēs* for the poor man and where he uses *euporos* for the well-to-do man and *aporos* for the indigent man.[13] Our own linguistic intuitions help us to understand Aristotle here, since we can say, 'He is rich, but he doesn't have much to contribute', or 'He is poor, but he still has something to contribute'. This is the case of using one pair in English where there are two pairs with different senses in Greek. For Aristotle, as Ostwald saw,

---

11. Despite 1293b5–7, where he is discussing the composition of the regime.

12. M. Schofield, "Sharing in the Constitution," *Review of Metaphysics* 49 (1996): 831–839.

13. M. Ostwald, *Oligarchia* (Stuttgart: Franz Steiner Verlag, 2000), 52–68.

someone could be well-to-do but not rich and indigent but not poor, and vice versa. Aristotle had gotten beyond rich and poor, as important as they are for him and for us.

Hermann Bonitz's *Index Aristotelicus* of 1870, now available electronically, remains an important aid to understanding Aristotle's political terminology. Bonitz's index, though less than exhaustive, not only includes a sizable range of occurrences of words in Aristotle but also attempts to classify and give examples of the different senses and uses of these words. Thus it provides a sort of analysis of Aristotle's terminology which goes some way toward giving a thorough treatment of Aristotle's language. A further aid appeared with the Thesaurus Linguae Graecae at the University of California, Irvine, in 1972 and especially with its migration to the web in 2001. The TLG enables scholars to search electronically all occurrences of important words in their contexts. Bonitz and the TLG have become indispensable resources for studying the *Politics*. The chapters that follow take extensive advantage of both Bonitz and the TLG, the latter of which was not available in the period when many still enduring scholarly impressions of the *Politics* were formed.

The book begins with a chapter on Aristotle's use of *phuō*, meaning 'grow', and the cognate *phusis*, the results of which will be important for subsequent chapters. Although many modern thinkers have viewed *phusis*, conventionally rendered by 'nature' in English, as simply the inborn and so have looked to the cradle argument to find out what was *phusei* or *kata phusin* (conventionally natural or by nature), as did some ancients, Aristotle saw *phusis* throughout life, and especially at maturity. Thus when Aristotle speaks of something as *phusei* or *kata phusin*, the reader would do well to ask whether he has in mind the whole life cycle, or maturity, or perhaps both, or something else. One focus of this first chapter is the third-person singular perfect active indicative of *phuō—pephuke*, meaning 'it has grown', since it and the different ways it has been handled by translators and interpreters are especially revealing.

The differences that go with different answers to the question of Aristotle's meaning in using *phusei* or *kata phusin* can be dramatic, and one of them is considered in chapter 2 in connection with *doulos*, often rendered by 'slave', in Aristotle's treatment of the household. Despite the impression that can be gathered from some writers, the expression *phusei douleia*, which might be rendered by 'natural slavery', does not occur in the *Politics*, though the expression *phusei doulos*, often 'natural slave', does occur. Aristotle identifies *phusei douloi* as those who lack foresight though they have bodily ability. Of course the immature are expected to lack both foresight and bodily ability and to require appropriate care, as are the superannuated, in ancient times as in modern ones; if Aristotle intended one or both of these two groups, there would be little purpose in his bringing up the point about lacking foresight or having bodily ability the way he does. So he apparently intends by *phusei* not the immature or the superannuated but the mature, who should have acquired foresight and bodily ability, if they ever will, and should not have lost them yet. Some scholars (e.g., Heath[14]) suggest that there are no chronologically mature people who lack foresight, others (e.g., Nussbaum[15]) suggest that there are. Perhaps these people are like the ones for whom modern governments provide counseling services and other programs of different kinds. If there are such people, they might be the ones that Aristotle has in mind. What Aristotle intends by foresight (*prohoran*) here also requires some attention, since it does not fit into his regular language for practical reasoning and is not deliberation, as some have thought it to be.[16] Likewise for *ktēma* (possession, often rendered by 'property' even today[17]) and *archē* (rule), which figure prominently in Aristotle's discussion of the household; it is not unusual to find it asserted that, for Aristotle, the *phusei doulos* is the property of the *despotēs*, who ordinarily exercises *archē* in the household.

Caution is called for in treating Aristotle's discussion of the household and his use of *ktēma* and its cognates and related expressions—the subject of chapter 3. This chapter addresses the translation of *ktēma* by 'property' and 'possession' in the *Politics*. The modern notion of property is easily contrasted with that of possession, since one can possess things that are not one's property, as in the case of stolen goods. Here the one whose property the goods are does not possess them while the one whose property they aren't does possess them. Aristotle regularly uses language

---

14. M. Heath, "Aristotle on Natural Slavery," *Phronesis* 53 (2008): 243–270.

15. M. Nussbaum, "Aristotle on Human Nature and the Foundations of Ethics," in *World, Mind, and Ethics: Essays on the Philosophy of Bernard Williams*, ed. J. E. J. Altham and R. Harrison (Cambridge: Cambridge University Press, 1995), 117, suggests that Aristotle's natural slaves are the people we would now think of as suffering from "mental retardation."

16. For example, P. Pellegrin, *L'Excellence menacée: Sur la philosophie politique d'Aristote* (Paris: Classiques Garnier, 2017), 147, 153; M. Schofield, "Ideology and Philosophy in Aristotle's Theory of Slavery," in *Aristoteles "Politik": Akten des Xi. Symposium Aristotelicum*, ed. G. Patzig (Göttingen: Vandenhoeck und Ruprecht, 1990), 14.

17. See for example B. Hennig, "Aristotle on Ownership," *Phronesis* 69 (2024): 1–21, especially section 4.

that indicates possession—*ktēma* and *ktaomai*—whereas he lacks language that is clearly for property as moderns understand it, involving property qualifications and property rights. Chapter 4 is on *timēma*, often rendered by 'property qualification' or the like, with the suggestion that the *timēma* is designed for political exclusion such as one might find in an oligarchy.[18] An inventory of occurrences in the *Politics* and the *Politeia of the Athenians* suggests, however, that Aristotle has in mind the process of assessment of output, as from a farm. He finds assessment in democracies as well as in oligarchies, and he recommends it to place a heavier burden of public service on the more successful, leaving the less successful the time to work on their holdings and to become more successful. Chapter 5 considers *dikaion*, sometimes rendered with 'right' (*vide supra*). While some scholars may profess to find property and other rights in Aristotle in some modern sense of 'right' where the expression *dikaion* occurs, the text of the *Politics* suggests that Aristotle does not use *dikaion* this way. This chapter looks to Lysias and Thucydides along with Aristotle to show that, in ancient Greek claim-making situations, in both peace and war, the opposed parties would offer reasons to support the enforceability of their claims rather than relying on the ontology of putative rights or on the emotive meaning of any Greek equivalent of 'right'.

Modern authors sometimes write of a conflict of rights with what they name the common good. Chapter 6 reviews the occurrences of *sumpheron*, of which no analysis is given in the *Politics*, to determine what Aristotle might mean by it, especially in the phrase *koinēi sumpheron*, as an alternative to considering *koinon agathon* (conventionally common good), which occurs only twice in the work and not in a sense that suggests the mediaeval and postmediaeval common good.

Chapter 7 considers Aristotle's treatment of the citizen by focusing on the meaning of *haplōs* in *Politics* 3, where Aristotle is explaining how he will get to his analysis of the *politeia*, a word with many meanings, often rendered by 'constitution', by starting with the *politēs*, regularly and appropriately rendered by 'citizen'. The citizen *haplōs* is, as Aristotle shows by example, the citizen without verbal qualification, rather than, as David Keyt would have it, a "full citizen."[19] Thus Aristotle here is making a terminological and logical point rather than a point of some other kind.

---

18. Aristotle's account here differs from that in *Republic* 550C11–D1, where the *timēma* is associated with oligarchies and where translations sometimes suggest property qualifications.

19. In Robinson, *Aristotle's Politics: Books III and IV*, 130.

Chapter 8, which is a revised and expanded version of a chapter in the 2015 Cambridge volume *Aristotle's Politics: A Critical Guide*,[20] addresses *politeia*, often and sometimes appropriately rendered by either 'constitution' or 'regime', in the three Aristotelian works where it is more frequent—the *Politeia of the Athenians*, the *Nicomachean Ethics*, and the *Politics*, sometimes with the sense of 'citizenship' or 'citizen body'. With four senses (as well as several uses) of *politeia* in play and 522 occurrences in the *Politics* alone, the selection of a translation here or there can have a considerable impact on understanding the texts as wholes and so Aristotle's political thought. A table which shows how all 522 occurrences have been treated by a number of translators and by Bonitz and in preparing this chapter is available online and illustrates the value of looking at all occurrences of the expression under study in a defined universe.

The following three chapters address questions that have been connected with the *politeia* in previous scholarship. Chapter 9 is devoted to showing that and why, while Aristotle hardly if ever uses the language of kinds or forms of *politeia*, though it occurs frequently in translations, sometimes in 'forms of government', he does mention kinds of democracy, kinds of oligarchy, and so on. Chapter 10 updates articles published in *Phronesis* in 1972 and *Polis* in 2007 to address work subsequently done along comparable lines by Aubenque and Pellegrin as well as criticisms by Keyt and Destrée. It takes up what Aristotle means when he observes in book 5 of the *Nicomachean Ethics* that *pantachou* there is only one [*politeia*] that is *aristē* (correctly rendered by either 'best' or 'excellent') *kata phusin*; it appears that he intends that, for every place, there is only one that is best or very good for it in its current stage of development rather than that there is only one and the same that is best for every place at every time—the established universalist understanding. Chapter 11 documents what Aristotle has to say in all the places in the *Politics* where he uses *kat' euchēn* (variously given by 'ideal', 'according to wish', and 'according to prayer') and the cognate verb, where he has in mind the men and the places that are the material for the legislator and statesman rather than the *politeia* itself, which is a matter for deliberation and choice rather than for prayer or wish.

---

20. Portions of chapter 8 were originally published in "*Politeia* in Greek Literature, Inscriptions, and in Aristotle's *Politics*: Reflections on Translation and Interpretation," in *Aristotle's Politics: A Critical Guide*, ed. Thornton Lockwood and Thanassis Samaras (Cambridge: Cambridge University Press, 2015), © Cambridge University Press 2015. Used with permission.

In preparing some of the chapters, but not all, evaluating Aristotle's language was made easier by collecting and displaying it in tabular form, especially where occurrences in the text were numerous or widely spread out and where it might prove useful to consider the understandings reflected in alternative renderings. The tables were designed in each case to help with the material in question in a certain chapter, and so they differ in design and substance from one another. The resulting worksheets have been referenced in or appended to the appropriate chapters where it seemed advisable or, in the case of chapter 8, made available electronically elsewhere. These worksheets allow the reader to replicate the author's procedure and so to correct for any bias in the author's selection of passages for comment in the chapters. Readers can supplement the information in the worksheets easily by consulting Bonitz or the TLG for themselves. The worksheets also indicate just how much or how little has changed among translators from Jowett in 1885 to the present day. Many of the cited translations remain in print or otherwise available, and often they contain valuable information even where they call for modification. Each of them has contributed something to the established interpretation of Aristotle, and so some are more germane than others to the subject of this or that chapter. In some cases they show that there has been a lack of consensus about the details of Aristotle's meaning, which does not sit well with the rough consensus about Aristotle's *Politics* as a whole. These tables may help readers to see where more work remains to be done.

Some readers may wonder why certain expressions were chosen for treatment and not others. It has been suggested already that those chosen figure importantly in Aristotle's work. They also sometimes affect the way other expressions are understood and, as will become clear, have been challenging for scholars to address. Other expressions still need to be addressed. Another example which the author has addressed is that of *ponos* and *poneō*, an example which shows that Aristotle's view of work is more sophisticated than many have thought rather than being a matter of mere ideology.[21] It is to be hoped that other scholars will treat other expressions comprehensively and in detail.

Readers who wish to see a summary of one way of interpreting the results of this study so far may proceed directly to the epilogue.

---

21. J. J. Mulhern, "ΠΟΝΟΣ and ΠΟΝΕΩ in Aristotle," in *Valuing Labour in Greco-Roman Antiquity, Mnemosyne Supplement* 481, ed. M. Flohr and K. Bowes (Leiden: Brill, 2024), 41–61.

Chapter 1

Growth (*Phusis* and *Phuō*)

'Nature' and 'natural' are expressions in common use, and so it may seem that what people mean when they use them would be obvious and that there would be agreement about what nature is and what is natural, so that using them in translations and interpretations of Aristotle would be informative to the reader. Yet people conceive nature differently and disagree about what is natural. The three most available books in English on the concept of nature—those of Whitehead (1920), Collingwood (1945), and Habgood (2002), though Habgood depends to some extent on Collingwood and Collingwood on Whitehead—are books on different subjects. Still, all suggest that 'nature' has many meanings and that the concept of nature and the things considered natural have changed over time. Whatever people mean by these expressions descriptively, though, to call something natural ordinarily is taken to be a sign of approval; that is to say, 'natural' has a favorable emotive meaning. As advertisers know, one way to promote a product or service is to characterize it as having to do with nature or as being natural. Since there are multiple descriptive senses, if one is to use 'nature' and 'natural' informatively in translations, it is advisable to say what one means descriptively by them.

So it was also in antiquity, when *phusis* had many meanings. The Presocratic works *peri phuseōs* of the sixth and fifth centuries, though their distance from the present makes interpretation challenging, offer a variety of views on what is natural. The current project *Phusis kai phuta: On Nature and Plants in Ancient Greece*[1] is shedding further light on this subject from Homer forward. Again, the fifth-century Sophistic contrast of

---

1. https://phusiskaiphuta.wordpress.com/

phusis with *nomos* gave the primitivist interpretation of *phusis* a relatively secure place in the history of ideas, though not an exclusive one. Because *phusis* might be used for different things and in different ways, Aristotle had to go to some lengths to say what he meant by it, or how it was said, to use his idiom, which he did in both the *Physics* and the *Metaphysics*.

Aristotle wanted to give a sense of the different ways in which *phusis* was used not only by himself but by others, one of which is *genesis*, as he says in 193b12–13.[2] Ross explains in his commentary that *phusis* "in the sense of generation is a process toward φύσις,"[3] to which it should be added that the latter *phusis* indicates the condition when *genesis* is complete. As Aristotle goes on to explain, to the extent that the beginning is the shape or form, as he says it is, it is not the from which genesis proceeds but the to which genesis proceeds. Aristotle gives his first glossary definition of *phusis* in the *Metaphysics* at 1014b16–17: "In one way nature is said to be the coming to be of growing things, as if someone would speak stretching the u."[4] Here Aristotle is connecting the noun with the verb. Burnet discounted this passage in defending his treatment of *phusis* as stuff in *Early Greek Philosophy* on the grounds that Aristotle had difficulty with *phuomai*'s having a long υ in some forms while *phusis* has a short one, adding "We need not discuss the question whether Aristotle's difficulty is a real one or not."[5] Collingwood also discounted Aristotle's first definition, interpreting it as "origin or birth," invoking Sir David Ross, who gives instead ad loc. "the genesis of growing things" and later " 'birth' or 'growth,'" which in English are not the same.[6] But Collingwood's reasoning is different from Burnet's; it is that "Aristotle has a characteristic method in philosophical lexicography. . . . he arranges his meanings in a series like shots on a target which gradually creep in and find the bull."[7] While this observation may be correct as far as it goes, it is only a simile; and

---

2. ἔτι δ' ἡ φύσις ἡ λεγομένη ὡς γένεσις ὁδός ἐστιν εἰς φύσιν.

3. W. D. Ross, *Aristotle's Physics* (Oxford: Clarendon Press, 1936), 350.

4. Φύσις λέγεται ἕνα μὲν τρόπον ἡ τῶν φυομένων γένεσις, οἷον εἴ τις ἐπεκτείνας λέγοι τὸ υ. W. D. Ross, *Aristotle's Metaphysics*, 2 vols. (Oxford: Clarendon Press, 1924; repr. 1970 [of 1953 corr. ed.]). Retrieved from the *Thesaurus Linguae Graecae* December 16, 2015.

5. J. Burnet, *Early Greek Philosophy*, 4th ed. (London: Macmillan, 1930), 364. See now G. Naddaf, *The Greek Concept of Nature* (Albany: State University of New York Press, 2009).

6. Ross, *Aristotle's Metaphysics*, 1: 295, 296.

7. R. G. Collingwood, *The Idea of Nature* (Oxford: Clarendon Press, 1945), 80.

Aristotle does not leave aside other meanings when he finishes his list. And so, when he gets to what Collingwood considers his seventh and final definition (Ross enumerates six, five in his translation), Aristotle says, "and processes of becoming and growing are called nature because they are movements proceeding from this [scil. the substance of things which have in themselves, as such, a source of movement]" (trans. Ross).[8] Here Aristotle reaffirms the connection of the noun with the verb. And so, as Collingwood sums up: "Nature as such is process, growth, change."[9]

Since the translation of Aristotle's *Politics* into Latin by William of Moerbeke in the thirteenth century, *natura*, with words derived from it, and despite its failings, has served as the dominant rendering of *phusis* in this work. The failings come from *natura*'s being associated with the verb *nascor* (*gnascor*) and its participle *natus*, in which the sense of becoming, or growing, associated with the Greek *gignomai* (*geno, gigno*), has been largely overcome by the sense of being born. Over the centuries, further, 'nature' has taken on new and different meanings, and so its utility as a translation for Aristotle has become further reduced. This difficulty has not been lost entirely on scholars. In 1885, Jowett observed that "the word nature was ambiguous in ancient no less than in modern times, and was variously used to signify 1) the undeveloped or inchoate, 2) the final or perfect nature."[10] Newman, a few years later, seemed to be reflecting something of Jowett's view, though adding something of his own about *phusis* as process, when he wrote, "The real being, . . . , of Nature is rather to be found in the end than in the process, and rather in the process than in the starting-point."[11] In his Wesleyan lectures of 1925–1926, Sir John Myres shifted the focus to the sequence of growth.[12] Sir Ernest Barker acknowledged Myres in the prefatory note on the vocabulary of the *Politics*, which preceded his translation of the work, published first in 1946 and again in 1948. His discussion merits quoting at some length:

> It would almost need a volume, or at any rate a whole essay, to explain the origin and significance of his [Aristotle's] general conception of *physis*. Here it can only be noticed that an English

---

8. λέγεται φύσις, καὶ αἱ γενέσεις καὶ τὸ φύεσθαι τῷ ἀπὸ ταύτης εἶναι κινήσεις.

9. Collingwood, *The Idea of Nature*, 82.

10. Jowett, *The Politics of Aristotle*, 1: xviii.

11. W. L. Newman, *The Politics of Aristotle*, 4 vols. (Oxford: Clarendon Press, 1887–1902), 1: 19.

12. J. L. Myres, *The Political Ideas of the Greeks* (New York: Abingdon Press, 1927), 301.

> translator is bound to render *physis* and *physikos* by the Latin words "nature" and "natural," and that he is equally bound to alter the exact significance of the Greek by using those Latin terms. The Latin *natura*, connected with a verb which indicates the idea of birth, suggests the primitive; the Greek *physis*, connected with a verb which indicates the idea of growing (and which may be used, in the transitive sense, of "growing" a family, or teeth, or an understanding), suggests the whole process that leads from the first inception of growing, through all the stages of "growth," to the completion of the "grown" thing. . . . We have, as it were, to unhook the word [nature] from the Latin *natura*, and to hitch it to the Greek *physis*, in order to become aware of its associations and echoes, and to see that it includes the process of "growth" and the condition of being "grown" as well as the beginnings of "growing."[13]

Phusis in Aristotle still sometimes is thought to be the original or the primitive or, in the case of human beings, the inborn. Kraut, for example, writes of "the nature that inheres in a living thing at the beginning of its existence," for which see the following note.[14]

At *Politics* 1252b32–34, in the second column of book 1, Aristotle observes that one sees *phusis* best in the mature example since, when the coming to be is complete (*geneseōs telestheisēs*), we say this is the *phusis* of each, as man, horse, household [rather than infant, foal, occasional liaison].[15] This stage of growth is the stage at which something will be able to do all the things that it ever will be able to do and before it loses that ability. Indeed, Aristotle seems to see nature, or growth, throughout life,

---

13. E. Barker, *The Politics of Aristotle* (Oxford: Clarendon Press, 1948), xxiii.

14. R. Kraut, "Nature in Aristotle's Ethics and Politics," *Social Philosophy and Policy* 24 (2007): 207. On 213, Kraut gestures at the position developed in the present chapter, though without following up: "when he [Aristotle] uses the word *phuein* (*pephukamen*) in the passage quoted above [1109b2], we should take him to mean that certain desires have grown into us and in that sense have become natural to us (cf. *EN* VII.3.1147a22)." See also, for example, T. Engberg-Pedersen, "Justice at a Distance: Less Foundational, More Naturalistic: A Reply to Pierre Aubenque," in *Aristotle and Moral Realism*, ed. R. Heinaman (London: UCL Press, 1995), 56, for whom by nature, in this case *kata phusin*, "presumably means by birth and in accordance with human (genetic) nature."

15. οἷον γὰρ ἕκαστόν ἐστι τῆς γενέσεως
τελεσθείσης, ταύτην φαμὲν τὴν φύσιν εἶναι ἑκάστου, ὥσπερ
ἀνθρώπου ἵππου οἰκίας.

even to aging and dying.[16] Since Jackson it has been customary to render the beginning of this passage with "many natural processes" (Ross, Rackham, Ostwald, Brown).[17] Perhaps it would be more informative to render by 'many of the things belonging to us by growth . . . for example aging and dying'. Of course Aristotle does not limit nature or growth to maturity, perhaps since the mature condition can be understood properly only if the growth from the beginning is understood. And so Aristotle is concerned also with the beginning, including birth. When Aristotle speaks of birth, he sometimes uses more precise language, or perhaps contrasting language, as with *genetē* in 1254a23 and in 27 other places in the corpus. Since he has this language ready to hand, there is no need to assume that he always intends an original state or the state at birth, which for Aristotle would not be quite the original state or undeveloped or inchoate, as is clear from his embryology, when he uses *phusis*, as he does 147 times in the *Politics*.

The cognate verb *phuō*, English 'grow', especially in the perfect active *pephuka*, which is intransitive,[18] should help to fill out the sense of *phusis*, but it has been a trial to interpreters and translators of Aristotle's *Politics*, as the accompanying table (1.1) shows. Sometimes they translate it with an adjective, sometimes with an adverb, sometimes with a prepositional phrase. Sometimes they translate the plural as a singular. They don't always fit it syntactically into its surroundings very well. Sometimes they ignore it entirely, as if it didn't mean anything or added nothing to the sense.

The grammarians and lexicographers give uncertain guidance here. Smyth gives both *natus sum* and "am by nature" as renderings for *pephuka*,[19] though the primary association of *nascor* and *natura* with birth makes them seem narrower in meaning than *phuō* (grow) and *phusis*. According to LSJ, the perfect active has the sense of grow, wax, spring up or forth; with the infinitive, it means to be formed or disposed by nature to do so and so; used impersonally, it means it is natural, it happens naturally, citing Aristotle *Politics* 1261b7 and *Poetics* 1450a1; and used absolutely, it means as is natural. There is a transition in LSJ from the language of growth to the language of nature in English, but this transition is not explained, though

---

16. πολλὰ γὰρ καὶ τῶν φύσει ὑπαρχόντων . . . οἷον τὸ γηρᾶν ἢ ἀποθνῄσκειν, *EN* 1135a33–b2.

17. H. Jackson, *ΠΕΡΙ ΔΙΚΑΙΟΣΥΝΗΣ: The Fifth Book of the Nicomachean Ethics of Aristotle* (Cambridge: Cambridge University Press, 1879), 45.

18. H. W. Smyth, *Greek Grammar*, rev. G. M. Messing (Cambridge: Harvard University Press, 1956), 224.

19. Smyth, *Greek Grammar*, 224, 434.

things that grow, an economy, say, or a tumor, may not be natural in one usual English sense. The second sense in LSJ might be closer to the mark if "by nature" were deleted and "formed or disposed to do so and so" were left.

Kraut goes part of the way toward growth in explaining *EN* 1109b2: "when he [Aristotle] uses the word *phuein* (*pephukamen*) in the passage quoted above [1109b2, which Kraut renders "different people have natural tendencies toward different goals"], we should take him to mean that certain desires have grown into us and in that sense have become natural to us (cf. *EN* VII.3.1147a22)."[20] The explanation would be sufficient if it came to an end at "have grown into us." *Pephukamen* occurs here in a terse parenthesis, in which Aristotle says only that we different people have developed with respect to different things; it is difficult to see how Aristotle would say in his own language that "certain desires have grown into us and in that sense have become natural to us" without being redundant, and in any case he does not say that here. It may be possible to get a better view of what Aristotle has in mind when, as here, he uses inflections of *pephuka* in the *Politics* by looking at some of the occurrences shown in the table. A few examples will suggest the possibility that, in using *pephuke* rather than *esti* or a finite form of another verb without *pephuke*, Aristotle intended to invite his audience's attention to a conceptual complication that has to do with growth, as the language would suggest. Perhaps he wanted to point out that someone or something may have grown simply or may have grown to the stage at which it can do what the infinitive suggests rather than being moved by chance or compulsion. This possibility can be confirmed or disconfirmed by working through the whole table.

1261b6–9

According to Aristotle, "It is clear then from these things that it has not come about (developed, *pephuke*) that the city is one as some say, and [it is clear] that what has been spoken of as the greatest good in the cities destroys the cities."[21] He is involved here in his critique of Socrates on sharing in the *Republic*. LSJ cites this occurrence as an example of the impersonal

---

20. Kraut, "Nature in Aristotle's Ethics and Politics," 213.

21. φανερὸν τοίνυν ἐκ τούτων ὡς
οὔτε πέφυκε μίαν οὕτως εἶναι τὴν πόλιν ὥσπερ λέγουσί τινες,
καὶ τὸ λεχθὲν ὡς μέγιστον ἀγαθὸν ἐν ταῖς πόλεσιν ὅτι τὰς
πόλεις ἀναιρεῖ (1261b6–9)

use, rendering "it is natural" or "it happens naturally" with the infinitive, but the translators take several different lines. Jowett treats *pephuke* as if it were the prepositional phrase "by nature" (1: 29),[22] Sinclair-Saunders renders *pephuke* as an adjective and gives "natural unity" (105),[23] Simpson also treats *pephuke* as if it were a prepositional phrase, offering "by nature a unity" (36),[24] and Barker suggests "it is not the nature of the polis to be a unit" (51), and so on, as if *pephuke* were a noun in the nominative singular. The reader might well find this diversity in translations confusing. Clearly, good scholars have come to no agreement here. Some sense of what *pephuke* might mean here can be derived from "these things" to which Aristotle refers, where Aristotle has explained that in a city, the elements differ in kind, doubtless having in mind the historical portions of his collection of *politeiai*. Thus his point seems to be that actual cities have not grown up to become one in the way Socrates suggests that they should; it would take some forcible action to make them become one this way, and then they would devolve, since the result of forcible action would not be sustainable. It probably was not lost on Aristotle that the fictional and putatively unified city of the *Republic* devolves almost immediately in book 8. So a workable translation might be 'it has not grown up' or 'it has not developed', and a translation of this kind leads one back to the context of the passage, which is required to construe it well.

1262a21–24

Aristotle notes, "There are some women and other animals, as mares and cows, who have grown to produce offspring very like their sires, as the mare in Pharsalus called Dikaia."[25] In these lines, Aristotle continues to discuss Socrates on sharing, and here he has in mind the situation of women who have more than one sexual partner. These women, as the females of other species, for example mares and cows, *pephukasin* to deliver children who look very much like their fathers. The bodily reference is not inobvious

---

22. After this, page numbers for frequently cited translations will be given in the text.

23. T. A. Sinclair and T. J. Saunders, *Aristotle: The Politics* (London: Penguin, 1992).

24. P. L. P. Simpson, *The Politics of Aristotle* (Chapel Hill: University of North Carolina Press, 1997).

25. εἰσὶ δέ τινες καὶ
γυναῖκες καὶ τῶν ἄλλων ζῴων, οἷον ἵπποι καὶ βόες, αἳ
σφόδρα πεφύκασιν ὅμοια ἀποδιδόναι τὰ τέκνα τοῖς γονεῦ-
σιν, ὥσπερ ἡ ἐν Φαρσάλῳ κληθεῖσα Δικαία ἵππος.

here; the female does grow during gestation. Aristotle mentions Dikaia also in *Historia Animalium* 586a13 in the same connection. Most of the translators have used 'tendency' here but not elsewhere, although Barker has used it elsewhere as well.

1288a8–15

Aristotle begins to address kingship thematically at 1284b35, and eventually he gets to using *pephuke* in his discussion. In 1288a8, 10, and 13, there are three parallel occurrences of *pephuke* with the infinitive. They address the citizens' being suited to the kingly or to the aristocratic or to the mixed. The kingly people is such that it has grown to bear (*pephuke pherein*) a race or family that exceeds (*huperechon*) in excellence at ruling over the citizens (a8);[26] the aristocratic is such that it has grown to bear (same phrase) a multitude capable of being ruled with respect to the rule of the free by those who are dominant in excellence at political rule (a10); the mixed is one in which the populace has grown to become (*pephuke enginesthai*) capable of being ruled and of ruling according to law (or custom) while assigning the positions of initiative and command to the well to do according to merit (a13).[27] Here Aristotle pretty clearly is calling attention to how different cities have developed to produce a certain political culture, as we might say and as Pellegrin has pointed out.[28] Analogues of these different political cultures may be able to be observed in the different sections of, for example, the United States.[29] Sinclair-Saunders (230) and Robinson (63) render *pephuke* in 10 by the adverb "naturally," Barker by "naturally tends" and "there naturally exists" (176–177). That Aristotle has in mind in the first occurrence the devel-

---

26. Newman ad loc. refers the reader to 1: 290, n. 1, where he gives "is so constituted [as to produce]" and cites Plutarch's *Dion*, 58.

27. βασιλευτὸν μὲν οὖν τὸ τοιοῦτόν ἐστι πλῆθος ὃ πέφυκε φέρειν
γένος ὑπερέχον κατ' ἀρετὴν πρὸς ἡγεμονίαν πολιτικήν, ἀρι-
στοκρατικὸν δὲ πλῆθος ὃ πέφυκε φέρειν *genos* ἄρχεσθαι (10)
δυνάμενον τὴν τῶν ἐλευθέρων ἀρχὴν ὑπὸ τῶν κατ' ἀρετὴν
ἡγεμονικῶν πρὸς πολιτικὴν ἀρχήν, πολιτικὸν δὲ πλῆθος ἐν
ᾧ πέφυκε ἐγγίνεσθαι *genos* πολιτικὸν δυνάμενον ἄρχεσθαι καὶ ἄρχειν κατὰ νόμον τὸν κατ' ἀξίαν διανέμοντα
τοῖς εὐπόροις τὰς ἀρχάς.

28. Pellegrin, *L'Excellence menacée*, on *EN* 1135a5.

29. D. J. Elazar, *The American Mosaic: The Impact of Space, Time, and Culture on American Politics* (Boulder: Westview Press, 1993).

opment of a kingly family over time is clear from what follows, and he is advising his intended audience (*hoi tas politeias kathistantes*, 1288a21) to see whether such a family has developed or has produced an outstanding figure. If it hasn't, trying to establish a kingship will be a matter of force, or perhaps deceit, and probably will not produce the desired stability.

1296b24–26

Here Aristotle gets to the causes of the growth of democracy and of each kind of democracy: "Wherever the multitude of the indigent exceeds the stated proportion, here *pephuken* for a democracy to be." Robinson gives "there democracy is natural" (104), as if 'democracy' were in the nominative as the subject of the clause. It is, however, in the accusative. Newman (4: 223) is unusually but revealingly confused. He notes: "Though Aristotle uses the word πέφυκεν here, he does not probably intend to imply that democracy or oligarchy exist by nature under any circumstances (cp. 3. 17. 1287 b 39 sq.)," which suggests that Newman was concerned that Aristotle might have said what he did not mean. Aristotle is not doing that. He is addressing the conditions under which a democracy is likely to appear—"here it has developed for a democracy to be."[30]

1310a39–40

In these lines, reminiscent of 1289b26 and 1296b26, Aristotle is considering monarchy, "the things from which it is destroyed and the things through which *pephuken* to be preserved." His account of what preserves the monarchy might help to clarify *pephuken*. This account begins at 1313a18, and it suggests that a process of moderating the monarchic rule preserves it, as in the case of Sparta. Rackham gives "the natural means of its preservation" (436). An alternative might be 'the things through which it has grown to be preserved', since Aristotle's emphasis is on the process of moderation. Then the whole sentence would be: "It remains to address monarchy, the things from which it is destroyed and the things through which it has grown to be preserved."[31]

---

30. ὅπου
    μὲν οὖν ὑπερέχει τὸ τῶν ἀπόρων πλῆθος τὴν εἰρημένην ἀνα- (25)
    λογίαν, ἐνταῦθα πέφυκεν εἶναι δημοκρατίαν,

31. Λείπεται δ' ἐπελθεῖν καὶ περὶ μοναρχίας, ἐξ ὧν τε
    φθείρεται καὶ δι' ὧν σῴζεσθαι πέφυκεν.

1329a13–16

Here Aristotle observes: "It is left then for the regime to be given in both respects to the same people but not at the same time, as capacity *pephuken . . . einai* in the younger, practical wisdom in the elder."[32] Jowett's approach was to give "but in the order prescribed by nature" (222), as if *hōsper pephuken* were a separate clause. Barker elegantly gave, "The order of nature gives vigour to youth and wisdom to years" (354); Sinclair-Saunders offered, "Rather we should follow nature" (416), and so on; Simpson used, "just as by nature power exists in the younger and prudence in the older" (130). But if Aristotle wanted to say 'by nature power exists', for example, why didn't he just say *esti* rather than going to the trouble to use *pephuken . . . einai*? The reason seems clear enough. Aristotle just has been speaking of the warriors and the deliberators as parts of the city; they are the same people but at different stages of their lives. Thus he is concerned here with growth, which occurs in more or less regular ways, though of course there could be unusually prudent younger people, like Cyrus, and unusually vigorous older people, like Nestor. And so a translation such as 'has grown to be' or 'has developed' seems to be indicated here, reflecting the fact that there are different stages of growth in human life, which are characterized by different advantages. Aristotle comes back to this point in *Rhetorica* 1361b7–14, where he notes that what it means to be beautiful varies with age. The young are beautiful if they have grown (*pephukasin*, 11, the only occurrence in this passage) in relation to speed and force, like the pentathletes; the mature in relation to the works of war; the elderly in relation to necessary labors and to avoiding the painful infirmities that age brings.[33]

1334b22–25

A little further along, Aristotle is concerned with the development of human children. He observes that spirit and wish and desire belong to children straightaway as they come to be, though the stage is not indicated, but "reasoning and insight *pephuken* to come to be as they

---

32. λείπεται τοίνυν τοῖς αὐτοῖς μὲν ἀμφότερα ἀποδιδόναι τὴν
    πολιτείαν ταῦτα, μὴ ἅμα δέ, ἀλλ' ὥσπερ πέφυκεν ἡ
    μὲν δύναμις ἐν νεωτέροις, ἡ δὲ φρόνησις ἐν πρεσβυτέροις (15)
    εἶναι·

33. Newman is the source of this reference.

go forward."[34] Sinclair-Saunders left *pephuken* untranslated ("reasoning and intelligence come into their possession as they grow older"), as if *huparchei* were repeated, and Barker gave "as a rule." Jowett's "but reason and understanding are developed as they grow older" (237) comes closer. The translation might be: For spirit and wish and again desire belong to children straightaway as they come to be, but reasoning and insight grow to come to be as they go forward.

While it is customary to render *pephuke* by adjectives and adverbs and even nouns or separate clauses to get a version that sounds familiar in modern English, doing so may obscure a subtlety in Aristotle's way of explaining things—namely, that he is calling attention to the way things grow or develop rather than talking about nature as some understand it today, which is colored by the Latin tradition of Roman Law and by the modern use of the expression 'nature' for a regular and orderly system with Newtonian or other laws. In Greek it is clear that *phusis* is connected with *phuō*—to grow. Latin also has appropriate cognates—*natura* and *nascor*, both of which, however, are focused on birth and thus are narrower in focus than their Greek counterparts. English currently has no verb cognate with 'nature'. It had such a verb in the late Middle Ages, since 'nature' itself was used as a verb, from the scholastic Latin verb *naturare* and Middle French *naturer*, according to the *OED*. But in current English the connection of the noun and verb is lost, and only a transliteration of the Latin *natura* remains when one must translate Aristotle. Hence the tendency to use 'nature' itself or to slip in such English cognates as we have in the translations—'natural', 'naturally'. The difficulty is compounded by our sometime belief that nature is something fixed—some thing, in any case, rather than a going-on of some sort or its completion, and that it is to be opposed as the undeveloped to the developed. It seems, though, that, for Aristotle, *phusis* can indicate growth at any stage, and *pephuke* indicates that something has grown to some stage or other, whether that stage be early, middle, or late.

Several of these passages have growth in view—the growth and decline of cities, the growth of the female during gestation, the growth and decline of institutions, the growth of adults and elders as they go through life, the growth of human children.

---

34. θυμὸς γὰρ καὶ βού-
λησις, ἔτι δὲ ἐπιθυμία, καὶ γενομένοις εὐθὺς ὑπάρχει τοῖς
παιδίοις, ὁ δὲ λογισμὸς καὶ ὁ νοῦς προϊοῦσιν ἐγγίγνεσθαι
πέφυκεν.

While this concludes my remarks on *pephuke*, perhaps these remarks may suggest something further about the way Aristotle uses *phusis* in the *Politics*.

The nominative singular of the noun *phusis* occurs 15 times in the *Politics*, and 2 of these occurrences are especially revealing. In 1332a40, Aristotle identifies three things that make men good, and these things are *phusis*, *ēthos*, and *logos*. Aristotle goes on to say that first it is necessary to be born as a man but not any of the other animals. And thus a certain sort of body and soul (a41–42). One might suppose that Aristotle is interpreting *phusis* in the sense of being born here, and Sinclair-Saunders apparently takes this view (429); but it seems more likely that he is viewing *phusis* as the sort of growth that includes birth and accommodates habituation for better or worse at some point and even accommodates reason eventually; and that his view is that these three must harmonize with one another (b5–6), even though people may do many things counter to their habituation and their growth because of reason (b6–7). 'Counter to their growth' here renders *para phusin*. Clearly Aristotle does not intend a sharp break of *ēthos* and *logos* with *phusis* here, since his regular view is that people can grow into their habits and into reason, given proper tutelage, unless something prevents them; but he does allow the case in which, despite one's past, one acts because of becoming convinced.[35] After all, he is considering education here.

The second occurrence, in 1332b36, is found in Aristotle's discussion of how people who are similar can share ruling and being ruled in turn, even though the superior rule, which is desirable. The Greek practice was for people to be eligible to share in rule as citizens simply speaking during their years of maturity; before that and after that, they were citizens only with a qualification—immature citizens or superannuated citizens[36]—and so were restricted with respect to holding office and in other ways. Those who are immature and those who are growing old notoriously falter in judgment and in other ways; Aristotle is describing growth here. And so he says, as I would translate it, that growth has given us the selection by making the younger and the older in the same family, of whom it is appropriate for the former to be ruled and for the latter to rule. The

---

35. For discussion of this topic, see C. Chamberlain, "The Meaning of *Prohairesis* in Aristotle's Ethics," *Transactions of the American Philological Association* 114 (1984): 147–157.

36. 1275a17

translators often say that nature has given us the selection or something of the kind, but it is quite clear here that Aristotle is talking about growing through the ages through which men grow.

Of *phusei* there are fifty-eight occurrences to consider in the *Politics*. Here I shall consider a couple of revealing texts in their contexts. The first is 1252a32, which is part of a discussion in which Aristotle has recommended that we look at things as they grow. Aristotle just has said that those who are not able to get by without one another pair off together. And so they do, as they grow. Then he gives two examples, that of the woman and the man who pair off together for the sake of procreation, even though that may not be on their minds at the moment, and that of the one who takes the initiative and the one who follows who pair off together for the sake of preservation, presumably preservation of both of them, even though that may not be on their minds at the moment. The former case is only somewhat controversial, the latter case is more so. We know how the woman and the man pair off, but how about the one who takes the initiative and the one who follows the initiative? Aristotle says that the one who, as a result of growth or development is capable of foresight by understanding, takes the initiative and directs, whereas the one who, as a result of growth or development, is able-bodied [but not more], takes direction and is dependent on the one who has foresight. Note that the woman and the man pair off together only at a state of relative maturity. Aristotle's parallel suggests that the others also pair off at a state of relative maturity. Here again, the immature and the superannuated are not in question. What happens with someone who, despite having become mature in years, lacks the foresight that one would expect of a mature individual? We expect young children and the elderly to lack foresight and to be dependent. We expect that the mature will be independent and will be able to take care of themselves. But sometimes they cannot; they can't look ahead; they lack foresight and so don't know how to provide for themselves. These are the people of whom Aristotle is speaking at this point when he uses *phusei*. Despite growth, or *phusei*, they lack foresight. They are the mature dependent (see chapter 2).

The second text is 1253a3, where Aristotle says that the man is *phusei politikon zōion*, which means that when grown the man is a live thing adapted to be a citizen, or approximately that. *Politikos* as an adjective means related to the citizen or something of the kind rather than the very vague modern 'political'. As will be discussed more fully in chapter 7, for Aristotle, one is a citizen simply speaking only at a mature stage of life.

Aristotle is saying here that the human being, when grown, is adapted to citizenship—that is, to deliberating about matters of joint interest and to assessing the results of any choices and actions that are taken that follow on this deliberation. Here again he has growth in mind.

It might be objected to the foregoing, based on book 1, chapter 2, that, according to Aristotle, the *polis* is natural or by *phusis* because it is the human partnership that is self-sufficient, and it is more sufficient than a village or a kingdom because it allows us to live well (1252b30), as if only the *polis* were *phusei*. Actually, what Aristotle says here is: "From several villages the city is a complete partnership, already having reached the limit of autarky, so to speak, having developed for the sake of living, but being [continuing to be] for the sake of living well. Therefore every city is *phusei*, since [*epei* causal] also the first partnerships [are *phusei*]. For their end is the same, and *phusis* is an end. For as each is when its growth is complete, this we say to be the *phusis* of each, as of man, horse, and household. Moreover the for the sake of which and the end is best. And autarky is the end and best" (1252b27–1253a1). He concludes: "From these it is clear (*ek toutōn oun phaneron*) that the city is *phusei* and that man is an animal fitted to be a citizen" (1253a1–3). *Phaneron* has a logical force here, not a psychological one. It is fatal to the objection that Aristotle states here that the first partnerships—that is, the family and the village—are *phusei*, and that the *polis* is because they are. Thus the life we live in a *polis* enables us to live well because a human being is of a certain sort rather than the other way round, though this is not true of all human beings, as he indicates quoting Homer in 1253a5. He goes on to explain that men are more political—more citizenlike—than bees and so on because they have language, which allows them to deal with the just and the unjust, which citizens must do in deliberation and judgment. He wraps up this part of his discussion by saying, in so many words, that partnership in these [perception of the just and unjust and so on] makes household and *polis* (1253a18). His point is that because men are political—that is, capable of being citizens and so of deliberating and judging—they can live and live well in cities. Of course they may not have the opportunity to do that, as Aristotle recognizes, even though they might be able to if the opportunity presented itself.

Or it might be objected further that the account given here does not address Aristotle's remarkable claim in 2.1252b1–3 that *phusis*/nature makes each kind of thing for one purpose, as if *phusis*/nature were a thinking, godlike creator. Aristotle is terse here, as he often is, and so it is useful to look at the rest of the corpus to see what he has to say. Pellegrin noted of the dictum Nature intends one agent for one function: "Sometimes Aristotle says the opposite. Cf. *Parts of Animals* 2.16 659b35, but both positions may be reconciled."[37] Aristotle does say in *de anima* 432b21–23 that nature makes nothing in vain and leaves out no necessary things except in the disabled and incomplete, which may not seem very godlike. It is not sufficient to quote the first part of this sentence and leave out the qualification, which is required for Aristotle to make his point. He realizes that the cause he recognizes as *phusis* sometimes fails.

Finally, it might be objected in a similar vein that there is insufficient attention here to *phusis* as a fixed and lasting order, based on Aristotle's use of the phrase *hōs epi to polu*, as it occurs in the *Physics* and *Metaphysics*. This phrase, however, is meant to qualify his express treatment of *phusis* by noting that its operation can be and sometimes is thwarted by external obstacles rather than to present *phusis* as a fixed and lasting order.

To conclude: *Phuō* sometimes has the sense of 'grow', and *phusis* sometimes has the sense of 'growth', in the *Politics*. To say that something has grown is to say something temporally indefinite, since it can be said of the growing thing at any stage of its growth. At any stage, some growth has been completed and its effects remain. And so to say that something *pephuke* may mean that it has just begun growing, that it has been growing for a long time, or that it has completed its growth and has perished, though Aristotle often is concerned to indicate maturity. Likewise, to say that something is *phusei* is to say that it has grown without some foreign obstruction, such as chance or force or deceit. Some things develop without these obstructions, and their condition can be said to be *kata phusin*, while others have their growth obstructed, and their condition can be said to be *para phusin*. Thus *phusis* in Aristotle is more than the original condition which nature sometimes has been thought to be. The next chapter will illustrate how this approach to *phuō* and *phusis* can clarify important lines in book 1 on the so-called natural slave.

---

37. P. Pellegrin, *Endangered Excellence: On the Political Philosophy of Aristotle*, trans. A. Preus (Albany: State University of New York Press, 2020), 120, n. 25. Pellegrin provides the reconciliation in *Animals in the World*, trans. A. Preus (Albany: State University of New York Press, 2023), 259.

Table 1.1. Translations of *Pephuka* in the *Politics*

	Jowett 1885	Rackham 1932	Barker 1948	Robinson 1962 (III–IV)	Sinclair-Saunders 1981	Simpson 1997	Reeve 2017
1.1255b8 *pephukasin*	[which] nature intended them to have	[for which] they are by nature fitted	[for which] he is naturally intended		[for which] he is fitted by nature	[for which this second] is naturally fitted	[that is] natural
2.1260b37 *pephuken*	natural	is the natural	is the natural		natural	is the natural	natural
1261a26 *pephuken*	untranslated	the essential object . . . is	formed by its very nature		Is	the nature . . . is	naturally exist
1261b7 *pephuke*	is . . . by nature	is . . . an outcome of nature	is . . . the nature		is . . . a natural	is . . . by nature	in nature
1262a23 *pephukasin*	have a . . . tendency	have a . . . natural tendency	show a . . . natural tendency		have a . . . natural power	have a . . . natural tendency	have a . . . natural tendency
3.1279a11 *pephuken*	in the order of nature	under the natural system	this is the natural system	in the proper manner	in a natural and proper manner	according to what was natural	as is natural
1288a8[1] *pephuke*	by nature capable	to be naturally capable	naturally tends	naturally	naturally	naturally	naturally
1288a10 *pephuke*	untranslated[2]	naturally	naturally tends	naturally	naturally	naturally	naturally
1288a13 *pephuke*	there naturally [exists]	there naturally grows up	there naturally [exists]	there naturally [arises]	there naturally grows up	there naturally [emerges]	there naturally [arises]

	Jowett 1885	Rackham 1932	Barker 1948	Robinson 1962 (III–IV)	Sinclair-Saunders 1981	Simpson 1997	Reeve 2017
1288a26 *pephuke*	naturally	in the order of nature	is . . . intended by nature	it is . . . natural	is . . . naturally	does . . . by nature	it is . . . natural
1288b4 *pephuke*	untranslated	it is natural	does it tend	it naturally [arises]	naturally	it naturally	it naturally [arises]
4.1289b26 *pephuken*	untranslated	it is . . . natural	tend	natural	naturally	naturally	naturally
1296b26 *pephuken*	there will naturally be	it is natural	there will naturally be	is natural	naturally arises	it is natural	it is natural
5.1310a40 *pephuken*	untranslated	the natural means	untranslated		untranslated	naturally	naturally
7.1323b19 *pephuken*	untranslated	are in their nature	are		Are	are by nature	are naturally
1329a14 *pephuken*	prescribed by nature	in the natural order of things	the order of nature gives		we should follow nature	by nature	natural
1334b25 *pephuken*	are developed	it is the nature	as a rule		untranslated	naturally	naturally
8.1337a30 *pephuken*	untranslated	it is natural	naturally		naturally	naturally	it is natural
1339a9 *pephuke*	untranslated	it is the nature	tend naturally		naturally	naturally	naturally

1. Newman ad loc. refers to his 1, 290, n. 1 on φέρειν in the sense of 'breed', instancing Plutarch, *Dion*, 58, and translates: "A people is a fit subject for Kingship, if it is so constituted as to produce (πέφυκε φέρειν, 1288a8) a family excelling in virtue and in capacity for political leadership." Newman, *The Politics of Aristotle*.

2. Jowett does not translate here because he regards the text as dittographic.

Source: The author.

Chapter 2

The Mature Dependent (*Phusei Doulos*)

Scholars sometimes use the phrase 'natural slavery' in connection with *Politics* 1, as in Malcolm Heath's "Aristotle on Natural Slavery."[1] The first point to be noted is that the putative Greek for 'natural slavery' does not occur in the *Politics* (indeed, *douleia* itself occurs only six times in this work), although much of the scholarship has developed as if it did occur. I shall consider what Heath has to say about the *phusei doulos*, which is the actual subject of his article, along with a passage that he dismisses and a passage that he omits from what Aristotle has to say. This will require me to say something about what Aristotle means when he uses 'foresight' (*prohoran*), since foresight is an indispensable part of Aristotle's treatment of the *phusei doulos*, and something about what he means when he uses 'rule', which also is indispensable to his treatment.

Heath has suggested some revisions to the traditional view of Aristotle's description of the *phusei doulos*. For Heath, Aristotle's *phusei doulos* does not "suffer from a comprehensive failure of autonomous rationality" (246). He "need not lack a conception of intrinsic value" (252). He "may be extremely intelligent" (253). He is not "subhuman" (258–259). Still, one of these "lacks the capacity to make reasoned judgements about what he should do consistently with his conception of living well in general. And this renders him incapable of living a worthwhile human life" (253). The individual in question, according to Heath's Aristotle, has a limited impairment that affects practical reasoning alone, not scientific or technical reasoning; it affects "global deliberation" and detaches "an individual's

---

1. Heath, "Aristotle on Natural Slavery," 243–270. Page references to this article are given in the text in parentheses.

conception of intrinsic value from executive control of his behaviour" (253). Perhaps there is more to be said.

Heath dismisses one passage that might be instructive—1252a30–34—and fails to mention another—1327b33–36. In the first passage, Aristotle says that there must be "the ruler *phusei* and the ruled because of *sōtēria*. For the one who is able to foresee with the intelligence must be the ruler *phusei* and the one who gives direction *phusei*, and the one who is able to work with the body must be the ruled and the *phusei doulos*."[2] Newman found somewhat similar sentiments in *Laws* 690B1–2 and in Isocrates *Antidosis* 180 and, most strikingly, in the perhaps Isocratean *Ad Demonicum* 40, where the author is advising Demonicus on looking out for himself (*prohoran*). This usage goes back to Herodotus.[3] Heath observes that, in 1252a30–34, Aristotle "grounds the distinction between natural ruler and natural subject in the slave's lack of foresight with regard to *survival*. But the context refers to the earliest stages of social development, and we should be cautious about extrapolating these comments to larger social organizations" (246, n. 8). Cautious always, yes, but perhaps no more than that. Heath's argument seems to be that survival becomes unimportant in larger or more advanced social organizations; yet in fact, the issue of

2. [ἀνάγκη] ἄρχον δὲ φύσει καὶ
 ἀρχόμενον διὰ τὴν σωτηρίαν. τὸ μὲν γὰρ δυνάμενον τῇ
 διανοίᾳ προορᾶν ἄρχον φύσει καὶ δεσπόζον φύσει, τὸ δὲ
 δυνάμενον [ταῦτα] τῷ σώματι πονεῖν ἀρχόμενον καὶ φύσει
 δοῦλον

Ross departs from Bekker's text here. W. D. Ross, *Aristotelis Politica* (Oxford: Clarendon Press, 1957; repr. 1964). Retrieved from the *Thesaurus Linguae Graecae* December 16, 2015.

3. Newman, *The Politics of Aristotle*, 2: 107. LSJ gives the usual spatial sense for προορᾶν but also the temporal sense and a more revealing sense—make provision for oneself, or approximately that—which goes back to Herodotus 5.39, where the case under discussion is that of the Spartan king Anaxandrides, who married a woman who seemed to be barren, though later events would show otherwise. The ephors met with him to tell him that if he would not provide [a successor] for himself, still they could not let the dynasty perish. Anaxandrides was happy with his wife, but the ephors thought that he was wrong in not looking to having children, which was important for the Greeks. Anaxandrides was failing to provide for himself; the failing to provide for the city was not on his mind, and so the ephors spoke up. Foresight here appears first to regard one's own condition rather than that of the city. For Isocrates, *Ad Demonicum*: É. Brémond and G. Mathieu, *Isocrate: Discours*, vol. 1 (Paris: Les Belles Lettres, 1929; repr. 1963). Retrieved from the Thesaurus Linguae Graecae. For Herodotus: Ph.-E. Legrand, *Hérodote: Histoires*, 9 vols. (Paris: Les Belles Lettres, various dates). Retrieved from the Thesaurus Linguae Graecae.

survival never goes away in any stage of social development or in any size of social organization, any more than does the distinction of those who have foresight from those who lack it. Jowett thought that "the preservation of the subject or inferior" was intended by Aristotle, perhaps because the preservation of the ruler would not be in question;[4] the ruler has enough foresight *ex hypothesi* to look out for himself. Of course, Heath's "survival" may be a misleading translation because too narrow. Perhaps 'welfare' or the like would be more to the point—something closer to the Latin *salus*.

This word *prohoran* occurs only in this form in the *Politics* and only in this place. Overall it occurs in the corpus with reference to seeing something in front of one in three biological contexts (*HA* 524a14, *PA* 656b31, *Pr.* 892b7) and perhaps with a more complex intent in a fourth such context—*HA* 614b26 (see later discussion); it occurs with reference to seeing something ahead of time on twenty-seven occasions, including here in the *Politics*. What is intended by in front of one or *emprosthen* is explained in *PA* and *Pr.* as the direction of movement—*eph' ho hē kinēsis*. For assessing what Aristotle may mean in the *Politics*, one is well advised to look to the places in which the sense clearly is temporal.

Of these, fourteen are in the *Topics*, *Sophistici Elenchi*, and *Rhetoric*, where all seem to have to do with appreciating in advance where an argument is going—what may happen (*Top.* 148b9 and 155b13, *to sumbēsomenon*; 156a18, *ek tinōn sumbainei*), or failing to appreciate it. To foresee where an argument is going is difficult, as Aristotle notes in *Rh.* 1419a23–24; and it is more difficult to deal with an argument while it is going on, he observes in *SE* 177a6–8, for it is hard to foresee then, though it is easy to see when one has the leisure. In the competitive situations addressed in all three works, the speakers are under various pressures, including time pressures; not all people will deal with these pressures equally well, and some may fail entirely.

Reason may be involved in these cases, but not deliberative reasoning, which is, as Greenwood observed long ago, of *prakta* only—things to be done.[5] Those involved are trying to see what might happen to them

---

4. Jowett, *The Politics of Aristotle*, 1: xvi.

5. L. H. G Greenwood, *Aristotle Nicomachean Ethics Book Six* (Cambridge: Cambridge University Press, 1909), 23. The lack of scholarly interest in foresight even in the *Topics* and so on is illustrated by the absence of *prohoraō* from the *index verborum* of the Third Symposium Aristotelicum and by the absence of texts in which it occurs, and so of comments on these texts, from the index of texts cited there. G. E. L. Owen, ed., *Aristotle on Dialectic: The Topics*. Proceedings of the Third Symposium Aristotelicum (Oxford: Clarendon Press, 1968).

rather than trying to choose a course of action to take. Aristotle perhaps makes clearest what he has in mind in *EN* 1150b23 while discussing *akrasia*, where, in considering tickling, he observes that those who perceive in advance or foresee that someone will try to tickle them are not tickled. They have foreseen what might happen and have set themselves. The phrase *kai proaisthomenoi kai proïdontes* reminds the reader that to foresee is to be understood along the lines of perceiving (*aisthēsis*) rather than of reasoning, whether deliberative or other reasoning. Perceiving involves no reasoning or discursive thought; the apprehension and the thought involved are immediate.[6] So also, arguably, foresight.

There are six occurrences in the *De Divinatione per Somnia* and one in the *De Somno et Vigilia*—all associated with divining the future in a way that apparently differs from Aristotle's more prosaic foresight, though they also are concerned with what will happen (e.g., *Div.Somn.* 464a18–19, *Somn.Vig.* 453b21, *ta mellonta*). The five others are in the *Historia Animalium* (1), *Eudemian Ethics* (1), *Nicomachean Ethics* (2), and *Poetics* (1), along with the one in the *Politics*.

All in all, it appears that the foresight of the *despotēs* in 1252a32 is not deliberation or reasoning but is rather an intuitive grasp, perhaps developed from experience, of what might happen and thus of what needs to be guarded against. That may be why Aristotle treats foresight in connection with *sōtēria* in 1252a31–32, which may be reflected in *HA* 614b26, where Aristotle describes the behavior of cranes and the leader's foresight for the safety of the flock; he will go on to generalize a few lines later (b31–32) about wild birds and the *sōtēria* of their offspring.

In what sense would lack of foresight be spoken of as *phusei*? The text at 1252a30–34 contains the fourth, fifth, sixth, and seventh occurrences of φυ- in the *Politics*. The immediate context begins in 1252a24–26, where Aristotle says that, if one would look at the growing things from the beginning, as in other things, one would observe best of all in these.[7] Note *phuomena* in 24—the first occurrence of φυ- in the *Politics*. This is the beginning of the immediate context. Von Fritz and Kapp rendered "as

---

6. H. H. Joachim, *Aristotle: The Nicomachean Ethics* (Oxford: Clarendon Press, 1955), 103, *ad* 1112b34–1113a2.

7. Εἰ δή τις ἐξ ἀρχῆς τὰ πράγματα φυόμενα βλέψειεν,
ὥσπερ ἐν τοῖς ἄλλοις, καὶ ἐν τούτοις κάλλιστ' ἂν οὕτω
θεωρήσειεν.

they grow."[8] Aristotle could have said *en archē*—at or in the beginning, suggesting a snapshot of the original condition, as in St. John—rather than from the beginning, suggesting continuous observation; but he did not. Thus Aristotle's emphasis here is not on the original condition of something but on its growing or growth, from beginning presumably to end.[9] When he goes on to speak of *phusis*, it is likely that he has growth in mind. This is clear, as noted in chapter 1, from his first definition of *phusis* in *Metaphysics* 1014b16–17: "In one way *phusis* is said to be the coming to be of things as they grow, as if someone would speak stretching the u."[10]

In 1252a31–34, there are two conditions mentioned for the *phusei doulos*—that he lack foresight and that he be able to work with the body.[11] Both foresight and the ability to perform bodily work are associated with mature people then as now. Thus the *phusei doulos* is not the chronologically immature nor the superannuated, both of whom notoriously lack foresight, as recognized in law, and neither of whom is capable of much in the way of work. Indeed, Aristotle points out that children should not work (1338b38–1339a10) and that, when they get older, they take care of their aged parents, who cannot work any longer (*Oec.* 1343b15–23). As if to make sure that his point would not be missed, he shortly observes that, as noted earlier, as each is when its *genesis* is complete, this we say to be the nature of each, as man, horse, household, 1252b32–34),[12] not of child, foal, occasional liaison. Thus when he says shortly after in 1253a1–3 that from these it is clear that the city is among the things that are *phusei*, and that man is a *politikon zōon*,[13] he is stressing that

---

8. K. von Fritz and E. Kapp, "The Development of Aristotle's Political Philosophy and the Concept of Nature," in *Essays on Aristotle*, ed. J. Barnes, M. Schofield, and R. Sorabji (London: Duckworth, 1977), 124.

9. Aristotle does not use the dative singular of ἀρχή in this work. He does use the genitive, though, and sometimes elsewhere with ἐξ in the sense of 'from the beginning,' as at 1255a31, 1256b10, 1258a19, 1269b39, 1273a32, 1280a30, 1284b17, and 1287b10.

10. Φύσις λέγεται ἕνα μὲν τρόπον ἡ τῶν φυομένων γένεσις, οἷον εἴ τις ἐπεκτείνας λέγοι τὸ υ.

11. τὸ μὲν γὰρ δυνάμενον τῇ διανοίᾳ προορᾶν ἄρχον φύσει καὶ δεσπόζον φύσει, τὸ δὲ δυνάμενον [ταῦτα] τῷ σώματι πονεῖν ἀρχόμενον καὶ φύσει δοῦλον

12. οἷον γὰρ ἕκαστόν ἐστι τῆς γενέσεως τελεσθείσης, ταύτην φαμὲν τὴν φύσιν εἶναι ἑκάστου, ὥσπερ ἀνθρώπου ἵππου οἰκίας.

13. ἐκ τούτων οὖν φανερὸν ὅτι τῶν φύσει ἡ πόλις ἐστί, καὶ ὅτι ὁ ἄνθρωπος φύσει πολιτικὸν ζῷον.

the city belongs to a mature stage of human partnership and that the mature man is adapted or disposed to live in it and to be a citizen simply speaking, as he underlines in book 3, 1275a11–23, where he points out that the immature citizen and the superannuated citizen are not citizens simply speaking. Thus, in using *phusei*, Aristotle is not making the cradle argument of his Stoic and Epicurean successors. Maturity is the thought elsewhere as well. In his will, for example, as given by Diogenes Laertius 5.15, he directs that his attendants, when they reach the appropriate age, shall have their freedom if they merit it; no one will know whether they merit it until they approach maturity.

Heath notices the "complexity of Aristotle's use of 'nature'" (260) but does not explain it (see chapter 1). I infer that, at least in some cases, Aristotle intends growth when he uses *phusis* and that growth throughout the life of the individual is intended. I would add that Aristotle lays special emphasis on maturity. If this is correct, then Aristotle in speaking of the *phusei doulos* may have in mind first of all the chronologically mature individual who lacks foresight and who would benefit from direction by someone who has it. Many people would agree, after all, that the immature individual and the superannuated individual cannot be depended upon for foresight; they obviously need direction. Further, neither the immature nor the superannuated is capable of much in the way of work with the body, as the *phusei doulos* must be in Aristotle's account. Aristotle's point thus can't be about the immature and the superannuated. It can be only about the mature individual.

Unlike Nussbaum, Heath professes to believe that there are no people who fit this description (244, n. 4), but that Aristotle thought that there were such people for empirical rather than ideological reasons, unlike Schofield, who thinks that Aristotle's reasons were ideological (244, n. 2). Whatever one may think of Heath's view that there are no people who meet Aristotle's description of the *phusei doulos* as lacking foresight, modern society is organized in part for the purpose of looking after chronologically mature people who seem, whatever the cause or causes, to lack foresight about how they should take care of themselves, whatever their other abilities, and who may be helped by direction from social workers and others, sometimes using court orders, whose foresight about them is presumed to be better than their own. Of course society is organized with the purpose of dealing with the immature and the superannuated who lack foresight as well, though the results are mixed.

Here is a modern example of organizing to deal with mature individuals who seem to lack foresight: In very cold weather, some American city governments collect people and put them in shelters so that they won't suffer frostbite or freeze to death; these people know that the shelters are there, but they don't go to them. As the official City of Philadelphia website says, for example: "During extremely bitter cold conditions (this is when the temperature, wind chill and precipitation combined together result in real feel temperatures near or below 20 degrees Fahrenheit), the City implements extraordinary measures to preserve the lives of chronically homeless individuals."[14] I recall being in the Philadelphia underground near City Hall on a very cold night some years ago when an acquaintance of mine, now deceased, who was a city councilman at the time, also a boxer and labor union official and afterward a member of Congress, came through the tunnel with a group of assistants and collected a sizable group of men who were resting there to convey them to a shelter. We exchanged greetings. Those being collected were men of roughly middle age who might have been expected to have developed foresight but who appeared to lack it.

At the state and national level, governments organize programs for people who may be presumed to lack foresight involving environmental conditions, nutrition, hygiene, financial management, and so on. These people, even when they come of age, are assumed to lack foresight even though some of them are competent at performing scientific or technical or bodily work. There seems to be a consensus in many countries that there are people who fit the description of chronologically mature people who lack foresight in approximately Aristotle's sense, though they have other abilities, and so might benefit from being given direction—people who might benefit from having someone else exercise foresight on their behalf since they don't exercise it themselves.

Although, in Aristotle's time, some elements of the welfare state were present, including redistribution, public-service employment, and public contracts for infrastructure, the city had not become the modern welfare state; failing that, the Greek system might address the situation of the mature dependent in the household, and that apparently was what Aristotle had in mind.[15]

There might be more than one cause for lack of foresight in the chronologically mature. Heath, having dismissed inability to foresee, has asked, "How did the natural slave get that way?" He has answered, "By

---

14. http://www.phila.gov/codeBlue.html, retrieved November 17, 2015

15. D. B. Nagle, *The Household as the Foundation of Aristotle's Polis* (New York: Cambridge University Press, 2006).

living in the wrong place" (253). That is to say, he has argued that, in Aristotle, the cause of the putative natural slavery not mentioned in the *Politics* is climate (253–258), which affects the psyche, so that those in unfavorable climates are *phusei douloi*. Heath's discussion of the role of climate is drawn mainly from 7.7, which has no immediate connection with the argument of *Politics* 1. In *Politics* 1, Aristotle is concerned with a phenomenon that we still can observe—that some people lack foresight while other people have it, to a greater or lesser extent, when they are of mature age. Heath urges that, in 7.7, Aristotle argued that the Greeks were superior to the Europeans, who are deficient in *dianoia*, and to the Asiatics, who are deficient in *thumos*, because of Greece's central location and its climate—warmer than that of Northern Europe, cooler than that of Asia. This aetiology is supposed to provide Aristotle's "empirical" reasons. Heath does not mention 1327b33–34, which is in this chapter, where Aristotle says that there is the same difference [in psychic makeup] among the Greek nations with respect to one another.[16] An explanation by lack of *thumos* in whole peoples is hardly the same as an explanation by lack of foresight in individuals in households—the subject in book 1, to which it doesn't seem germane. The phenomenon remains; some people lack foresight while other people have it, to a greater or lesser extent, when they are mature, whatever the explanation. The climate explanation is not needed to explain lack of foresight.[17]

---

16. τὴν αὐτὴν δ' ἔχει διαφορὰν καὶ τὰ τῶν Ἑλλήνων ἔθνη πρὸς ἄλληλα

17. Aristotle's seeming to view foresight mainly as a matter of individual welfare—what individuals can do for themselves, as relatively short term, and as practical rather than detached, contrasts with much of the modern literature, in which foresight is concerned instead with the ability or inability of large organizations including governments to foresee on behalf of others and into the far future in a rather detached way. An example of this modern literature is L. S. Fuerth, "Foresight and Anticipatory Governance," *Foresight* 11, no. 4 (2009): 14–32. An exception is an article by S. Stark, "Executive Foresight: Definitions, Illustrations, Importance," *Journal of Business* 34 (1961): 31–44. Stark's work drew on mainstream thinkers from Aristotle to Henri Fayol, William James, and Peter Drucker as well as on the specialist thinkers in business and psychology from his own day. He quoted Fayol, who died in 1925 but who has remained influential in organization theory, to the effect that to foresee "means both to assess the future and make provision for it" and that "it is not given to mortals to do either of these well" (32). C. E. Lindblom would be making similar points with respect to policy analysis in his classes at Yale in political science and in his books in the middle of the century and after. See *The Policy-Making Process*, 2nd ed. (Englewood Cliffs: Prentice-Hall, 1980), chapter 3, "Limits of Analysis as an Alternative to Politics." In chapter 5, "Making the Most of Analysis," he observed,

Heath observed early in his treatment of this subject that while, in addressing parts of the corpus other than the treatment of the *phusei doulos*, "scholars work hard to fill gaps and resolve inconsistencies," here "ideological repugnance has proved a deterrent" (244). Part of the explanation for this repugnance may be the emotive meaning of the translation 'slave'—that is to say, the emotional response or range of responses that hearers and readers have on being presented with the translation 'slave'.[18] This response may be compounded by discomfort with Aristotle's discussion of rule, ruling, and being ruled in this context, since, in the passage cited at the outset of this chapter (1252a30–34), Aristotle speaks of the *doulos* as *archomenos* and of the *despotēs* as *archōn*. And so it may prove useful to address what Aristotle apparently has in mind by rule.

Archē and *archō* are frequent in the *Politics*—338 occurrences for the noun and 368 for the verb, according to the TLG. The senses of these words are multiple in the corpus. Bonitz distinguishes four senses for the noun—*initium, principia cognoscendi* and *principia realia* both in the plural, and, fourth, a definition Aristotle himself gives—"the *archē* by the choice of whom moving things are moved and changing things are changed, as in cities the magistracies and the dynasties and the kingships and tyrannies are called *archai* and the arts, and of these the architectonic ones most of all" (1013a10–14). Bonitz's fourth, with examples drawn mostly from the *Politics*, is the item of interest here. Bonitz divides it into *imperium/ dominatio/principatus*, his initial example being the rule of the sea; and then *magistratus*, conventionally magistracy, magistrate by metonymy. For the verb Bonitz gives *incipere* and *imperare*.

Aristotle tells us elsewhere what he means by *archē*. At the beginning of *Metaphysics* Δ, Aristotle says that *archē* has six senses. The six senses are, as Ross gives them:

1. The starting point of [one's] movement (e.g., the beginning of a road)

2. The best starting point (e.g., for learning a subject)

3. That part of a thing from which genesis proceeds (e.g., the keel of a ship)

"At any given time our cognitive capacity always remains limited, still not up to the complexity of the problems we face in policy making" (34).

18. Discussed by C. L. Stevenson in *Ethics and Language* (New Haven: Yale University Press, 1944), 59 and following.

4. The external starting-point of genesis or movement (efficient cause)

5. That which moves something else at its will (e.g., the *archai* in cities)

6. That from which knowledge of a thing starts (*causa cognoscendi*)[19]

Ross's fifth sense corresponds to Bonitz's fourth.

In the *Politics*, Aristotle explains the fifth sense in more detail. In his section on the division of the *archai*, he notes that "it is not easy to distinguish this, what sort it is necessary to call *archai*" (1299a14–15), before giving his answer: "But as to speak most of all in an unqualified way, it should be said that these are *archai* to which it is given to deliberate about certain things and to judge and to command, and most of all this last. For to give orders is the more appropriate for ruling" (1299a25–28). Where Aristotle mentions speaking without qualification (*haplōs*, not generally or roughly), he may be giving us a sign that he is going beyond his immediate concern to indicate not just the rule of citizens in a city but rule in other settings as well, such as the household but also, presumably, in other Greek associations such as armed forces, choruses, and the like. In all of these there is place for deliberation and judgment as well as for giving orders, just as in modern times; modern readers expect people such as air traffic controllers, musical conductors, CEOs, mayors, governors, football quarterbacks, parents, emergency room physicians, traffic police, and so on to deliberate, make judgments, and tell people what to do, since different people have different responsibilities that require coordination. In any organization in which responsibilities differ and must be coordinated, directing and being directed will be distinguished. Thus rule, ruling, and being ruled, or directing, giving directions, and being directed, are normal parts of human life. Or so, at least, Aristotle apparently believed. Although moderns also may have these expectations and act on them in daily life, reactions to the language of ruling and being ruled sometimes fail to reflect these expectations.

When Aristotle uses inflections of *archē* and *archō* in book 1, he may well have this sense in mind and be distinguishing those who command or direct and those who are commanded or directed in the household.

---

19. Ross, *Aristotle's Metaphysics*, 1: 291.

There has been some disagreement over whether Aristotle is talking about the magistracies or the magistrates here. Jowett came down on the side of magistracies and rendered by "offices," and Newman followed him with "posts," and Rackham and Barker and Simpson with "offices"; but Robinson gives "officers" and Sinclair-Saunders "officials," doubtless in the belief that the occupants of the offices rather than the offices themselves deliberate and judge and give orders.

In this chapter I have observed that Aristotle does not use the putative Greek for 'natural slavery' in the *Politics*. I have suggested that Aristotle may mean it when he says that "the one who is able to foresee with the intelligence must be the ruler *phusei* and the one who gives direction *phusei*, and the one who is able to work with the body must be the ruled and the *phusei doulos*." I have noted that the *phusei doulos* must be for Aristotle the mature individual who lacks foresight, and that modern societies acknowledge the presence of large numbers of such people by enacting costly programs to look out for them and provide them with guidance (counseling). I have recalled that Aristotle acknowledged the presence of such people in Greece as well as outside it and that his discussion of climate in book 7 does not seem intended to bear on his discussion of foresight in book 1. And I have argued that using one's foresight to give direction is a normal part of organizational life. The fact that one gives direction to other people does not mean that they are one's property—another issue that can be clarified in Aristotle's case by looking at the language that sometimes is rendered, incorrectly, by 'property', as the next chapter will show.

Chapter 3

Possessions (*Ktēmata, Pol.* 2.1260b27–1274b28)

According to LSJ, *ktaomai* in all but the perfect and pluperfect has the sense of procure, get, or acquire, while in the perfect and pluperfect it has the sense of possess or hold; and the cognate nouns reflect this sense. *Ktēma* is given as anything gotten, piece of property, possession, with the plural as possessions, while *ktēsis* is given as possession (from the perfect). It has become customary, however, to speak of Aristotle's views on property rather than possession and to use 'property' in translations for *ktēma*, as in Sinclair-Saunders, with respect to book 2, as if the language of possession indicated the kind of object possessed or its status.[1] But 'property' and 'possession' do not have the same sense in English. That is to say, one can distinguish property as that to which one has an enforceable claim even if one doesn't possess it. We talk (correctly) about stolen property, lost or unclaimed property, or property held in trust as property that people own, in the sense that they have an enforceable claim to it, but that they do not possess at the moment. Further, what people possess, or have gotten some way, might not be their property at all. They might have filched it and not have an enforceable claim to it. Justice tries to safeguard property or to restore property to its rightful possessors. But people always are in danger of losing their property.

In this chapter I suggest that Aristotle often has in mind possessions rather than property in book 2 where he uses *ktēma* and its cognates in discussing the treatment of the household in the *Republic* and perhaps elsewhere, and I discuss two other pertinent expressions that occur in

---

1. All references to Sinclair-Saunders in this chapter are to Sinclair and Saunders, *Aristotle: The Politics*. The Greek texts cited are from Ross, *Aristotelis Politica*.

Politics 2—*idios* and *ousia*, the former of which sometimes appears in translations to indicate private property in contrast with the somewhat oxymoronic public property; *ousia* is used by Aristotle to indicate wealth or estate even where possession is not in question. Distinguishing property from possessions in considering book 2 shifts the overall focus of interpretation somewhat from the status of things possessed to the mere possession of them.

First, the key sentence that orients the discussion: "These things being so, it is necessary to consider possession (*ktēseōs*), in what way it is necessary to prepare the *politeia* about to become excellent, whether possession (*tēn ktēsin*) is to be shared (*koinēn*) or not shared" (1262b37–40). Aristotle is preoccupied here with possession and with sharing. He starts from these and not from the individual, and so from possession and its varieties rather than from one's own, or property as moderns understand it. Here he uses *koinos*, perhaps best rendered 'shared' in discussions of this kind. In what follows, most but not all of the references will be to chapter 5 (1262b37–1264b25).

Ktēma

Aristotle uses *ktēma* three times in this book and seventeen times in the work as a whole, as confirmed by a lemma search of the TLG. The word means something that one has gotten, cognate with the Greek for getting or acquiring (*ktaomai*). As the grammarians say, words formed with the *-mat* suffix, as *ktēma* is (genitive *ktē-mat-os*), signify "the result or effect of an action" (Smyth, §841). 'Possession' would be all right here, since, in English, possession is the effect of the action of getting or acquiring.

Sinclair-Saunders uses "pieces of property" for the first occurrence of *ktēma* at 1261a5: "It is certainly possible for citizens to go shares with each other in children, in wives, and in pieces of property, as in the *Republic* of Plato." We don't know from the text, however, that the *ktēmata* are the possessors' property or anything else about their status. We know only that the possessor has them. A less supposititious translation might be '[other] possessions'. In the next occurrence, Aristotle says that the work of the liberal man is in the use of possessions (*en tēi gar chrēsei tōn ktēmatōn*, 1263b13)—things that he has, presumably. One can't use things that one does not have. One hopes that these possessions are possessed rightfully. Sinclair-Saunders gives the singular "property," though Aristotle has a plural here. And in 1264a33, Aristotle says that Socrates makes the farmers lords of their possessions even though (if the participle is being used concessively) they pay rent. Again a plural in Aristotle, and again Sinclair-Saunders gives the singular "property." Even renters can possess things, though their claims to them might be provisional or conditional. Renters may be said to possess the houses they live in; they have acquired a place to live. *Ktēmata* are possessions, whoever owns them as property.

It may be useful to see how Aristotle uses this language elsewhere. Early in book 3 (1277b24–25), he discusses economy, which for him is the management of the household, the Greek productive unit. His view here is different from the modern one, in which the individual often is the productive unit. The individual in modern thought sometimes might come from no household, have no household, produce no household, and act with only number one in mind. Quite different from Aristotle's view, and perhaps not faithful to most modern experience. In any case, here Aristotle observes that the household management of the man and the woman is different, for the role of the man is to get (*ktasthai*) while the role of the woman is to guard (*phulattein*). This is an instance in which *ktasthai* is understood to be acquiring whatever the household possesses, since no object is given. The sense is simply that the man gets, the woman guards. What she guards is their possessions, whatever they may be, or perhaps the possessions of the household rather than of individuals, since individuals were limited in what they could do with the household's possessions. These possessions are held separately by the household and so are *idia*.

Idios

Idios, whose neuter is used elsewhere for the logical property (*Topics* 102a18–19), occurs twenty-nine times in this book, as shown in table 3.1, but arguably not as the logical property. It occurs several times with *ktēsis*—the cognate of *ktēma* with the suffix -*si*, indicating an action (Smyth §840), thus the act of possessing or possession, though the distinction of the action from the result of an action is permeable. In one of these places Sinclair-Saunders gives:

Each man has his own possessions (*idian . . . ktēsin*), part of which he makes available for his friends' use, part he uses in common with others. For example, in Sparta they use each others' slaves practically as if they were their own, and horses

> and dogs too; and if they need food on a journey, they get it
> in the country as they go. Clearly then it is better for property
> (*ktēseis*) to remain in private hands (*einai men idias*); but we
> should make the use of it communal (*koinas*). (1263a33–39)[2]

This passage exemplifies Aristotle's expository care. There is no "man"
here or close by in the Greek, just an "each" (*hekastos*); each what is
left unstated, and there is no "his." It seems likely to be each household
(*oikos*). In its first occurrence *ktēsis* would have been rendered more
faithfully if the singular had been kept. And, in the Greek, Aristotle adds
something to 'possession'—*idian* to qualify it as possessed in a certain
way. The distinction is that of a possession *haplōs* from a possession to
which something has been added, as with *prostithentas* at 1275a17 where
Aristotle is defining the *haplōs politēs*; this is a distinction that Aristotle
knows (see chapter 7). In the second occurrence, it would be much better
to be consistent with the first and, instead of using "property," to say that
it is better for possessions (plural) to be separate. One still could make
their use shared as a matter of generosity or liberality—a basic concern
of Aristotle's. In this example, the beneficiaries of sharing use what they
do not separately possess. One might revise the translation as follows:
"Each having separate possession makes some useful to friends while some
it uses as if by agreements, as in Sparta they use *douloi* of one another
[which are] separate, so to speak, and again horses and dogs, and if there
is a need of supplies in the farms throughout the country."

Another passage as rendered in Sinclair-Saunders:

> But none of these things [charges and countercharges, trials,
> sucking up to wealthy owners] is due to the absence of com-
> munal ownership; they arise out of the depravity of human
> character. In fact we find more disputes arising between those
> who own and share property in common than we do among
> separate holders of possessions, even though, as we can see,

---

2. ἰδίαν γὰρ ἕκαστος τὴν κτῆσιν
ἔχων τὰ μὲν χρήσιμα ποιεῖ τοῖς φίλοις, τοῖς δὲ χρῆται
κοινοῖς, οἷον καὶ ἐν Λακεδαίμονι τοῖς τε δούλοις χρῶνται (35)
τοῖς ἀλλήλων ὡς εἰπεῖν ἰδίοις, ἔτι δ' ἵπποις καὶ κυσίν, κἂν
δεηθῶσιν ἐφοδίων, [ἐν] τοῖς ἀγροῖς κατὰ τὴν χώραν. φανερὸν
τοίνυν ὅτι βέλτιον εἶναι μὲν ἰδίας τὰς κτήσεις, τῇ δὲ χρή-
σει ποιεῖν κοινάς·

> the number of those who quarrel over partnerships is small
> as compared with the great multitude of private owners [those
> having possessed possessions separately—*kektēmenous idiai*
> (dat.) *tas ktēseis*]. (1263b22–27)[3]

At the least, this passage suggests that possessions can be held separately
in the household and can be shared. I shall come back to this passage in
connection with *ousia*.

Again, Aristotle says, adverting to the *Republic*: "But as for the
farmers, if they were expected to provide maintenance for those possessing arms, then it would have been reasonable for them to be a part
of the state. But actually that is not so: the land they work is their own
(*idian*) and they work it for their own benefit (*idiai*, dat.)" (1268a32–35,
trans. Sinclair-Saunders).[4] Besides these occurrences where *idios* is in the
feminine because it modifies the feminine *ktēsis* or perhaps *onēsis* (benefit) understood, it occurs also in the neuter as a substantive. In one of
these occurrences, Aristotle says: "There are two which most of all make
men be concerned and love—the separate (*to idion*) and the lovable (*to
agapēton*)" (1262b22–23). Aristotle appears to be using *idion* for what is
held separately, though one might not possess it at the time, even as one
might not possess the lovable at the time when one was concerned about
it. Another example occurs at 1263a29, which Sinclair-Saunders gives
as follows: "Responsibility for looking after property, if distributed over
many individuals, will not lead to mutual recriminations; on the contrary,
with every man busy with his own (*idion*), there will be increased effort
all around."[5] A sparer translation of this passage might be: 'Cares being

---

3. ὧν οὐδὲν γίνεται διὰ τὴν ἀκοινωνησίαν ἀλλὰ
   διὰ τὴν μοχθηρίαν, ἐπεὶ καὶ τοὺς κοινὰ κεκτημένους καὶ κοι-
   νωνοῦντας πολλῷ διαφερομένους μᾶλλον ὁρῶμεν ἢ τοὺς χωρὶς
   τὰς οὐσίας ἔχοντας· ἀλλὰ θεωροῦμεν ὀλίγους τοὺς ἐκ τῶν κοι- (25)
   νωνιῶν διαφερομένους, πρὸς πολλοὺς συμβάλλοντες τοὺς κεκτημένους ἰδίᾳ τὰς κτήσεις.

4. οἱ δὲ γεωργοὶ πορίζοντες μὲν τοῖς τὰ
   ὅπλα κεκτημένοις τὴν τροφὴν εὐλόγως ἂν ἦσάν τι τῆς
   πόλεως μέρος, νῦν δ' ἰδίαν ἔχουσιν καὶ ταύτην ἰδίᾳ γεωρ-
   γήσουσιν.

5. αἱ μὲν γὰρ ἐπιμέλειαι διῃρημέναι τὰ ἐγκλήματα
   πρὸς ἀλλήλους οὐ ποιήσουσιν, μᾶλλον δ' ἐπιδώσουσιν ὡς πρὸς
   ἴδιον ἑκάστου προσεδρεύοντος·

divided do not make for claims against one another, rather they will devote themselves, each being attentive, to what is held separately".

There are a few examples outside chapter 5 at the end of the book in which Aristotle is considering lawgivers and whether anything is *idios* in the sense of being peculiar to them, including Phaleas (1274b9), Draco (1274b16), Pittacus (1274b19), and Androdamus (1274b25). Here Aristotle seems to be saying that what he attributes to these figures occurs only with them. The sense seems to be that, if you knew what had been done, you would know as well who did it.

Overall, where *idios* occurs with *ktēsis* in book 2, Aristotle appears to have in mind the possession of something, as by the household, which might or might not be shared. *Idios* is unlikely to mean private here, and *idia ktēsis* is unlikely to mean private property as that is thought of today.

Ousia

Ousia (substance or wealth) occurs twenty-eight times in this book, which is extraordinary, since it occurs only sixty-five times in the work as a whole. Bonitz gives *opes* (resources) and *divitiae* (wealth) as the first sense. Aristotle seems to be concerned here with something other than current possession; one's substance might go beyond what one currently possesses, such as an inheritance that will provide a future income stream.[6] Aristotle seems to understand this. In 1263b19–20, Aristotle is addressing the position of Socrates in the *Republic*, who attributes evils in the *politeiai* to substance's not being shared (*dia to mē koinēn einai tēn ousian*). For Sinclair-Saunders this is "the absence of communal ownership of possessions." Aristotle's point has been lost, since one's substance might not be in one's possession. In 1263b23–25, noted earlier, Aristotle is careful to keep everything in its place. Sinclair-Saunders gives, "we find more disputes

---

6. Greek inheritance law appears to confirm that *ousia* is to be conceived in terms of the multigenerational household. See, for example, L. Foxhall, "Female Inheritance in Athenian Law," https://classics-at.chs.harvard.edu/wp-content/uploads/2021/05/ca1.2-foxhall.pdf. Foxhall concludes that "property [I would say possessions] and households were intertwined" in the context of "reproduction of households over time." See also a revised version of Foxhall's paper: "Household, Gender, and Property in Classical Athens," *Classical Quarterly* 39, no. 1 (1989): 22–44.

arising between those who own and share property in common than we do among separate holders of possessions." It would be more accurate to render 'we see those possessing common things and partnering differing more than those holding their substances separately'. Here the Greek gives *ousias* where Sinclair-Saunders gives "possessions."

Ousia, often in the singular, is much like our 'substance' in the sense of 'wealth' or 'estate', as in the phrase 'an individual of substance', where it seems that possessions held separately are not distinguished from others. So Aristotle uses three words in his discussion, distinguishing possessions simply from possessions held separately and substance or wealth from both.

Conclusion

My conclusion, having gone through all the occurrences in book 2 of *ktēma* and its cognates, of *idios*, and of *ousia* is that Aristotle was careful to distinguish among these three. 'Property' in our language has to do with the status of an object—the legal status—in a way that 'possession' does not. While perhaps only certain sorts of things can be possessed, the variety is very great, and something's being possessed does not tell us what sort of thing it is or whether it is one's property. Rendering by 'property' where Aristotle has just *ktēma* or *ktēsis* risks obscuring what Aristotle apparently has in mind.

The translators' confusion of 'possession' with 'property' has helped to throw off, among other things, the ongoing discussion of *douleia*, conventionally rendered by 'slavery', in Aristotle. Aristotle's discussion of *douleia* is couched partly in terms of possession, since everything in the household has been acquired, including the people. One gets a wife or husband, one gets or begets children, one acquires staff, one acquires beasts of burden, and so on. Aristotle's discussion of these matters is not couched in terms of property. Yet when the translators render *ktēma* and *ktēsis* 'property', they give the impression that something other than acquiring or possession is at stake.

Interestingly, in book 1, Aristotle does associate *douleia* with being a *ktēma* but not with being *idios*. The pertinent texts are 1254a2, 11, 16, 1255b32, and 1256a2. Sinclair-Saunders regularly gives "property," which suggests that the *doulos* is untouched by law, which is not correct, according to my colleague Professor Cohen, who has recorded the legal protections afforded to *douloi*.[7] Of course it is true that the *doulos*, like everything else in the household, is possessed by the household. But since everything in the household is possessed, simply being possessed does not tell us very much about the status of the item possessed.

While possessions can be held separately in the household and not shared, they also can be shared outside the household. *Ousia*, however, is rather 'substance', and at any given time it may not be possessed. One may have to go to court to claim and recover *ousia* if it has been lost, as illustrated in some speeches of Lysias (see chapter 5). Clarity about Aristotle's use of *ktēma* and its cognates will shed light on his discussion of the assessment or *timēma* in chapter 4.

---

7. E. E. Cohen, *The Athenian Nation* (Princeton: Princeton University Press, 2000), 160.

Table 3.1. Translations of *Idios* in *Politics* 2

Line	Text	Jowett	Rackham	Sinclair-Saunders
1261b34	τῶν γὰρ ἰδίων μάλιστα φροντίζουσιν, τῶν δὲ κοινῶν ἧττον	Every one thinks chiefly of his own, hardly at all of the common interest;	men care most for their private possessions, and for what they own in common less,	People are much more careful of their personal possessions than of those owned communally;
1262a13	κρεῖττον γὰρ ἴδιον ἀνεψιὸν εἶναι ἢ τὸν τρόπον τοῦτον υἱόν.	and how much better it is to be the real cousin of somebody than to be a son after Plato's fashion!	For it is better for a boy to be one's own private nephew than one's son in the way described.	Anybody would rather be a cousin who really was someone's own personal cousin, than a son in the manner described.
1262b23	δύο γάρ ἐστιν ἃ μάλιστα ποιεῖ κήδεσθαιτοὺς ἀνθρώπους καὶ φιλεῖν, τό τε ἴδιον καὶ τὸ ἀγαπητόν·	the two qualities which chiefly inspire regard and affection — that a thing is your own and that you love it —	For there are two motives that most cause men to care for things and be fond of them, the sense of ownership and the sense of preciousness;	There are two impulses which more than all others cause human beings to cherish and feel affection for each other: 'this is my own', and 'this is a delight'.
1263a6	τὴν μὲν γῆν κοινὴν εἶναι καὶ γεωργεῖν κοινῇ, τοὺς δὲ καρποὺς διαιρεῖσθαι πρὸς τὰς ἰδίας χρήσεις	the soil may be common, and may be cultivated in common, but the produce divided among individuals for their private use;	the land be common and farmed in common, but the produce be divided for private use	the land is communally held and communally worked but its produce is distributed according to individual requirements.
1263a26	λέγω δὲ τὸ ἐξ ἀμφοτέρων τὸ ἐκ τοῦ κοινὰς εἶναι τὰς κτήσεις καὶ τὸ ἐκ τοῦ ἰδίας.	would have the advantages of both systems.	I mean the advantage of property being common and the advantage of its being private.	it will have the advantages of both systems, both the communal and the private.

continued on next page

Table 3.1. Continued.

Line	Text	Jowett	Rackham	Sinclair-Saunders
1263a27	δεῖ γὰρ πὼς μὲν εἶναι κοινάς, ὅλως δ' ἰδίας.	Property should be in a certain sense common, but, as a general rule, private;	For property ought to be common in a sense but private speaking generally.	For, while property should up to a point be held in common, the general principle should be that of private ownership.
1263a29	μᾶλλον δ' ἐπιδώσουσιν ὡς πρὸς ἴδιον ἑκάστου προσεδρεύοντος·	because every one will be attending to his own business.	because each will apply himself to it as to private business of his own;	on the contrary, with every man busy with his own, there will be increased effort all round.
1263a33	ἰδίαν γὰρ ἕκαστος τὴν κτῆσιν ἔχων	For, although every man has his own property,	for individuals while owning their property privately	Each man has his own possessions,
1263a36	οἷον καὶ ἐν Λακεδαίμονι τοῖς τε δούλοις χρῶνται (35) τοῖς ἀλλήλων ὡς εἰπεῖν ἰδίοις	The Lacedaemonians, for example, use one another's slaves . . . as if they were their own;	For instance in Sparta people use one another's slaves as virtually their own,	For example, in Sparta they use each other's slaves practically as if they were their own.
1263a38	φανερὸν τοίνυν ὅτι βέλτιον εἶναι μὲν ἰδίας τὰς κτήσεις	It is clearly better that property should be private,	It is clear therefore that it is better for possessions to be privately owned,	Clearly then it is better for property to remain in private hands;
1263a40	ὅπως δὲ γίνωνται τοιοῦτοι, τοῦ νομοθέτου τοῦτ' ἔργον ἴδιόν ἐστιν.	the special business of the legislator is to create in men this benevolent disposition.	and to train the citizens to this is the special task of the legislator.	It is a particular duty of a lawgiver to see that citizens are disposed to do this.

Line	Text	Jowett	Rackham	Sinclair-Saunders
1263a41	ἔτι δὲ καὶ πρὸς ἡδονὴν ἀμύθητον ὅσον διαφέρει τὸ νομίζειν ἴδιόν τι.	Again, how immeasurably greater is the pleasure, when a man feels a thing to be his own;	And moreover to feel that a thing is one's private property makes an inexpressibly great difference in one's pleasure;	Moreover there is an immense amount of pleasure to be derived from the sense of private ownership.
1263b7	ὃ γίνεται τῆς κτήσεως ἰδίας οὔσης.	which can only be rendered when a man has private property.	a condition of this is the private ownership of property.	this happens when people have property of their own.
1263b27	πρὸς πολλοὺς συμβάλλοντες τοὺς κεκτημένους ἰδίᾳ τὰς κτήσεις	compared with the vast numbers who have private property.	compared with the total number of private owners.	compared with the great multitude of private owners.
1264a16 (2)	καὶ τοῖς γεωργοῖς κοινὰς εἶναι δεῖ τὰς κτήσεις ἢ καθ' ἕκαστον ἰδίας, ἔτι δὲ καὶ γυναῖκας καὶ παῖδας ἰδίους ἢ κοινούς.	are the husbandmen, too, to have their property in common? Or, besides the common land which he tills, is each individual to have his own? and are their wives and children to be individual or common?	whether the Farmers also are to have their property in common or to hold it in private ownership, and also whether community of wives and children is to apply to them or not.	whether the farming class are to have communal or individual private possessions, whether of property or of wives and children.
1264b2	εἴ γε τὰς μὲν γυναῖκας ποιήσει κοινὰς τὰς δὲ κτήσεις ἰδίας	if Socrates makes the women common, and retains private property,	if Socrates intends to make the Farmers have their wives in common but their property private,	if he means to make wives shared and property privately owned,

continued on next page

Table 3.1. Continued.

Line	Text	Jowett	Rackham	Sinclair-Saunders
1265a25	εἰ δέ τις μὴ τοιοῦτον ἀποδέχεται βίον, μήτε τὸν ἴδιον μήτε τὸν κοινὸν τῆς πόλεως,	Even if the life of action is not admitted to be the best, either for individuals or states,	and if one does not accept such a description whether for the life of the individual or for the common life of the state,	And if one rejects such a life, both for individuals and for the state at large,
1267b34	διήρει δ' εἰς τρία μέρη τὴν χώραν, τὴν μὲν ἱερὰν τὴν δὲ δημοσίαν τὴν δ' ἰδίαν·	He also divided the land into three parts, one sacred, one public, the third private:	He divided the land into three parts, one sacred, one public and one private.	The territory also was to be divided into three parts, a sacred, a public, and a private;
1267b37	οἱ προπολεμοῦντες βιώσονται, κοινήν, τὴν δὲ τῶν γεωργῶν ἰδίαν.	the second was to support the warriors, the third was the property of the husbandmen.	common land to provide the warrior class with food, and private land to be owned by the farmers.	the defenders out of the common land, and the private land would belong to the farmers.
1268a34 (2)	νῦν δ' ἰδίαν ἔχουσιν καὶ ταύτην ἰδίᾳ γεωργήσουσιν.	they are supposed to have land of their own, which they cultivate for their private benefit.	as it is they have private land of their own and farm it for themselves.	the land they work is their own, and they work it for their own benefit.
1268a38	εἰ δ' ἔτεροί τινες ἔσονται τῶν τε τὰ ἴδια γεωργούντων καὶ τῶν μαχίμων,	If, again, there are to be other cultivators distinct both from the husbandmen, who have land of their own, and from the warriors,	while if the cultivators of the common land are to be a different set of people from both those who cultivate the private farms and the soldiers,	if there are to be certain others, different from the fighters and from those farmers working their own property,

Line	Text	Jowett	Rackham	Sinclair-Saunders
1268a41	ἀλλὰ μὴν εἴ τις τοὺς αὐτοὺς θήσει τούς τε τὴν ἰδίαν καὶ τοὺς τὴν κοινὴν γεωργοῦντας,	Or, if the same persons are to cultivate their own lands and those of the public as well,	But yet if one is to make those who cultivate the private and the common land the same people,	Or again, if one makes the same people cultivate the private and the common land,
1274b6	Χαρώνδου δ᾽ ἴδιον μὲν οὐδέν ἐστι πλὴν αἱ δίκαι τῶν ψευδομαρτυριῶν	In the legislation of Charondas there is nothing remarkable, except the laws about false witnesses.	There is nothing special in the code of Charondas except the trials for false witness	As for Charondas, there is nothing peculiar to him except the suits for false witness
1274b9	Φαλέου δ᾽ ἴδιον ἡ τῶν οὐσιῶν ἀνομάλωσις,	Characteristic of Phaleas is the equalization of property;	Peculiar to Phaleas is the measure for equalizing properties;	The feature peculiar to Phaleas is his equalization of possessions;
1274b16	ἴδιον δ᾽ ἐν τοῖς νόμοις οὐδὲν ἔστιν ὅ τι καὶ μνείας ἄξιον,	there is no peculiarity in them which is worth mentioning,	there is nothing peculiar in his laws which is worthy of mention,	There is nothing peculiar to them worth mentioning
1274b19	νόμος δ᾽ ἴδιος αὐτοῦ	he has a law which is peculiar to him,	a special law of his is that . . .	a law peculiar to him states . . .
1274b25	οὐ μὴν ἀλλὰ ἴδιόν γε οὐδὲν αὐτοῦ λέγειν ἔχοι τις ἄν.	but there is nothing remarkable in them.	however one cannot mention any provision that is peculiar to him.	but I cannot mention any point that is peculiar to them.

Source: The author.

Chapter 4

Assessment (*Timēma*)

In this chapter, I consider Aristotle's use of *timēma* in the *Politics*. I shall be concerned in particular with the translation of *timēma* by 'property qualification', or sometimes just 'qualification' for short, by which is intended an amount of property that qualifies certain people—a "census class"—for some desired role in society for which those who lack that amount of property are not eligible.[1] Translated this way, *timēma* might suggest a hurdle designed to exclude the poor from participation in an oligarchy. I shall suggest instead that the *timēma* is not about property and is not a qualification. Aristotle has in mind the result of a procedure for getting those who have had a successful period on their farms or in business to spend a certain amount of time in service to the city,

---

1. Thoughtful readers of these translations might suppose that Aristotle, when he speaks of the *timēma*, has in mind what we would speak of as landed property or perhaps monetary property, which could be inherited, and so a class or caste society with minimal social mobility, and that other authors have the same sort of thing in mind. This perspective shows up when, in translating *Resp.* 550D1, for example, Shorey renders "the poor man is excluded" where Socrates observes of the oligarchy simply that the poor man does not share in rule. See P. Shorey, *Plato: The Republic*, 2 vols. (London: William Heinemann, 1937). According to the *Oxford English Dictionary* online: "property qualification n. a qualification for office (e.g., as a member of parliament), or for the exercise of a right (e.g., that of voting), based on the possession of a certain amount of property." "Census class" goes back at least to Glotz's *classe censitaire*. G. Glotz, *Le Travail dans la Grèce ancienne* (Paris: Alcan, 1920), 204. Guía and Gallego suggest "capital" and even "declared capital" for *timēma*, but without giving a reason. M. V. Guía and J. Gallego, "Athenian *Zeugitai* and the Solonian Census Classes: New Reflections and Perspectives," *Historia: Zeitschrift für Alte Geschichte* 59 (2010): 273, especially n. 81.

perhaps unpaid, whether they want to or not, and some apparently did not want to, while relieving the poor of that responsibility so that they can improve their condition, in democracies, oligarchies, and mixtures. Thus the citizen of a Greek city would be likely to respond to *timēma* differently from the way one might react to 'property qualification', since the *timēma* could increase the citizen's responsibilities and costs even if it opened up opportunities for gaining honor, and it made the citizen liable to changes in social standing, both up and down.

'Property-qualification' and other compounds of 'property' are poor choices in any case. In 1968, Robin Harrison pointed out in his two-volume work *The Law of Athens*,[2] "Now not only had the Athenians no general term to describe the law of property; they had no abstract word for ownership."[3] It would seem, then, that one should be doubly cautious about using 'property' in translating or discussing the *Politics*, since ownership and property, as the *OED* reminds us, are mutually entailing. Some translators nonetheless persist in rendering *ktēma* by 'property', though Aristotle typically intends what we would mean by 'possession' and though 'property' in English has a different sense from 'possession' (see chapter 3). Briefly, as previously noted, we might possess something that is not our property if we have borrowed it or stolen it; or we might not possess our property because someone has borrowed it and has not given it back or perhaps has stolen it. If 'property' is an inadvisable rendering for *ktēma* in the *Politics*, 'property-qualification' and other compounds are not likely to be much better for *timēma*. The defects of 'qualification' will be treated later in connection with book 6.

The word *timēma* is formed from the same stem as *timē*, which indicates adjudged worth of some kind and even sometimes a position conceived as an honor, and *timaō*, which indicates making some sort of evaluation, as honoring or estimating a price; and from the root of *tiō*, which has the sense of *timaō* in older literature; and from the

---

2. A. R. W. Harrison, *The Law of Athens: Vol. 2, The Family and Property* (Oxford: Clarendon Press, 1968), 200–205. Also now, S. C. Todd and P. C. Millett, "Law, Society and Athens," in *Nomos: Essays in Athenian Law, Politics and Society*, ed. P. A. Cartledge, P. C. Millett, and S. C. Todd (Cambridge: Cambridge University Press, 1990), 5. Also the more extensive discussion by S. C. Todd, *The Shape of Athenian Law* (Oxford: Clarendon Press, 1993), which is critical of Harrison but ultimately inconclusive.

3. Harrison, *The Law of Athens*, 2: 201.

suffix -*mat*, which indicates the result of action. Thus 'assessment'—in the sense of the result of assessing—would be one good rendering in some cases.[4] The cognate *timēsis*, with the suffix -*si*, indicates the action itself—assessing; it is used three times in the *Politics*. The *timētēs* is an assessor. *Timēma* often occurs in the *Politics* without any word that gives the object of assessment, and so one must look further to see what is being assessed.

We may get a hint about what is being assessed from the *Politeia of the Athenians*, which is one of the preliminary studies for the *Politics*[5] but which had not been discovered when Jowett published his translation in 1885; Jowett's translation with its supplementary material helped to give the notion of a property qualification its currency in later work on the *Politics* (see table 4.1). In 7.3–4 of the historical part, the author says of Solon (trans. Rhodes modified):

> He divided it [the citizen body] by assessment into four classes, as it also had been divided before: the 500-*medimnos* class, the cavalry, the ox drivers, and the laborers. He distributed among the 500-*medimnos* class, the cavalry, and the ox drivers the major offices, such as the nine archons, the treasurers, the sellers of taxes, the eleven commissioners of police, and the paymasters, giving to each the rule proportional to the size of the assessment. To those registered in the laborers he gave only sharing in the assembly and the jury courts. [7.4] He was registered in the 500-*medimnos* class who made from his holdings 500 dry and liquid measures taken together, in the cavalry if it amounted to 300. . . . The ox drivers were those whose produce amounted to 200 measures in both kinds; the remainder belonged to the laborers and had no share in office holding. For this reason, even today (*kai nun*), when a candi-

---

4. H. Bonitz, *Index Aristotelicus* (Berlin: Walter de Gruyter, 1870), does not give a translation. D. F. Ast, *Lexicon Platonicum*, 3 vols. (Leipzig: Weidmann, 1835–1838), gives *aestimatio* and *census* with reference mainly to the *Republic* and *Laws*.

5. Whether this work was written by Aristotle or by one of his students has interested some scholars but will not be addressed here. Authorship then may not have worked quite the way it does today. The work was cited as Aristotelian in antiquity.

> date for allotment to any office is asked to which he belongs,
> no one will reply that he belongs to the laborers.[6]

Here the object of the assessment was the output of one's household or estate, in this case one's farm or farms, and the result was assignment to one or another pool from which one might be selected for offices. Property in our sense would not be in question, since the assessment does not include the whole estate, just its output over a defined period. Though referring to the early sixth century, this is the most explicit evidence we have in the corpus Aristotelicum for the object of the *timēma* in relation to appointment to office, and it is not controverted in the *Politics*.[7] Indeed, the author remarks on its continuing pertinence in his own day—something about which he was not likely to be mistaken—with the phrase *kai nun* (even today).

There were advantages to using direct measures of output such as *medimnoi* (fifty-five liters dry) for the *timēma*. They provided good evidence for how the farmers were doing currently, whereas acreage, for example, would be a less direct and less sensitive indicator, since the same farmers might produce more or less from their acreage in different years, and different farmers might produce more or less from the same acreage in the same year, as the Greeks knew by Hesiod's time. That the Greeks were able to deal with measures is clear from 53.2, where the

---

6. τιμήματι διεῖλεν εἰς τέτταρα τέλη,
    καθάπερ διήρητο καὶ πρότερον, εἰς πεντακοσιομέδιμνον
    καὶ ἱπ[πέα] καὶ ζευγίτην καὶ θῆτα. καὶ τὰς μὲ[ν ἄλλ]ας
    ἀρχὰς ἀπένειμεν ‖ ἄρχειν ἐκ πεντακοσιομεδίμνων καὶ ἱπ-
    πέων καὶ ζευγιτῶν, τοὺς ἐννέα ἄρχοντας καὶ τοὺς ταμίας (5)
    καὶ τοὺς πωλητὰς καὶ τοὺς ἔνδεκα καὶ τοὺς κωλακρέτας,
    ἑκάστοις ἀνάλογον τῷ μεγέθει τοῦ τιμήματος ἀποδιδοὺς
    τὴν ἀρχήν· τοῖς δὲ τὸ θητικὸν τελοῦσιν ἐκκλησίας καὶ
    (4) δικαστηρίων μετέδωκε μόνον. ἔδει δὲ τελεῖν πεντακοσιο-
    μέδιμνον μέν, ὃς ἂν ἐκ τῆς οἰκείας ποιῇ πεντακόσια μέτρα
    τὰ συνάμφω ξηρὰ καὶ ὑγρά, ἱππάδα δὲ τοὺς τριακόσια
    ποιοῦντας. . . . ζευγίσιον δὲ
    τελεῖν τοὺς διακόσια τὰ συνάμφω ποιοῦντας. τοὺς δ' ἄλ-
    λους θητικόν, οὐδεμιᾶς μετέχοντας ἀρχῆς. διὸ καὶ νῦν (15)
    ἐπειδὰν ἔρηται τὸν μέλλοντα κληροῦσθαί τιν' ἀρχήν, ποῖον
    τέλος τελεῖ, οὐδ' ἂν εἷς εἴποι θητικόν.

7. The description with the four is summarized in *Politics* 1274a18–21. Aristotle will use the language of dividing (*dihaireō*) in the *Politics* as well, though not in this summary.

author mentions the ten *metronomoi* or measure overseers at Athens, five in the upper city and five in the Peiraeus.[8] Although Gustave Glotz a century ago converted these direct measures to currency (drachmas), doing so is chancy, since the currency-denominated value of real output can change over time.[9] Further, wealth is not as good a basis for assessing one's condition as output is, since wealth can be hidden, as it was at Athens, especially as time went on.[10] Indeed, there were arguments about how wealthy different people were, especially when the city tried to force contributions from them.

In 8.1, the author says that the law on the treasurers is "a sign that he [Solon] made appointments by lot from the assessments, which remains in use even today." That is to say, once the assessments were made, people would be selected by lot from the resulting pools for offices. This second occurrence of "even today" (*kai nun*) suggests that Aristotle was indicating some continuity here. The author repeats in 47.1 that this law still (*eti*, perhaps)[11] was in force in late fourth-century Athens.

Some scholars have tried to discredit the *Politeia of the Athenians* as evidence for output as the object of the *timēma* and for the *timēma* as assessment in the fourth century, when the *Politics* was written. While Glotz, for example, conceded long ago that "Les distinctions établies par Solon parmi les citoyens eux-mêmes ne furent jamais abrogées par un texte formel. Officiellement, les classes censitaires existaient toujours," he then went on to say: "Peu à peu, presque sans lois nouvelles, par l'action combinée des forces économiques et politiques, le régime des classes se

---

8. On the technique for measuring grain, see R. S. Stroud, *The Athenian Grain-Tax Law of 374/3 B.C.* (Princeton: American School of Classical Studies at Athens, 1998). That different measures are used in wholesale and retail markets is suggested in *EN* 1135a1–3. Aristotle writes as if the well-to-do can be distinguished from the indigent from the rolls without difficulty, as one sees in 1297a24–29.

9. Glotz, *Le Travail dans la Grèce ancienne*, 204: "Pour les pentecosiomédimnes, le cens était fixé à cinq cents mesures ou, dans la pratique, à cinq cents drachmes," and so on. Glotz did not give a source. W. T. Loomis, *Wages, Welfare Costs, and Inflation in Classical Athens* (Ann Arbor: University of Michigan Press, 1998), treats mainly wage inflation; but see 2, n. 3, on price changes for wheat per *medimnos* around 330.

10. E. E. Cohen, *Athenian Economy and Society: A Banking Perspective* (Princeton: Princeton University Press, 1992), 193–194.

11. Chambers indicates that he is not completely certain of this reading. M. Chambers, ed., *Aristoteles Athenaion Politeia* (Stuttgart: B. G. Teubner, 1994).

tranforma."[12] It is well known that the laws of Solon were revised in the fifth and fourth centuries, though they still might be called the laws of Solon.[13] Guía and Gallego recently have done something similar to Glotz in suggesting that "the Solonian classes were remodeled in the new legal code of 403–399 (before the restructuring of 378) for the purpose of levying taxes, which established, on the basis of landownership, that those who produced more than 500 measures would be included in the *pentakosiomedimoi*, those between 300 and 500 measures, in the *hippeis*, and those between 200 and 300 measures, in the *zeugitai*" but that, after 403, "and particularly with the reorganization of the *eisphora* in 378, the Athenian census classes completely lost their political, military and fiscal role."[14] This is to confuse land ownership, if 'ownership' is the right

---

12. Glotz, *Le Travail dans la Grèce ancienne*, 204.

13. See, for example, K. Clinton, "The Nature of the Late Fifth-Century Revision of the Athenian Law Code," *Hesperia Supplements* 19 (1982): 27–37; also, P. J. Rhodes, "Athenian Democracy After 403 B.C.," *Classical Journal* 75 (1980): 305–323. Rhodes observes: "In the first half of the century the usual last resort was *eisphora*, a property tax levied on all who admitted to owning more than a certain amount" (311). The taxpayers' admission would not provide a very promising basis for a tax system—not nearly as promising as a measured amount of some commodity.

14. Guía and Gallego, "Athenian *Zeugitai* and the Solonian Census Classes," 271, 278. Guía and Gallego appear to take some of the conclusions of V. J. Rosivach, "The Requirements of the Solonic Classes in *AP* 7.4," *Hermes* 130 (2002): 36–47, at face value; but there are difficulties in the arguments. Rosivach, in an attempt to show that the pertinence of the four bodies and assessment of output had disappeared by Aristotle's day and that *timēma* might be translated by 'tax-assessment', argued that Aristotle's numbers must have been wrong. His argument was that the "evidence is contradictory," since it suggests both that the ox drivers were "part of the broad mass of the Athenian population" and that Aristotle's numbers and his assertion at 1274a18–21 make the ox drivers "part of the élite" (38). While Rosivach does not say what he is rendering by 'élite', he appears to have in mind the *gnōrimoi* and *euporoi* of 1274a18–21, which he apparently thinks of as the *plousioi*; but, as Ostwald has shown, Aristotle in the *Politics* distinguishes the *euporoi* from the *plousioi*. Ostwald, *Oligarchia*, 52–68. There need not be a contradiction here. Rosivach also argues that there is a conflict where Aristotle says that it is more reasonable to define the cavalry by the production of their farms than by the ability to raise horses and that these "conflicting inferences drawn from different kinds of evidence" provide "very good evidence that by Aristotle's day Solon's law defining membership in the hippic class no longer physically existed to be consulted" (39). But these two inferences need not conflict—some people, such as horse breeders, might think of a farmer in terms of his possessing horses while others, such as grain buyers, might think of the same farmer

word, with land output. Our question is whether there is any evidence in the *Politics* for a change in the object of *timēma* in connection with appointment to office.[15]

There are forty-six occurrences of *timēma* in the *Politics*, of which thirty-seven are in books 4 through 6, with five in book 2[16] and four in book 3.[17] Thus most of them are in discussions mainly of democracies and oligarchies and of the ways to make or keep them stable by avoiding or quelling *stasis* or internal war—the motive also behind Solon's division of the citizen body. *Timēma* is used in the *Politics* almost exclusively in describing entry into the *archai*—positions of initiative or command, often given as 'offices' or 'magistracies'—with the possible exception of 1318a37.[18]

In book 4, the main concentration of occurrences is in 1294b1–14—six of the sixteen occurrences in this book. Here Aristotle describes

---

in terms of the output of his farm. Further, Aristotle may have been commenting on usage here rather than on the law. And perhaps the law was common knowledge and didn't need to be mentioned. So the argument goes nowhere. Rosivach, in the space of a few pages, proceeds from his more cautious and probabilistic assertion about "very good evidence" to the stronger assertion that "the nature of the arguments in AP 7.4 makes the conclusion unavoidable that by Aristotle's day this particular law no longer existed to be consulted" (41) and then to the categorical "the actual law defining membership in the classes was itself, for whatever reason, lost" (46). But *a posse ad esse non valet consequentia.* And then he must deal with "scattered references to these [census] classes in Athenian public life late into the fourth century and probably to the end of the democracy" (41). Among these is the speech of Isaeus on Apollodorus in the middle of the century, where Rosivach renders "declared a small amount of property for tax-assessment" (44) when the Greek gives only "registered a small assessment" in connection with being placed in the cavalry pool for offices.

15. The *Politeia of the Athenians* illustrates other contexts in which *timēma* was used in the later fourth century. The text at 39.6 has to do with the aftermath of the Thirty, 48.4 with examination of accounts, and 53.1 with private suits; but none of them is clear on the object of the *timēma.*

16. The five in book 2 occur in a discussion of the *Laws.*

17. The four in book 3 are part of the discussion of citizenship.

18. A *timēma* is associated with the position one may be required to assume. It apparently was thought that people should be required to assume the most demanding positions they were capable of discharging given their current resources, though sometimes they might not want to assume these positions because doing so would be a drain on their resources. There was the matter of avoiding liturgies and trierarchies, of taking an oath to avoid financial responsibility, and of avoiding offices that carried risk but no financial gain. Aristotle associates the dignity of the office with the amount of the *timēma.*

his second and third ways of mixing democracy and oligarchy to avoid *stasis* (trans. Robinson):

> (2) Another way is to take the middle between what they [the democracy and the oligarchy] both ordain. Thus to sit in the Assembly no assessment or a very small one is required by the one side [the democracy], but a great assessment by the other [the oligarchy]. The joint thing is to require neither of these, but the middle assessment.
>
> (3) A third is, given two sets of ordinances, to take some from the oligarchic law and some from the democratic. I mean, for example, it is thought democratic to appoint officers by lot and oligarchic to do it by election. It is also thought democratic not to require an assessment, and oligarchic to require one [an assessment]. It is aristocratic and 'constitutional', therefore, to take one from each, making the officers elected as in oligarchy but without assessment as in democracy. Such is the mode of mixture.[19]

Although it is not obvious from the translation, the genitive singular of *timēma* with *apo* occurs in five of the six occurrences here.[20] This phrase

---

19. ἕτερος δὲ τὸ ≤τὸ≥ μέσον λαμβάνειν ὧν ἑκάτεροι τάττουσιν, οἷον ἐκκλησιάζειν οἱ μὲν ἀπὸ τιμήματος
οὐθενὸς ἢ μικροῦ πάμπαν, οἱ δ' ἀπὸ μακροῦ τιμήματος, κοινὸν δέ γε οὐδέτερον, ἀλλὰ τὸ μέσον ἑκατέρου τίμημα τού- (5)
των. τρίτον δ' ἐκ δυοῖν ταγμάτοιν, τὰ μὲν ἐκ τοῦ ὀλιγαρ-
χικοῦ νόμου τὰ δ' ἐκ τοῦ δημοκρατικοῦ. λέγω δ' οἷον δοκεῖ
δημοκρατικὸν μὲν εἶναι τὸ κληρωτὰς εἶναι τὰς ἀρχάς, τὸ
δ' αἱρετὰς ὀλιγαρχικόν, καὶ δημοκρατικὸν μὲν τὸ μὴ ἀπὸ
τιμήματος, ὀλιγαρχικὸν δὲ τὸ ἀπὸ τιμήματος· ἀριστοκρα- (10)
τικὸν τοίνυν καὶ πολιτικὸν τὸ ἐξ ἑκατέρας ἑκάτερον λαβεῖν,
ἐκ μὲν τῆς ὀλιγαρχίας τὸ αἱρετὰς ποιεῖν τὰς ἀρχάς, ἐκ δὲ
τῆς δημοκρατίας τὸ μὴ ἀπὸ τιμήματος.
> ὁ μὲν οὖν τρόπος τῆς (13)
μίξεως οὗτος·

Robinson is unusual in using "assessment" fairly consistently. His break with tradition is explained in part by his having "always composed a version of each of Aristotle's sentences before looking at the version of any other translator." Robinson, *Aristotle's Politics: Books III and IV*, xxx.

20. It occurs nine times in the *Politics*, while the genitive plural occurs with *apo* ten times.

is formulaic with Aristotle in both the singular and the plural and means from assessment(s) or on the basis of assessment(s). Getting people to serve from assessment is contrasted with other ways of getting people to serve—from family connection or from membership in a political club or because of virtue (1292b5, 1298b3–4, 1300a16–17, 1305b31–32). Thus the *timēma* is only one basis for pools for office in the cities Aristotle knew; there were others, and the *timēma* was distinctive.

Book 4 also adverts repeatedly to acquisition of the assessment and its consequences. Addressing one kind of democracy, in 1291b39–41, Aristotle observes that it is necessary for someone acquiring (*ktōmenōi*) [the assessment] to be allowed to share [perhaps in the offices] and for someone who loses it not to share. Going on to the first kind of oligarchy, in 1292a39–41, he says that, based on the assessments, the indigent will not be allowed to share, but anyone who acquires (*ktōmenōi*) [the assessment] shares in the citizenship. In 1292b29–30, he observes that it is allowed for the others (along with those with productive farms) to share whenever they acquire (*ktēsōntai*) the assessment defined by the laws. He expands on this in 1297a19–21, observing that, with respect to oligarchies, those who have (*echousi*) the assessment are not allowed to decline office by oath, but those without resources are. In 1297b1–3, Aristotle says (trans. Robinson): "The political community [probably the citizen body] should consist of those who have heavy arms only. On the other hand, it is not possible to define absolutely the amount of the assessment that a man should have." At this point Aristotle indicates how the assessment should be set, giving guidelines for a procedure that will achieve its aim in different circumstances. In 1298a34–40, in treating oligarchies where some of the citizens make all of the decisions, he observes that one who acquires (*ktōmenōi*) the assessment is allowed to participate, perhaps in the council. Aristotle uses the phrase 'acquire the *timēma*' in four of the seven occurrences of the accusative singular in the *Politics*. Thus acquiring and losing the assessment play important parts in his account, which suggests that the changes could be frequent.

In book 5 the key passages are 1306b6–14 and 1308a35–b10. In the former passage, which includes three of the twelve occurrences in this book, we might illustrate Aristotle's argument this way: Suppose that the division of the citizen body by assessment associated with pools for offices was set, as in the *Politeia of the Athenians*, at five hundred, three hundred, and two hundred *medimnoi* of farm output for the upper three pools. That division organizes the citizens in four groups with respect to selection for office and assures that the appropriate people are in the pools and the others not, so that, in Solon's case, the agrarian democracy is maintained by mixing it with an oligarchic element—a high assessment for the high offices. But if there follows a period of peace instead of the usual war, the farms become more productive and some of the now more prosperous farmers (except those at the top) are ratcheted up a notch or two at the next assessment, and perhaps some of the fourth body acquire the lowest assessment. As Aristotle says, the same possessions—farm output in this illustration—become worth a much higher assessment, so that everyone shares in all [the pools for offices]. A similar sort of reconstruction would work with an economy that has shifted further away from agriculture to industry and trade as long as it associates different assessments with different pools for offices, though it seems that most Greeks still were engaged in agriculture in the fourth century.

In the latter passage, which includes four more of the twelve occurrences in book 5, Aristotle says:

> With respect to the change from oligarchy and the mixture's coming about because of the assessment: whenever this happens with the [levels of] assessment remaining the same while the money supply has increased (*euporias nomismatos gignomenēs*), it is advantageous to look over the amount of the new[21] assessment in relation to the past. In some cities they are assessed annually based on this [annual] period, in other larger cities they are assessed every three or five years; and if the assessment is much greater or much smaller than it was when they set up the [levels for] assessments of the citizen body, it is the law to tighten or loosen the [levels for] assessments—if it is greater, tightening [the assessment] according to the magnitude of the increase, and if it is smaller, loosening and making the [levels for] assessment less. In the oligarchies and mixtures if they do not make it so, it will happen thus: in the one case [if the money supply declines] it happens that an oligarchy or dynasty

---

21. Reading *kainou* with Dreizehnter following Coraes. A. Dreizehnter, *Aristoteles' Politik* (Munich: Wilhelm Fink, 1970). Keyt claims to have translated Dreizehnter's text in his Clarendon version and to have departed from it in only five places; he departs from it here ("total amount . . . of the community" = *koinou* with Ross rather than "new assessment" = *kainou* with Dreizehnter) but does not list this instance. D. Keyt, *Aristotle Politics: Books V and VI* (Oxford: Clarendon Press, 1999), xvii.

comes into being [from a mixture], in the other [if the money supply increases] from a mixture comes a democracy or from an oligarchy comes a mixture or a democracy.[22]

An expansion of the money supply, as Cohen points out, could occur through the banks.[23]

Jowett probably was approximately correct in suggesting: "The object is to preserve the same number of qualified [I would say assessed] persons [for each pool], when the wealth [I would say output] of a city has increased or diminished."[24] So, for example, if output across the city increases, more will have the five hundred–*medimnos* assessment from the former three hundred–*medimnos* group, and the three hundred–*medimnos* group will have more from the former two hundred–*medimnos* group. The number of *thetes* will shrink accordingly, all other things being equal. The resulting imbalance, which would put more people into the top pool, can be forestalled by raising the levels of assessment to fit the increase, say to six hundred, four hundred, and three hundred. Raising the levels of assessment will keep the pool at the top from growing disproportionately

---

22. πρὸς δὲ τὴν διὰ τὰ τιμήματα γιγνομένην (35)
μεταβολὴν ἐξ ὀλιγαρχίας καὶ πολιτείας, ὅταν συμβαίνῃ
τοῦτο μενόντων μὲν τῶν αὐτῶν τιμημάτων εὐπορίας δὲ
νομίσματος γιγνομένης, συμφέρει τοῦ τιμήματος ἐπισκο-
πεῖν τοῦ κοινοῦ τὸ πλῆθος πρὸς τὸ παρελθόν, ἐν ὅσαις μὲν
πόλεσι τιμῶνται κατ' ἐνιαυτόν, κατὰ τοῦτον τὸν χρόνον, (40)
(1308b) ἐν δὲ ταῖς μείζοσι διὰ τριετηρίδος ἢ πενταετηρίδος, κἂν ᾖ
πολλαπλάσιον ἢ πολλοστημόριον τοῦ πρότερον, ἐν ᾧ αἱ τι-
μήσεις κατέστησαν τῆς πολιτείας, νόμον εἶναι καὶ τὰ τιμήματα ἐπιτείνειν ἢ ἀνιέναι, ἐὰν μὲν ὑπερβάλλῃ, ἐπιτείνον-
τας κατὰ τὴν πολλαπλασίωσιν, ἐὰν δ' ἐλλείπῃ, ἀνιέντας
καὶ ἐλάττω ποιοῦντας τὴν τίμησιν. ἐν μὲν γὰρ ταῖς ὀλιγαρ-
χίαις καὶ ταῖς πολιτείαις, μὴ ποιούντων [μὲν] οὕτως ἔνθα
μὲν ὀλιγαρχίαν ἔνθα δὲ δυναστείαν γίνεσθαι συμβαίνει,
ἐκείνως δὲ ἐκ μὲν πολιτείας δημοκρατίαν, ἐκ δ' ὀλιγαρχίας πολιτείαν ἢ δῆμον.

23. Cohen, *Athenian Economy and Society*, 12–14; "the fifth century had seen a revolutionary expansion in liquid wealth," 153. See also R. Thomsen, *Eisphora* (Copenhagen: Glydendalske Boghandel, 1965), 32, on the "great rise in prices since Solon."

24. Jowett, *The Politics of Aristotle*, 2: 1, 210.

large. The result is tighter, in a sense, since it assigns fewer people than otherwise to the high-output pools. Mutatis mutandis for the opposite case. Aristotle's use of plurals here suggests multiple assessments or a system of assessments.

That Aristotle does not think of the *timēma* as a qualification to exclude the poor or indigent to their detriment also comes out in this book. The point of the assessment is rather to identify those who currently have the resources that will permit them to devote some of their time to the city and to excuse, rather than to exclude, those who lack these resources, so that they will be able to improve their own condition. After all, as Aristotle says, "They are glad if someone allows them the leisure to look to their affairs (*pros tois idiois*, the affairs of their households)" (1308b35–36). He goes on after a few lines to expatiate: "Those who are indigent will not wish to rule and gain nothing by it, but rather to deal with their own things (*pros tois idiois*), but the well-to-do will be able because they need nothing from the common pool. So that it will come about that the indigent will become well-to-do by spending their time at their tasks, and the notables will not be ruled by any chance people" (1309a4–9). He then suggests a number of measures so that "estates [*ousiai*] may be more nearly even and more of the indigent will achieve plenty" (1309a25–26). In book 6, he will observe that, instead of distributing the excess to those without resources, "It is necessary for the true friend of the people to see how the multitude may not be too much without resources" (1320a33–34).

Three of the nine occurrences in book 6 can be found in 1320b22–30, where Aristotle, in discussing the preservation of oligarchies, begins with the first or most moderate oligarchy, saying:

> This is near the so-called mixture [of oligarchy and democracy], in which it is necessary [for the statesman] to divide the assessments, making some less and some greater, from the less of which they share in the necessary offices, from the greater of which [they share in] the more commanding ones. [It is necessary] for anyone who acquires the assessment to share in the citizenship, such a multitude of the [formerly] poor being introduced because of the assessment that they [those who share] will be stronger than the ones who don't share. But, always, it is necessary to introduce the better group of the

[formerly] poor. Likewise for the next oligarchy it is necessary in preparing it to tighten a little.[25]

Here Aristotle uses both the language of dividing (*dihaireō*), which was used in the *Politeia of the Athenians*, and the language of tightening (*epiteinō*) used in book 5. He comes back at 1320b25–26 to the point made in book 4 about acquiring the *timēma* in treating appointment to office with respect to the preservation of oligarchies, noting that someone who acquires (*ktōmenōi*) the assessment is allowed to share in the citizenship;[26] and in 1321a28, he asserts that a share in the regime is to be given to those who acquire the *timēma*.

What can one take away from reviewing these occurrences of *timēma*?

1. In the *Politics*, Aristotle continues to associate the distinctive *timēma* with appointment to office. He has in mind a procedure for putting people in pools for office, from which they might be selected by lot (1298b21–23 and 4.15), and for leaving them out of these pools, rather than a definite quantity of possessions.

2. This procedure is assessment. The assessment is carried out frequently, sometimes as frequently as annually, and its object is the output (or income) realized in the assessment period rather than, for example, the anticipated selling price of a family holding.

---

25. αὕτη δ' ἐστὶν ἡ σύνεγγυς τῇ καλουμένῃ πολιτείᾳ, <ἐν> ᾗ δεῖ τὰ
    τιμήματα διαιρεῖν, τὰ μὲν ἐλάττω τὰ δὲ μείζω ποιοῦντας,
    ἐλάττω μὲν ἀφ' ὧν τῶν ἀναγκαίων μεθέξουσιν ἀρχῶν,
    μείζω δ' ἀφ' ὧν τῶν κυριωτέρων· τῷ τε κτωμένῳ τὸ τί- (25)
    μημα μετέχειν ἐξεῖναι τῆς πολιτείας, τοσούτου εἰσαγομένου
    τοῦ δήμου πλήθους διὰ τοῦ τιμήματος μεθ' οὗ κρείττονες ἔσον-
    ται τῶν μὴ μετεχόντων· ἀεὶ δὲ δεῖ παραλαμβάνειν ἐκ τοῦ
    βελτίονος δήμου τοὺς κοινωνούς. ὁμοίως δὲ καὶ τὴν ἐχομένην
    ὀλιγαρχίαν ἐπιτείνοντας δεῖ μικρὸν κατασκευάζειν.

26. When Aristotle uses the present of *ktaōmai*, acquire, with *timēma* as its object, he apparently is pointing to cases in which people who did not meet the assessment at one point came to meet it later. Translators, as Sinclair-Saunders at 1321a28, sometimes use "possess" instead of 'acquire', which may obscure Aristotle's apparent point. 'Possess' would be more appropriate with a perfect ('have acquired' = 'possess') than with a present.

3. It was expected that, since output (or income) could change from year to year as the amount of land possessed might not, people could change pools or enter them or drop out, which would adjust their responsibilities and costs in the immediate future to the resources they currently had available.

4. It was recommended that the *timēmata* be changed as the money supply changed so as to maintain stability in the regime and the citizen body; if the *timēmata* changed in the same ratio as the money supply, more of the same people would be more likely to remain in the same pools for office, all other things staying equal, and the city would be more stable.

5. The *timēma* is contrasted with family membership and club membership as a source of citizens to be appointed to office; it is contrasted also with virtue.

Finally, against thinking of the *timēma* as if it were a tax: it should be noted that, while the *timēma* is not a tax, when the Athenians did tax, they tended not to use direct taxes on what we would call property;[27] they used excise taxes on transactions such as retail sales and duties on, for example, imports. The *eisphora* was the exception, and it apparently was less a tax than a forced contribution, since the criteria on which it was levied appear to have been unstable. The Athenians became practiced at measuring goods bought and sold, for which they had a bureaucracy, and perhaps they used self-assessments of the citizens or records of goods bought and sold, and perhaps both, in carrying out the *timēma*.

In any case, there is no suggestion in the *Politics* that the *timēma* consists in property, possessions, or capital, since Aristotle does not say what the object of the *timēma* is, though he does continue to associate it with appointment to office. In particular, Aristotle does not indicate that he is not thinking of agricultural output any longer. Thomsen has argued that there must have been "city-states where the *eisphora* was charged on

---

27. Thomsen, *Eisphora*, 11: "It was, in fact, considered irreconcilable with a citizen's dignity that taxes should be levied on his person, his income, or his capital." See now M. R. Christ, "The Evolution of the *Eisphora* in Classical Athens," *Classical Quarterly* 57 (2007): 53–69.

income, and where the citizens did not declare their fortune, but their annual income as a basis on which the tax was levied."[28] At one point (1292b23–30; see also 1318b9–10, 1319a4–6), Aristotle suggests that the agricultural citizens still make the best democracy because the law rules, though he compares others who acquire the *timēma* with them.

Scholars who look to the *Politics* for a new object for *timēma* in the fourth century may be confused by what has been learned about the development of the *eisphora* in Athens, our picture of which, however, still is incomplete. They sometimes may forget that, in books 4 through 6, Aristotle's intended audience is not limited to Athenians,[29] and he is not talking only about Athens nor only about his own age. In these books Aristotle is talking to a variety of people about many other places—Chalcis, Eretria, Magnesia, Apollonia, Thera, Colophon, Tarentum, Byzantium, Aegina, Chios, Tenedos, Carthage, Sparta, Malis, Miletus, Megara, Epidamnus, Argos, Rhodes, Thebes, Syracuse, Heraea, Sybaris, Thurii, Zancle, Clazomenae, Hestiaea, Delphi, Mytilene, Phocis, Cos, Cyme, Massalia, Istros, Heraclea, Cnidos, Erythrae, Larissa, Abydos, Amphipolis, Pharsalus, Elis, Corinth, Locri, Leontini, Gela, Rhegium, Mantinea, and Cyrene—and other times as well.

It seems, then, that in the *Politics*, as in the *Politeia of the Athenians*, when it is connected with appointment to office, the *timēma* is an assessment and that it does not have to do with property and is not a qualification. Almost as common as property qualifications in discussions of Aristotle is the appearance of property rights and other rights. The next chapter focuses on the language that some have supposed suggests a theory of rights in Aristotle.

---

28. Thomsen, *Eisphora*, 44.

29. J. J. Mulhern, "The *Aristē Politeia* and Aristotle's Intended Audience in the *Politica*," *Polis* 24 (2007): 297.

Table 4.1. Translations of *Timēma* in Aristotle's *Politics*

Bekker number	Jowett 1885 w/note indices[1]	Barker 1948	Robinson 1962	Sinclair-Saunders 1981	Reeve 2017
nom. & acc. sing. 1282a39	property	property qualification	property-qualification	property-qualifications	property assessment
1283a17	tax(-payers)	tax(payers)	taxable property	taxable property	assessed property
1292b30	qualification	property-qualification	assessment	property	property assessment
1294b5	property qualification	not trans.	assessment	assessment	assessment
1297a20	property	property qualification	ratable property	property-qualification	assessed amount of property
1298a39	qualification	property qualification	assessment	property level	assessed amount
1303a23	qualification	property qualification		property-qualification	property assessment
1306b9	qualification 5.6.17	property qualification		qualification	assessment
1318a33	qualification	property		property-assessment	assessed property
1318a37	qualifications	property		property-assessment	property assessment
1320b25	qualification	sufficient property to be put on an assessment roll		assessment of property	qualifying property

Bekker number	Jowett 1885 w/note indices[1]	Barker 1948	Robinson 1962	Sinclair-Saunders 1981	Reeve 2017
1321a28	property qualification	sufficient property to put him on the assessment roll		property-qualification	assessed amount of property
nom. & acc. pl. 1308a35	qualification 5.8.10	assessment connected with the requirement of a property qualification		property-qualifications	property assessments
1308b3	qualification	assessments		property-qualifications	assessment
1318a12	qualification 6.3.1	assessed properties		property-qualifications	assessed property
1320b23	qualification	sufficient property to be put on an assessment roll		property-qualifications	property assessments
dat. sing. 1300a16	property qualification	not trans.	assessment	property-group	property assessment
gen. sing. 1266a15	class 2.6.20	assessment class		property- class	property assessment class
1266a19	class	assessment class		property-class	assessment class
1294b3	property qualification	property qualification	assessment	property-qualification	property assessment

continued on next page

Table 4.1. Continued.

Bekker number	Jowett 1885 w/note indices[1]	Barker 1948	Robinson 1962	Sinclair-Saunders 1981	Reeve 2017
1294b4	not trans.	qualification	assessment	property-assessment	property assessment
1294b10	property qualification	property qualification	assessment	property-qualification	property assessment
1294b10	not trans.	not trans.	not trans.	property-qualification	not trans.
1294b13	qualification	property qualification	assessment	property-qualification	property assessment
1297b2	property qualification	qualification	assessment	property-qualification	property assessment
1298a37	qualification	property qualification	assessment	property-qualification	assessment
1306b8	money qualification	property qualification		property-qualification	property assessment
1306b13	property	assessed value		assessment	value
1307a28	qualification 5.7.9	property qualification		property-qualification	property assessment
1308a38	qualification 5.8.10	property qualification		valuation	assessment
1317b22	property qualification	property qualification		property qualification	property assessment

Bekker number	Jowett 1885 w/note indices[1]	Barker 1948	Robinson 1962	Sinclair-Saunders 1981	Reeve 2017
1320b27	qualification	not trans.		assessment	qualifying property
gen. pl. 1266a13	classes	assessments		property-classes	property assessment
1266a21	incomes	assessments		property-classes	assessment classes
1266b23	qualification				
2.7.7	qualification		property-classes	assessment classes	
1278a23	qualification	property qualification	assessments	property-qualifications	property assessments
1282a30	property qualification	property	property	property-qualifications	property assessments
1291b39	property qualification	property qualification	property qualifications	property-qualification	property assessments
1292a39	property qualification	property-qualification	property-qualification	property-qualification	property assessment
1292b1	qualification	property-qualification	property-qualification	property-qualification	assessment
1298a36	qualification	property qualification	assessments	property-qualification	property assessments
1305a30	property qualification	property qualification		property-classes	property assessments
1305b32	qualification	properties		property-qualification	property assessments

continued on next page

Table 4.1. Continued.

Bekker number	Jowett 1885 w/note indices[1]	Barker 1948	Robinson 1962	Sinclair-Saunders 1981	Reeve 2017
1308a37	qualification	property qualification		valuation	assessments
1318b31	qualification	property qualification		property-qualification	assessed property
1318b31	qualification	property qualification		property	property assessments

1. In the volume of notes (volume 2, part 1) published with his translation, Jowett used book, chapter, and division rather than Bekker lines to index the notes. He did not include *timēma* in the Greek index to the notes.

Source: The author.

Chapter 5

Making Claims (*Amphisbētēsis, Enklēma*, etc.)

The notion of a right does not enjoy in Aristotle's *Politics* and in his other works anything like the prominence that it has in modern theories of rights or in modern political rhetoric. Some scholars, including Martin Ostwald[1] and Malcolm Schofield,[2] have found it best to dispense with the language of rights almost entirely in their treatment of Aristotle and to anchor their treatment instead on sharing in the city or in citizenship. Their position has incontrovertible textual support. Other scholars, however, notably Fred D. Miller, Jr., have tried to show not only that Aristotle had a notion of a right, which Miller at least sometimes identifies as a just claim,[3] but also that this notion of a right was basic to Aristotle's work on ethics and politics. Since recent scholars have learned much from both sides, it is likely that there is some truth in both of them. My purpose in this chapter is, if possible, to draw it out.

Some progress on this question can be made by considering the way Aristotle and other Greeks made claims or spoke of making them. It probably will be more enlightening, after all, to talk about rights construed as claims in this context if we can get clearer about claims and claiming and how they worked for the Greeks. This approach is different

---

1. M. Ostwald, "Shares and Rights: 'Citizenship' Greek Style and American Style," in *Demokratia: A Conversation on Democracies, Ancient and Modern*, ed. J. Ober and C. Hedrick (Princeton: Princeton University Press, 1996), 49–61, especially 55–57.

2. Schofield, "Sharing in the Constitution," 831–839.

3. F. D. Miller, Jr., *Nature, Justice, and Rights in Aristotle's Politics* (Oxford: Clarendon Press, 1995), 97.

from the usual one, which proceeds as if the question could be decided in the main by finding or failing to find a word or phrase in Aristotle that might be translated more or less plausibly by 'right'. It is different also in giving more than the usual weight to nondescriptive meaning. Although some studies along word-substitution lines have been informative, the question goes beyond simply devising a translation that passes muster *salva veritate* to finding out whether the Greek discussion tended to produce the same impression as discussions containing the English 'right' or its counterparts in other languages tend to produce in the modern reader. Devising a translation theorem is not the same as capturing the impressions that words make.

Aristotle's discussion of the making of claims apparently follows earlier usage. It includes not only nouns such as *amphisbētēsis* (claim) and *enklēma* (claim or complaint) but also, prominently, cognate and other verbs such as *amphisbēteō* (lay claim to, with the genitive), *axioō* (make a claim, with several constructions), *enkaleō* (demand as one's due), and *nemō* (allocate, as to oneself in the middle voice); these at least are their senses in some contexts. Context helps to clarify both what is said and what is not said, and in this chapter it will be necessary to look at several extended passages.

Before looking at Aristotle's treatment of claims and claiming, it will be useful to consider both Thucydides and Lysias as representatives of earlier usage. Thucydides, in his history, provides a third-person report of the claims and counterclaims that cities made against one another during the great war of Greek against Greek. Lysias, in his speeches, presents first-person examples of the making of claims in the courts at Athens that followed the outrages committed in the years around the end of this war. It will appear that, while both authors recognize that some claims may be just, neither author treats the notion of a just claim as a simple or basic notion in the way that some modern writers tend to treat the notion of a right. Nor does their language for making claims have the emotive force that one often finds in modern assertions of rights.

Thucydides (ca. 460–ca. 400)

An informative passage in Thucydides about the making of claims appears in 5.41.1–2, where he is reporting on the summer of the twelfth year of the war concerning a long-standing difference of the Spartans with the

Argives about the disposition of a border land. In the background is the attempt that is being made to put in place a treaty that would call for fifty years of peace. Here Thucydides describes a somewhat complicated exchange that illustrates the making of claims and the language associated with it (in bold).

> On their arrival their [the Argives'] envoys made proposals to the Lacedaemonians as to the terms on which the treaty should be concluded. At first the Argives **claimed** that they should be allowed to submit to the arbitration of some city or private person the matter of the Cynurian territory—a district containing the towns of Thyrea and Anthene and **occupied** [allocated to themselves] by the Lacedaemonians—which being border ground they were always **disputing** [making claims against one another] about. Afterwards, however, although the Lacedaemonians would not permit them to make mention of that district, but said that, if they wished to make a treaty on the same terms as before, they were ready to do so, the Argive envoys did induce the Lacedaemonians to agree to the following terms: for the present that a treaty should be made for fifty years; that, however, either Lacedaemon or Argos, provided there were at the time neither pestilence nor war in either place, **might** [would be allowed to] challenge the other to decide by battle the question about this territory—just as once before, when each **had claimed** to be victorious—but pursuit **must not** [would not be allowed to] **be made** beyond the boundaries, between Argos and Lacedaemon.[4]

---

4. The translation, with modifications in brackets, is that of C. F. Smith, *Thucydides* (Cambridge: Harvard University Press, 1919; repr. 1962). The text is that of H. S. Jones and J. E. Powell, *Thucydidis historiae*, 2 vols. (Oxford: Clarendon Press, 1: 1942, 1st ed. rev.; 2: 1942, 2nd ed. rev.; repr. 1: 1970; 2: 1967). Retrieved from http://stephanus.tlg.uci.edu.proxy.library.upenn.edu/Iris/Cite?0003:001:0.

(1) καὶ οἱ πρέσβεις ἀφικόμενοι αὐτῶν
λόγους ἐποιοῦντο πρὸς τοὺς Λακεδαιμονίους ἐφ' ᾧ ἂν σφίσιν
(2) αἱ σπονδαὶ γίγνοιντο. καὶ τὸ μὲν πρῶτον οἱ Ἀργεῖοι ἠξίουν
δίκης ἐπιτροπὴν σφίσι γενέσθαι ἢ ἐς πόλιν τινὰ ἢ ἰδιώτην
περὶ τῆς Κυνουρίας γῆς, ἧς αἰεὶ πέρι διαφέρονται μεθορίας
οὔσης (ἔχει δὲ ἐν αὐτῇ Θυρέαν καὶ Ἀνθήνην πόλιν, νέμονται

This passage includes several expressions connected with the making of claims that might bear on the way the Greeks thought and responded. The initial claim reported here is made with the verb *axioō*. What is claimed is some decision—an arbitration (*epitropēn*) on the Cynurian territory, about which the Argives and the Lacedaemonians were always disputing or differing (*diapherontai*). The Lacedaemonians currently occupied it (allocated or claimed it for themselves, *nemontai*), and the Argives were urging a procedure to advance their counterclaim. The Lacedaemonians could not have occupied all of this territory uniformly, since there were not enough of them to do so, and so 'occupy' is an overtranslation, if we have in mind modern armies of occupation; but they could claim it for themselves by fortifying a few key positions—subject, of course, to successful counterattack. The uncertainty of the Spartan claim is reflected when, as the treaty is being made, the parties agree that each might be allowed (*exeinai*)[5] to challenge the other to do battle for the territory again to decide who owns it, though the previous battle had been less than decisive, since each side had claimed (*ēxiōsan*) the victory, presumably because neither had won it in a decisive way. And even in the foreseen battle they will not be allowed (*mē exeinai*) to carry forays into adjacent lands.

A key point to note in reading this passage is that the making of the claims to this territory does not give any hint of what either the protagonists or the historian thought about the merit of the claims. The language of Thucydides does not embed any information about or any attitude toward the legitimacy or justice of the claim in the making of the claim.

In modern English, by contrast, when rights are in question, the merit of the claim typically is asserted in the making of it, as in claims of the

---

δ' αὐτὴν Λακεδαιμόνιοι) ἔπειτα δ' οὐκ ἐώντων Λακεδαιμονίων (5)
μεμνῆσθαι περὶ αὐτῆς, ἀλλ᾽, εἰ βούλονται σπένδεσθαι ὥσπερ
πρότερον, ἕτοιμοι εἶναι, οἱ Ἀργεῖοι πρέσβεις τάδε ὅμως
ἐπηγάγοντο τοὺς Λακεδαιμονίους ξυγχωρῆσαι, ἐν μὲν τῷ
παρόντι σπονδὰς ποιήσασθαι ἔτη πεντήκοντα, ἐξεῖναι δ'
ὁποτεροισοῦν προκαλεσαμένοις, μήτε νόσου οὔσης μήτε (10)
πολέμου Λακεδαίμονι καὶ Ἄργει, διαμάχεσθαι περὶ τῆς γῆς
ταύτης, ὥσπερ καὶ πρότερόν ποτε ὅτε αὐτοὶ ἑκάτεροι ἠξίωσαν
νικᾶν, διώκειν δὲ μὴ ἐξεῖναι περαιτέρω τῶν πρὸς Ἄργος καὶ
(3) Λακεδαίμονα ὅρων.

5. Miller, *Nature, Justice, and Rights in Aristotle's Politics*, 106, includes this verb among the four that he suggests correspond to the four senses of 'right' in Hohfeld. Clearly, though, Thucydides has nothing like Hohfeld in mind.

form 'I have a right to x (or φ),' where the claim might be a claim either to have something or to do something. Locutions of this kind often are expected to create a presumption in favor of the claim. But Thucydides' language doesn't even try to link the claim and its merit to one another. So the language here does not suggest that the claim is just, much less that it is just without regard to circumstances. The Greek experience was that claims, whatever their merit, would be made and supported in any way they could be. If an argument could be made that a claim was based on justice, the claimant might well make it or try to make it, even though the Greeks had a great deal of difficulty saying what justice is, or rather had too many ways of saying what justice is, as one can see in the first four books of the *Republic.* But claims might be made on other grounds as well. Or it might be agreed that force alone should be allowed to prevail. Here one can see something that endures in Greek language and thought—that the making of the claims is quite separate from the support adduced for those claims. No claim carries its own support with it. No claim is, as a claim, intrinsically just or unjust, warranted or unwarranted, a right or a nonright. Indeed, there seems to be no verb for making a just claim. Certainly *dikazō* typically is not used this way. Although in the passive *dikazō* may be used for having a claim made against one, and in the middle it may be used for making a claim on one's own behalf, in the active it is used simply for deciding or giving judgment; and in none of these instances does it suggest grounds for the claim or decision—for example, that the claim is just.

Lysias (ca. 458–ca. 386)

If Thucydides reported speeches that use *axioō* and *nemō* and other expressions for the making of claims, Lysias, in his speechwriting, left us examples of the first-person use of *axioō* and *amphisbēteō* in the required sense as well as examples of *enkaleō*—a verb that Thucydides also used (cf., e.g., 4.123.1–2).

Lysias 17 "On the Goods of Eraton," which is a speech before a court, illustrates the speaker's attempt to recover money that his grandfather had lent to Eraton. The speaker's father had gone to court against one of the sons of Eraton, named Erasistratus. Despite a favorable ruling, however, other descendants of Eraton tried to hold on to what they had, which, after some time, was seized for deposit in the Athenian treasury.

The speaker now is suing the treasury to get back part of the estate. The following lines appear in the speech:

> [5] But now let me tell you how I have treated you, as distinct from private persons, in the conduct of this **dispute**. As long as the relatives of Erasiphon **were contesting** this property [these things], I **claimed** the whole as mine, because Erasistratus lost his case when he pleaded against my father's suit for the whole debt; and for the last three years I have let out the property at Sphettus, but over the property at Cicynna and the house there **I was at law** with the occupiers. Last year, however, they got my suit quashed by alleging that they were sea-traders; but at present, although I was permitted to bring proceedings in the month of Gamelion, the nautical court has not decided the case.
>
> [6] Now that you have seen fit to confiscate the property of Erasiphon, I relinquish two-thirds to the State and **claim** that the property of Erasistratus be adjudged to me, because it is this property that your previous decision has already made ours. So I have limited my share to one-third of their property, making no exact calculation, but leaving much more than two-thirds to the Treasury.
>
> [7] This is easily concluded from the valuation [assessment] which has been attached to the schedule of the property. For they have valued [assessed] the whole at more than a talent, whereas to one of the properties for which **I am suing** [perhaps "which I am claiming"] I attached five minae, and to the other a thousand drachmae: if they are worth more than those amounts, the surplus after they have been sold by auction will go to the State.
>
> [8] And to convince you of the truth of this I will produce to you, as witnesses, first the persons who rented from me the estate at Sphettus, then the neighbors of the place at Cicynna, who know that **we have been contesting** it for the last three years, and next the magistrates of last year, before whom the suits were authorized to be heard, and the present judges of the nautical court.
>
> [9] You will also have these inventories read to you: for they above all will convince you that **our claim** to this

property is no recent matter [perhaps 'not only recently have we claimed these things to be ours'], and also that today **we are contesting** with the Treasury an amount that compares favorably with that which we formerly contested with private persons. Please call witnesses.

Witnesses

[10] That there is no injustice, gentlemen, **in my claiming** your verdict on the property in question [perhaps 'I claim not unjustly that the object of the suit be decreed to me'], but rather that I have relinquished to the State a great part of my own property before **claiming** this restoration, has been clearly proved. And now I deem it just to lay my request before you and also before the Commissioners in your presence.[6]

---

6. The translation, with modifications in brackets, is that of W. R. M. Lamb, *Lysias* (Cambridge: Harvard University Press, 1930; repr. 1988). The text is that of C. Carey, *Lysiae orationes cum fragmentis* (Oxford: Oxford University Press, 2007), 172–175. Retrieved from http://stephanus.tlg.uci.edu.proxy.library.upenn.edu/Iris/Cite?0540:053:1762.

(5) ὡς δὲ τὴν
ἀμφισβήτησιν ἐποιησάμην πρός τε ὑμᾶς καὶ τοὺς ἰδιώτας, ἔτι
ἀκούσατε. ἕως μὲν γὰρ ἡμῖν οἱ Ἐρασιφῶντος οἰκεῖοι τούτων
τῶν χρημάτων ἠμφεσβήτουν, ἅπαντα ἠξίουν ἐμὰ εἶναι, διότι
ὑπὲρ ἅπαντος τοῦ χρέως ἀντιδικῶν πρὸς τὸν πατέρα ὁ (5)
Ἐρασίστρατος ἡττήθη· καὶ τὰ μὲν Σφηττοῖ ἤδη τρία ἔτη
μεμίσθωκα, τῶν δὲ Κικυννοῖ καὶ τῆς οἰκίας ἐδικαζόμην τοῖς
ἔχουσι. πέρυσι μὲν οὖν διεγράψαντό μου τὰς δίκας, ἔμποροι
φάσκοντες εἶναι· νυνὶ δὲ λαχόντος ἐν τῷ Γαμηλιῶνι μηνὶ οἱ
(6) ναυτοδίκαι οὐκ ἐξεδίκασαν. ἐπειδὴ δ' ὑμῖν τὰ Ἐρασιφῶντος
δημεύειν ἔδοξεν, ἀφεὶς τῇ πόλει τὼ δύο μέρει τὰ
Ἐρασιστράτου ἀξιῶ μοι ψηφισθῆναι, διότι ταῦτά γε ἤδη καὶ
πρότερον ἐγνώκατε ἡμέτερα εἶναι. ὡρισάμην οὖν ἐμαυτῷ τὸ
τρίτον μέρος τῆς ἐκείνων οὐσίας οὐ τὴν ἀκρίβειαν (5)
ἐπισκεψάμενος, ἀλλὰ πολλῷ πλέον ἢ τὼ δύο μέρει τῷ δημοσίῳ
(7) ὑπολιπών. ῥᾴδιον δὲ γνῶναι ἐκ τοῦ τιμήματος τοῦ
ἐπιγεγραμμένου τοῖς χρήμασιν. ἅπαντα μὲν γὰρ πλείονος ἢ
ταλάντου τετίμηνται, ὧν δ' ἐγὼ ἀμφισβητῶ τῷ μὲν πέντε μνᾶς
τῷ δὲ χιλίας δραχμὰς ἐπεγραψάμην· καὶ εἰ πλείονος ἄξιά ἐστιν
ἢ τοσούτου, ἀποκηρυχθέντων τὸ περιττὸν ἡ πόλις λήψεται. (5)

The speaker says that he claimed the amount of the debt as his because Erasistratus had lost a case for the whole debt brought against the speaker's father. Now that the treasury has seized all of the holdings of Eraton's descendants, the speaker claims one-third of the property, or the amount of the debt, based on the prior court ruling. He then goes on to speak of the market value of the properties he is claiming. He wraps up the speech by pointing out that his family did not initiate the claim only recently, that they are claiming a comparatively modest amount from the treasury, that he is not claiming the decree in his favor contrary to what is just, and that he has given up most to the treasury before making his own claim.

This passage offers an example of how claims were made in fact. Justice, though appearing twice, plays a small part. It appears first in a litotes—"that there is no injustice" (*ou para to dikaion*)—close to the end of the pleading. This litotes is important, however, because it uses a prepositional phrase as an adverb to express the manner of the claim—"not unjustly"—so that the claiming is separated linguistically from any assertion of the merit of the claim. Again, in the last sentence, the speaker asserts that it seems to him to be just to present his case to the court. This is a statement of protocol, a way of concluding the plea. Thus the case as a whole does not depend upon the notion of a right at all much less on the notion of a right as a basic, simple notion whose assertion would foreclose all reply.

---

(8) ἵνα οὖν εἰδῆτε ὅτι ταῦτα ἀληθῆ ἐστι, μάρτυρας ὑμῖν παρέξομαι
πρῶτον μὲν τοὺς μεμισθωμένους παρ' ἐμοῦ τὸ Σφηττοῖ
χωρίον, ἔπειτα τοῦ Κικυννοῖ τοὺς γείτονας, οἳ ἴσασιν ἡμᾶς ἤδη
<τρία ἔτη> ἀμφισβητοῦντας, ἔτι δὲ τούς τε πέρυσιν ἄρξαντας,
πρὸς οὓς αἱ δίκαι ἐλήχθησαν, καὶ τοὺς νῦν ναυτοδίκας. (5)
(9) ἀναγνωσθήσονται δὲ ὑμῖν καὶ αὗται αἱ ἀπογραφαί· ἐκ τούτων
γὰρ μάλιστα γνώσεσθε ὅτι οὔτε νεωστὶ ταῦτα τὰ χρήματα
ἀξιοῦμεν ἡμέτερα εἶναι, οὔτε νυνὶ τῷ δημοσίῳ πλεόνων
ἀμφισβητοῦμεν ἢ τῷ ἔμπροσθεν χρόνῳ τοῖς ἰδιώταις. καί μοι
κάλει μάρτυρας. (5)
(10) <ΜΑΡΤΥΡΕΣ, ΑΠΟΓΡΑΦΑΙ>
ὅτι μέν, ὦ ἄνδρες δικασταί, οὐ παρὰ τὸ δίκαιον ἀξιῶ μοι
ψηφίσασθαι τὸ διαδίκασμα, ἀλλ' αὐτὸς τῇ πόλει πολλὰ τῶν
ἐμαυτοῦ ἀφιεὶς τοῦτο ἀξιῶ μοι ἀποδοθῆναι, ἀποδέδεικται. ἤδη
δέ μοι δοκεῖ δίκαιον εἶναι καὶ δεηθῆναι ὑμῶν τε καὶ τῶν (5)
συνδίκων ἐναντίον ὑμῶν.

It will be observed that the translator gives "property" for *chrēmata, ousia,* and where there is no corresponding noun in the Greek.

Lysias uses other verbs as well for making claims, including *enkaleō*. The speech "Against Simon" (3.26), for example, provides LSJ with its principal example of *enkaleō* in its primary sense of 'demand as one's due,' as in the case of the return of a debt. Demanding as one's due, whether what is demanded is one's due or not, is about as close to asserting something as a just claim in modern English, or in Miller's view as a right, as one comes in the Greek. But it is not close enough. The action in this speech of Lysias has to do with the litigant's never having claimed any money when, presumably, he might have. The same language occurs in other speeches of Lysias that have to do with other claims in the courts. Rather than being sources for a theory of rights, these texts show that Lysias and his hearers were aware that the main purpose of asserting a claim was to get it enforced, whether it was just or not. Of course arguing that a claim was just might help to get it enforced, but it was not the only way or even always the most important way of getting it enforced; one might appeal to the interests of the council or the city or the demos instead.

So far, then, Greek prose keeps the making of a claim separate from the merit of the claim and from emotive responses to the claim, whereas the expression 'right' compacts the assertion or description of a claim and its evaluation into one expression, as if the notion of a right were a simple primitive such that anything asserted as a right should be favored automatically by everyone. Thus the Greek makes a very different impression on the reader from the impression that would be made by the language of rights. There is no simple primitive expression or notion of a right in the sense of just claim here in the way Thucydides and Lysias use *axioō* and *enkaleō*. Nor is there anything like it in the use of *enklēma*.

Although *enklēma*, which is cognate with *enkaleō* and can be translated by 'claim' (not 'just claim') in some contexts, is not included among the nouns examined by Miller, and although 'claim' does not appear in Miller's general index, *enklēma* probably deserves a place in this discussion. Lysias used it in a speech written for Polyaenus the soldier, so that Polyaenus might defend himself against claims on his possessions. So, in "For the Soldier" (9.13), Lysias writes of the cause of the claim against Polyaenus. Again in the first speech "Against Theomnestus" (10.23), Lysias asks what claim the dicasts have standing against his client and notes that his opponent Theomnestus would not claim that (*hoti*) he was a better man or from a better family. So one could make a claim of this kind that was grammatically a claim of pertinent fact as well as a claim directly for some object. Here the claim is not for possessions but for honor. The basis for the claim again is separate from the claim itself.

Thus Thucydides and Lysias illustrate that the Greek language for making claims dissociates the making of claims from any suggestion of the merit of the claims or expected emotive responses to the claims on the basis of justice, however conceived, or of anything else.

Aristotle

Aristotle appears on the scene after the language of claims and their making has been developed at length in ordinary speech and in the prose writers whose works survive, some of whom themselves, as Thucydides the general and Lysias the democrat logographer, were engaged in public life. Thus, when Aristotle reports on the making of claims in the *Ethics* and the *Politics*, he has linguistic conventions to observe as well as analyses to make.

His use of these conventions is visible in *EN* 4, where Aristotle is discussing the different kinds of claims, especially claims to honor. Here his discussion of the *megalopsuchos* is most enlightening, since it is largely about the making of such claims and their merit or lack of it. It seems that in most cases, for Aristotle, claims to honor are made falsely, since those who make them claim too much or too little honor for themselves (they deserve less or more honor than they claim). The *megalopsuchos* is an extreme in greatness though a mean in claiming as he should, since he claims honor according to his merit (1123b13–15).[7] This is for Aristotle a linguistic point as well as a substantive one. He contrasts those who possess the goods of fortune, preeminently honor, but lack virtue, with the *megalopsuchos*, since, unlike him, they do not claim such things justly, nor is it right to call them *megalopsuchos* (1124a26–28).[8] Here again, the claim fails to bear its merit on its face. One must ask whether the claim is made worthily (*kat' axian*) or justly (*dikaiōs*) or rightly (*orthōs*), anticipating that in many or most cases it will not be. The importance of this discussion of claims to honor for Aristotle's political writings appears when one realizes that, in the *Politics*, Aristotle identifies the positions of

---

7. ὁ μεγαλόψυχος τῷ μὲν μεγέθει ἄκρος, τῷ δὲ ὡς δεῖ μέσος· τοῦ γὰρ κατ' ἀξίαν αὐτὸν ἀξιοῖ.

8. οἱ δ' ἄνευ ἀρετῆς τὰ τοιαῦτα ἀγαθὰ ἔχοντες οὔτε δικαίως ἑαυτοὺς μεγάλων ἀξιοῦσιν οὔτε ὀρθῶς μεγαλόψυχοι λέγονται.

initiative and command in the city—the *archai*—with honors (1281a31). Claims about honor are claims to rule.[9]

In *EN* 5.2–3, Aristotle gives his thematic analysis of justice in distribution—that is to say, in allocating. After some rigorous tidying up of what his predecessors had said, Aristotle focuses on justice as a virtue of the same sort as the rest—thus a virtue that is concerned with (*peri*) something or other. That something or other in this case is the *merista*—the things, such as honor and wealth, that can be divided up either equally or unequally among those who share in the citizenship (1130b31–32). Having made this point, he works his way into the assertion that the just is the equal (1131a13) and so requires at least two values (a14–15) and then that, since there are both people and *merista* involved, the just must be in at least four (a18–19)—two for the *hois* or people and two for the *en hois* or *merista* (a20–21) or things. He clearly has in mind that justice consists in relations of people who are of different merit to the things that they might merit. Thus he has in mind something like: $\text{people}_a : \text{things}_a :: \text{people}_b : \text{things}_b :: \text{people}_c : \text{things}_c :: \ldots :: \text{people}_n : \text{things}_n$.[10] Where the merit of the people has the appropriate relation to the value of the things they might possess, one finds justice. So, in the preceding formula, if the things that people possess are appropriate to their merit, one has a condition of justice or equality among the ratios, even if the things possessed are unequal.

The just is *analagon ti* (a29); it is a certain proportion that reflects not just quantity in numbers but whatever admits of more and less. People and things can be spoken of as more or less this or that, and so as more or less meritorious, and that is what Aristotle apparently is addressing. Here the just is not the analysans or that to which others are reduced or by which they are explained. Rather, proportion is the analysans, and it is used in the analysis of the just. Presumably proportion could be used in the analysis of other things (see later discussion). Thus the notion of a right is very far from being fundamental for Aristotle if it is interpreted as a just claim, since even the notion of justice is not primitive or simple for him but must be analyzed itself using the notion of proportion.

This not fewer than four-term proportion plays a key part in Aristotle's analysis of justice in distribution. Some scholars have taken a four-term

---

9. Aristotle explains his position on the *archai* in this sense at the beginning of *Metaph.* Δ.

10. οἷς_a : ἐν οἷς_a :: οἷς_b : ἐν οἷς_b :: οἷς_c : ἐν οἷς_c :: . . . :: οἷς_n : ἐν οἷς_n.

proportion for the whole analysis, apparently. But Aristotle does not say that it is the whole analysis, or even that four is the limit of the terms. Quite the contrary. For him the proportion is in four terms at least (*en tettarsin elachistois*, 1131a31–32, 1131b4); so presumably there could be more than four, say six or eight or another number, depending on the circumstances, for example, on how many people were involved in the distribution. It might be many more, even thousands. Further, and more important, the analysis of justice is only part of the analysis of just action, to which Aristotle comes in 5.8–9, where he reintroduces his analysis of the circumstances of action that he had outlined already in 1111a3–5 and to which he had alluded here in speaking of the *hois* or people and the *en hois* or *merista*. Here again the justice of a claim or indeed of one's actually taking what one claims depends upon circumstances.

The *Nicomachean Ethics*, not the *Politics*, is the main source for the question of claims in Aristotle, but its approach to claims is reflected in the *Politics*. In the passage of the *Politics* that follows, for example, *axioō* sometimes is used with an infinitive (claim . . .), and the infinitive that follows it here is *archein* ([claim] to rule). The infinitive serves here as the object of *axioō*. *Amphisbēteō* also occurs in this passage, if in a compound participial form (*diamphisbētountas*, 1283b14), illustrating the relation to one another of the two parts of the language of making claims—the factual part (that the claim is made) and the evaluative part (that it is justified or not). In form, Aristotle here is leading up to and then offering a discrete unit of analysis—an *aporia* or apparent conceptual impasse ("there is some difficulty," 1283b13)—with a corresponding *lusis* or escape from the impasse, which begins at "Accordingly" (*oukoun*, b23). The claim to rule, of course, is a claim that different parties can make, and Aristotle notes that different parties do make it; they claim the honors for themselves.

1283b13–1284a1.

And there is some difficulty as regards all **the rival claimants** to political honours. **Those who claim** to rule because of their wealth **might seem to have no justice** in their proposal, and similarly also **those who claim** on the score of birth; for it is clear that if, to go a step further, a single individual is richer than all the others together, according to the same principle of justice it will obviously be right for this one man to rule over all, and similarly the man of outstanding nobility among **the**

claimants [20] on the score of free birth. And this same thing will perhaps result in the case of aristocratic government based on virtue; for if there be some one man who is better than the other virtuous men in the state, by the same principle of justice that man must be sovereign. Accordingly if it is actually proper for the multitude to be sovereign because they are better than the few, then also, if one person or if more than one but fewer than the many are better than the rest, it would be proper for these rather than the multitude to be sovereign. All these considerations therefore seem to prove the incorrectness of all of the standards on which men **claim** that they themselves shall govern and everybody else be governed by them. For surely even against **those who claim** to be sovereign over the government on account of virtue, and similarly against those who claim on account of wealth, the multitudes **might be able to advance a just plea**; for it is quite possible that at some time the multitude may be collectively better and richer than the few, although not individually.

Hence it is also possible to meet in this way the question which some persons investigate and put forward (for some **raise the question** whether the legislator desiring to lay down the rightest[11] laws should legislate with a view to the advantage of the better people or that of the larger number) in cases when the situation mentioned occurs. And 'right' must be taken in the sense of 'equally right,' and this means right in regard to the interest of the whole state and in regard to the common welfare [perhaps agreed advantage or benefit; see chapter 6] of the citizens; and a citizen is in general one who shares in governing and being governed.[12]

---

11. Here the 'rightest' is expressed by the superlative of ὀρθός rather than of δίκαιος. "Rightest" here should not suggest the modern theory of rights.

12. The translation is that of H. Rackham, *Aristotle: Politics* (Cambridge: Harvard University Press, 1932; repr. 1990). On the translation of 1283b42, see chapter 10. The text is that of Ross, *Aristotelis Politica*:

ἔστι δὲ ἀπορία τις πρὸς ἅπαν-
τας τοὺς διαμφισβητοῦντας περὶ τῶν πολιτικῶν τιμῶν. δό-
ξαιεν γὰρ <ἄν> οὐδὲν λέγειν δίκαιον οἱ διὰ τὸν πλοῦτον ἀξι- (15)
οῦντες ἄρχειν, ὁμοίως δὲ καὶ οἱ κατὰ γένος · δῆλον γὰρ ὡς εἴ

The rival claimants (*diamphisbētountas*), whatever the merit of their claims, are our entry into the process that Aristotle describes. They oppose one another because they subscribe to different standards of merit. Thus they make claims against one another that cannot be resolved in an agreeable way. Aristotle notes "the incorrectness of all of the standards (*tōn horōn*) on which men **claim** that they themselves shall govern and everybody else be governed by them." Here again Aristotle uses *archein* as the object of *axioō*. The people who make this claim "seem to say nothing just." The saying and its justice or lack of justice are completely separate. This passage illustrates what Thucydides and Lysias already have shown about the Greek ways of speaking about claims. For Aristotle, no claim carries its merit on its face. In his way of thinking, the merit of claims must be discerned from their circumstances. This text illustrates a position that can be found in many other texts and one that is maintained consistently in the surviving corpus.

τις πάλιν εἷς πλουσιώτερος ἁπάντων ἐστί, δηλονότι κατὰ
τὸ αὐτὸ δίκαιον τοῦτον ἄρχειν τὸν ἕνα ἁπάντων δεήσει,
ὁμοίως δὲ καὶ τὸν εὐγενείᾳ διαφέροντα τῶν ἀμφισβητούν-
των δι' ἐλευθερίαν. ταὐτὸ δὲ τοῦτο ἴσως συμβήσεται καὶ (20)
περὶ τὰς ἀριστοκρατίας ἐπὶ τῆς ἀρετῆς· εἰ γάρ τις εἷς ἀμεί-
νων ἀνὴρ εἴη τῶν ἄλλων τῶν ἐν τῷ πολιτεύματι σπουδαίων
ὄντων, τοῦτον εἶναι δεῖ κύριον κατὰ ταὐτὸ δίκαιον. οὐκοῦν εἰ
καὶ τὸ πλῆθος εἶναί γε δεῖ κύριον διότι κρείττους εἰσὶ τῶν
ὀλίγων, κἂν εἷς ᾖ πλείους μὲν τοῦ ἑνὸς ἐλάττους δὲ τῶν (25)
πολλῶν κρείττους ὦσι τῶν ἄλλων, τούτους ἂν δέοι κυρίους
εἶναι μᾶλλον ἢ τὸ πλῆθος. πάντα δὴ ταῦτ' ἔοικε φανερὸν ποιεῖν ὅτι τούτων τῶν ὅρων οὐδεὶς ὀρθός ἐστι, καθ' ὃν
ἀξιοῦσιν αὐτοὶ μὲν ἄρχειν τοὺς δ' ἄλλους ὑπὸ σφῶν ἄρχεσθαι πάντας. καὶ γὰρ δὴ καὶ πρὸς τοὺς κατ' ἀρετὴν (30)
ἀξιοῦντας κυρίους εἶναι τοῦ πολιτεύματος, ὁμοίως δὲ καὶ τοὺς
κατὰ πλοῦτον, ἔχοιεν ἂν λέγειν τὰ πλήθη λόγον τινὰ δί-
καιον· οὐδὲν γὰρ κωλύει ποτὲ τὸ πλῆθος εἶναι βέλτιον· τῶν
ὀλίγων καὶ πλουσιώτερον, οὐχ ὡς καθ' ἕκαστον ἀλλ' ὡς
ἀθρόους. διὸ καὶ πρὸς τὴν ἀπορίαν ἣν ζητοῦσι καὶ προβάλ- (35)
λουσί τινες ἐνδέχεται τοῦτον τὸν τρόπον ἀπαντᾶν. ἀποροῦσι
γάρ τινες πότερον τῷ νομοθέτῃ νομοθετητέον, βουλομένῳ
τίθεσθαι τοὺς ὀρθοτάτους νόμους, πρὸς τὸ τῶν βελτιόνων συμφέρον ἢ πρὸς τὸ τῶν πλειόνων, ὅταν συμβαίνῃ τὸ λεχθέν·
τὸ δ' ὀρθὸν ληπτέον ἴσως· τὸ δ' ἴσως ὀρθὸν πρὸς τὸ τῆς (40)
πόλεως ὅλης συμφέρον καὶ πρὸς τὸ κοινὸν τὸ τῶν πολι-
τῶν· πολίτης δὲ κοινῇ μὲν ὁ μετέχων τοῦ ἄρχειν καὶ ἄρ-
(1284a) χεσθαί ἐστι,

In *EN* 9, Aristotle uses *enkaleō* in a discussion of friendship that clearly presupposes a proportional analysis such as that of justice in distribution in book 5. In that analysis, as he had said, *to dikaion* is *analogon ti* (1131a29); that is to say, the just is [to be analyzed as] a certain proportion. His argument about love or friendship (*philia*) also uses the analysis by *analogon ti; philia* is *analogon* (1158b23, 1162a15, 1162b4, 1163b32), and this point is of some importance for the present study, for claims may be based on friendship as well as on justice. Neither justice nor friendship is the basic notion here, since both may be explained by or reduced to *analogon ti.* In 1164a3, *enkaleō* is used not in claiming x or in claiming to φ but in claiming that, with 'that' expressed in a clause beginning with *hoti,* a construction used also by Lysias, as previously noted. But here again the analysis by proportion is at work. This is a case in which the *erastēs* makes a claim that is without foundation because of his lack of merit, and the *erōmenos* makes a counterclaim that Aristotle may think is equally far-fetched, though merit is not addressed explicitly here. So in Aristotle as in Thucydides and Lysias, there is the making of claims, and the making of claims is kept separate linguistically from whether the claims have merit or not.

Why would Aristotle keep the claim and the merit of the claim separate, as we do not when we use the expression 'rights'? One answer is that, for him, the making of a claim is an act, and the evaluation of the act depends upon all the circumstances of the act, not just on what the act is. The what—the act itself—is only one of the pertinent circumstances. The other circumstances, including at least who performs the act—*tis*—and that for the sake of which the act is done—*heneka tinos,* also must be addressed in the evaluation of the act. As Joachim says of who does the act:

1105a17–b18. . . .

An act indeed is called just if it is such as a just man would do: but we cannot infer from the quality of the act the character of the agent, as we infer the goodness of the shoemaker from the goodness of the shoes. For an agent is not just unless his actions, besides being such as a just man would do, are actually done by him in the way in which the just man would do them. And the just man does what is just from a settled purpose, whose formation presupposes a long training in acting rightly,

and the kind of knowledge which involves a development of
the whole character of the man.[13]

Joachim expands on the notion of the purpose of the act if it is to
be virtuous—that it should be performed for the sake of the noble—*tou
kalou heneka*, which answers the question *heneka tinos*: "1115b12–13. τοῦ
καλοῦ ἕνεκα. The meaning of this phrase is made clearer, for example, in
the following passages: in 1116a11–12 Aristotle says that the courageous
man endures the fear-inspiring dangers ὅτι καλὸν . . . ἢ ὅτι αἰσχρὸν τὸ
μή ('because it is noble to do so, or because it is base not to do so')."[14]
Joachim goes on to cite other, similar passages. All point to Aristotle's
view that an act can't be virtuous unless its purpose is the noble. But *tou
kalou heneka* is only one of the circumstances, and it is not enough; all
circumstances must be assessed to evaluate the merit of the claims.

If a claim is an act, which indeed it is, then it will be just only if it
is appropriate to the circumstances. If a just claim in this sense is what is
meant by a right, then Aristotle does recognize rights. A point for Miller.
But this recognition of just claims will provide cold comfort to the modern
rights theorist or advocate, especially the advocate of natural or human
rights, since Aristotle's just claims are not claims that have the same force
everywhere and always for everyone. For Aristotle, there are no claims
that are just by themselves regardless of the circumstances.

Nor are just claims conceptually simple or primitive for Aristotle
as they must be for some modern rights theorists and advocates. Rather,
whether a claim is just must be determined by analysis using his more
fundamental concepts—act, virtue, and so on, and by considering the
circumstances that go with them. Certainly the notion of a just claim,
though Aristotle recognizes that some claims may be just, is not an
analytical concept for Aristotle—one to which others are reduced or by
which others are explained.

Aristotle's thinking is dominated by a concern for finding the correct analytical concepts—the starting points or *archai*. Analysis for him
is taking the things to be explained back to their appropriate *archai*. A
right or just claim, however, is not an *archē*. It is not in this way ultimate,
a starting place or ending place for argument. Thus Aristotle's notion of

---

13. Joachim, *Aristotle: The Nicomachean Ethics*, 79.

14. Joachim, *Aristotle: The Nicomachean Ethics*, 118 (English supplied).

a just claim offers something that is very far from lending itself to the rhetorical uses to which the modern language of rights is put.

If there were a single noun for 'just claim' in Aristotle's Greek that conveyed the ostensible simplicity and primitiveness and emotive force of the modern 'right,' it might be easier to suppose that the notion of a right were an analytical concept for Aristotle that was conceptually simple and primitive. The absence of a noun of this kind in Aristotle doesn't keep him from dealing with just claims, but it does tend to indicate that he did not use the notion of a just claim, spoken of as a right, in the modern emotively charged way.

Thus I cannot agree, for example, with statements like this one about the proportion that is used in the analysis of justice in the *Politica*: "The formal principle [proportion] of distributive justice generates political rights by means of the following general formula:"

$$\text{(PR)} \quad \frac{\text{Merit of X}}{\text{Merit of Y}} = \frac{\text{The Political rights of X}}{\text{The Political rights of Y}}$$

especially where this general formula represents the *en hois* or things in Aristotle's *analogon ti* with the phrases "The political rights of X" and "The political rights of Y."[15] These English phrases do not translate the *en hois* or *merista* as I have portrayed them earlier. The formal principle, by which I presume is meant the *analogon ti*, so far as I can see, generates nothing in the way of political rights in the modern sense, or just claims on the part of the citizen, though it is useful or perhaps even indispensable for the analysis of justice. The analysis of justice is but one contribution to the analysis of just actions, including just claims. In the analysis adopted by Miller, emphasis on this "formal principle"—I would not call it that, of course—tends to obscure the pervasive concern with circumstances in Aristotle's analysis even of just claims, which are not the only claims that the good man will honor.

These considerations suggest that it is, though not impossible, still not necessary and perhaps not desirable to discuss Aristotle's positions in ethics and politics using the modern language of rights, especially when a right is construed as a noncircumstantial, self-certifying claim that is

---

15. Miller, *Nature, Justice, and Rights in Aristotle's Politics,* 124–125.

conceptually simple and primitive and to which one can appeal to end a discussion because of the emotive meaning of 'right'. Of course it is possible to adopt a translation theorem according to which the relatively few claims that Aristotle expects to encounter as just in the circumstances will be named in English by 'rights'. Doing so, however, suggests an approach that hardly is Aristotle's. This point clearly goes to Ostwald and Schofield.

Conclusion

The foregoing review suggests strongly that Aristotle has no primitive or quasi-primitive notion of a right as a just claim to which other notions in the study of ethics and politics—the study of the things related to character and of the things related to the citizen—could be reduced or by which they might be explained. In fact, such a notion could not be analytically basic for him since it is not simple, being compounded of the notion of a claim and the notion of something else, such as justice on some readings. And justice itself is, for him, much in need of analysis itself as an *analogon ti*. So justice is not simple or basic, either.

But Aristotle is much concerned with the making of claims and sometimes with their justice or lack of it. In reviewing the practice of the courts and of other institutional arrangements, including war, in which claims are made, he could see which claims were enforceable and which were not. In some cases, he probably did not agree with the decisions of the courts any more than with those of the assembly or the council or of arbitrators or with those of conflicting armies; but there they were, these decisions in fact. It was of the first importance to know which claims were enforceable, or which were likely to be enforceable, whatever their merits. In the world of Aristotle, these enforceable claims sometimes were what some moderns would have in mind when they speak of rights, though in his world they would not have had the strong emotive valence that 'rights' gives to such claims in modern English.

As noted in the introduction to the present volume, modern authors sometimes write of a conflict of rights with what they name the common good. Analysis of Aristotle's language in the next chapter will suggest, however, that he was concerned with something very different from what mediaevals and moderns may have thought of when they were using the language of the common good, where they have been reasonably explicit.

Chapter 6

Shared or Agreed Advantage
(*Koinēi Sumpheron*)

It is not unusual to find casual statements in academic literature about the common good in Aristotle. An example is Smith's piece on Aristotle and the common good in the *American Political Science Review* for 1999,[1] which referred to much of the scholarship on the subject fashionable in its day. More recently, Muirhead, addressing the traditional understanding of partisanship in Aristotle's political theory, has distinguished rulers according to whether they rule for "the common good or their own private interest."[2] In this instance, translators for the most part have been more circumspect, though not uniformly, as the following examples will show.

If the common good actually were an important feature of Aristotle's discussion, one would expect to find it frequently in the *Politics* doing the work that Smith and Muirhead and others suggest that it does. In fact, however, any Greek that might be rendered by 'common good' (*koinon agathon*) occurs only twice in this work, and in neither case does it contribute to Smith's or Muirhead's program. In the first occurrence, in 1268b31, it is part of a discussion of the history of legislation by analogy with the other arts, including medicine. Aristotle apparently believed that medicine had improved over time, and he recognized that people would say that laws should be changed for the *koinon agathon*; perhaps people

---

1. T. W. Smith, "Aristotle on the Conditions for and Limits of the Common Good," *American Political Science Review* 93 (1999): 625–636.

2. R. Muirhead, *The Promise of Party in a Polarized Age* (Cambridge: Harvard University Press, 2014), 25.

used that expression as loosely in his day as they do 'common good' in ours. But of course medicine, even where its improvements may be shared, does not help everyone, and certainly not in the same way. At the least, a common good would be something that, because of its distinct ontology, sharing does not diminish, as a piece of knowledge or a virtue of character; one's knowing a theorem or being temperate, for example, does not diminish another's knowing the theorem or being temperate, and people can pursue these together. Or, to use a mediaeval example, a soldier's participating in the victory of an army. Aristotle shortly went on to point out that it might not be a good idea to change the laws even if a change would improve them. In the second occurrence, in 1284b6, Aristotle is considering the expulsion of the better people from society, which he says occurs not only in the deviant *politeiai* but also in those that look to the *koinon agathon*. Not everyone shares in the *koinon agathon* here, apparently, especially not those who are ostracized.[3]

More frequent in the *Politics*, with seven occurrences, is the conjunction of inflections of *koinos* with *sumpheron*—advantage or benefit—or the cognate verb. In three of these cases (1279a28, 33, and 37), all in 3.7, *koinos* is inflected to agree with *sumpheron*. Once this chapter is done, Aristotle indicates that it is provisional, an *endoxon*, saying, "We must say what each of these *politeiai* is at slightly greater length. For the matter has some *aporiai*," as it is easy to see that it does. Robinson was unsure whether, in 3.7, Aristotle had in mind the arrangement of offices (Robinson's "abstract" sense, the third sense in chapter 8 in the present volume) or the citizen body (Robinson's "concrete" sense, the second

---

3. In the absence of appropriate texts in the *Politics*, one might look elsewhere, as with the *aristē politeia* (see chapter 10). In *EN* 1.2.1094b7–10, Aristotle has been thought by some to identify the common good this way: "For even if the end is the same for a single man and for a state, that of the state seems at all events something greater and more complete whether to attain or to preserve; though it is worth while to attain the end merely for one man, it is finer and more godlike to attain it for a nation or for city-states" (trans. Ross). The ontology of the common good has been thought to be suggested in 1.6.1096b27–28, where Aristotle asks: "Are goods one, then, by being derived from one good or by all contributing to one good, or are they rather one by analogy?" These texts were appealing to the mediaevals, who interpreted them from their Neoplatonic standpoint of procession and return. See, for example, M. S. Kempshall, *The Common Good in Late Medieval Political Thought* (Oxford: Clarendon Press, 1999). *Koinon agathon* occurs in neither. A more promising text for this point of view may be 1162a28–29, where *koinon agathon* does occur, but without much in the way of ontology.

sense in chapter 8).[4] If Aristotle was merely introducing his analysis by citing an *endoxon*, as appears to be the case here, there is less reason to be concerned about what Aristotle may have meant; he is not reporting his own position. It is inflected this way also, perhaps, in 1283b41, if *sumpheron* is supplied from the preceding phrase as a substantive for *koinon* to modify.[5] Both Jowett and Barker do supply *sumpheron* from the preceding phrase—"to the advantage of the state and the common good of the citizens" and "for the benefit of the whole state and for the common good of its citizens"—and render it as if the text had *agathon*. In the four other occurrences it is inflected as the feminine dative singular *koinēi*—in common or by common consent (LSJ). But the literature has not paid much attention to *koinēi* in the *Politics*. Newman cites both *koinēi* and *koinon* in his index entry for *sumpherein/on*, but he does not discuss them in his notes. Schütrumpf mostly uses compounds of *gemein* in his translation and does not treat the differences in inflections analytically. Cooper notices the *koinēi/on sumpheron* but neither treats the differences in inflections analytically nor asks how the *sumpheron* so modified might differ from the *koinon agathon*.[6] Still, there are some hints in the *Politics*, where Aristotle's concern often is to show how consent or agreement may be achieved about what will be advantageous or beneficial, whatever the eventual outcome may be. In book 6, for example, before wrapping up his discussion of avoiding *stasis*, which turns on different notions of equality, Aristotle gives a hint about what he means in 1318a27, when he observes that whatever equality it would be on which both [rich and poor] agree (*homologēsousin*), one should look to that based on the [different] justices as both define them.

Since Aristotle does not provide an analysis of what he means by *koinēi sumpheron* in the *Politics*, there may be a point in looking at both words separately to see how they are used in other contexts. *Sumpheron* is the neuter singular present active participle of the verb *sumpherō*, which originally is a compound meaning bring together and which acquires

---

4. Robinson, *Aristotle's Politics: Books III and IV*, 21.

5. τὸ δ' ἴσως ὀρθὸν πρὸς τὸ τῆς (40)
   πόλεως ὅλης συμφέρον καὶ πρὸς τὸ κοινὸν τὸ τῶν πολιτῶν

6. J. M. Cooper, "Political Animals and Civic Friendship," in *Aristoteles' Politik, Akten des XI. Symposium Aristotelicum*, ed. G. Patzig (Göttingen: Vandenhoeck & Ruprecht, 1990), 220–241.

meanings in both middle and passive that range from giving battle to agreeing. The neuter singular present active participle acquired a life of its own in the sense of use, profit, or advantage (LSJ). *Koinos* is an adjective that occurs 152 times in the *Politics* and whose basic sense is given in LSJ as common; it also is used in a variety of ways and contexts.

First, *sumpheron*, since it is the substantive. A lemma search of the TLG gives forty-seven occurrences in the *Politics*. Some of the occurrences are revealing.

In 1253a14, in book 1, for example, in remarking that human speech is for making clear the *sumpheron* and the *blaberon* or harmful, as also the just and the unjust, Aristotle shows that the *sumpheron* has a contrary; and it may be possible to learn something from this and other contrasts that he draws, especially since the common good as usually understood does not have a contrary. In any case, speech can be used by those who differ about what is *sumpheron* or *blaberon*—a phenomenon as ordinary in ancient Greece as elsewhere.

In 1254a22, he observes that ruling and being ruled are among not only the *anankaia* or necessary things but also the *sumpheronta*. The use of 'not only, but also' (*ou monon . . . alla kai*) indicates that he has in mind two different things rather than the same thing under two different names. Here the necessary things presumably are the hypothetically necessary things rather than the objects of *epistēmē*; they certainly are not eternal and unchangeable.

In 1254b7, Aristotle argues that it is *kata phusin* and *sumpheron* for the body to be ruled by the soul. Here there is no contrast or contrariety but rather a suggestion that, as the individual grows to maturity, when its *phusis* is most obvious (see chapter 1), it is advantageous for the body to be ruled by the soul. In the very young and the superannuated, the body is ruled less effectively by the soul; the very young and the superannuated sometimes lack self-control, for example.

In 1282b17, in book 3, Aristotle is introducing a matter that looks easy on the surface but turns out to be difficult. He says that the good related to the citizen is the just and that this is the *koinēi sumpheron*. Then, however, he observes that it seems to everybody that the just is a certain equal, and he must go on to deal with what certain equal it is. In book 6 he will identify differences over equality as a cause of *stasis*. The present discussion continues until he takes up kingship in 1284b in the context of his observation (1283b13–14) that there is an *aporia* about all the claims to citizen honors—that is, that none of them is supportable simply speaking. See chapter 5. No wonder that there is disagreement about them. Which, then, is consistent with the *koinēi sumpheron*? Perhaps it all depends. This section of text, especially the last lines of 1283b, will be considered again in treating *koinēi*.

In 1296a35, now in book 4, Aristotle is considering why most *politeiai* are democratic or oligarchic in his own day. He observes that, when Athens and Sparta were dominant in Greece, the one set up democracies and the other oligarchies, "not looking to the *sumpheron* [here Robinson renders by 'good'] of the [other] cities but to their own" (1296b35–36). The suggestion is that Athens and Sparta interrupted the normal development of the other cities. This passage reveals something in addition to the ones that included contraries of the *sumpheron*, since it indicates that the *sumpheron* might not be the same thing in every case or for every city.

In 1297b38, a similar sentiment is expressed where Aristotle notes that all the *politeiai* have three parts (*moria*) about which the effective *nomothetēs* must examine the *sumpheron* for each. He goes on to say that having these parts well makes the *politeia* well and makes each of these differ from the others. The suggestion is that what is *sumpheron* for one part may not be *sumpheron* for the others.

Again, in 1299a14, Aristotle speaks of what sort of ways will be *sumpheron* (*sumpherousin*) for what *politeiai*. Here he is addressing ways of arranging the officeholders with respect to what the offices are, how long the offices can be held, how they might be filled, and so on. The suggestion is that one way will be *sumpheron* for one *politeia*, another for another.

In 1299b28, he still is considering the offices and officeholders and whether the same offices might be *sumpheron* for different *politeiai*.

In 1308a13, now in book 5, Aristotle is discussing the equal that the democrats seek, and he finds that in some cases it is not only just but also *sumpheron*—when there are more in the regime. There would be little point in recommending the democrats' equality to democrats, and apparently Aristotle has in mind the situation in oligarchies where many of the oligarchs are allowed to share in the regime, which is a stabilizing strategy, rather than having the share restricted to a few. Newman suggests along these lines: "Aristotle would probably recommend the adoption in aristocracies and oligarchies not only of the democratic practice which he here recommends for their adoption, but also of others, such as the prohibition of a repeated tenure of most offices and of the cumulation of offices."[7] Here what is *sumpheron* is highly circumstantial.

In 1316b39, at the beginning of book 6, he is going back over the kinds of democracy and of the other *politeiai* to consider what is familiar and *sumpheron* for each, again suggesting that what is *sumpheron* may differ for each.

In 1318b28, Aristotle observes that it is *sumpheron* for one of the democracies he has mentioned, perhaps Mantinea at one time, to fill the offices with election by all the citizens and to have all the citizens share in the scrutiny of the accounts when the officeholders' terms are over. The suggestion is that it might not be *sumpheron* for other democracies.

A little later, in 1318b39, in book 6, he notes that it is *sumpheron* not to be entitled to do whatever seems appropriate, for the entitlement to do what one wishes cannot guard against the base that is in each of men.

In 1328b14, Aristotle is listing the functions required to make a city, and here he mentions as most necessary of all judgment about the *sumpheronta* and the just things among one another. Apparently not everyone will see the *sumpheronta* the same way any more than the just things. A few lines down in 23, he will mention the judges of the necessary things and the *sumpheronta*.

In 1330b18, he is discussing the site of a city, which involves military considerations, and he observes about the fortified places that the *sumpheron* is not the same for all *politeiai*, presumably regimes here, and then he explains what is *sumpheron* for each.

What comes out of these statements is that the *sumpheron* is a circumstantial matter rather than a matter of ontology, unlike the *bonum commune* as one finds it in the mediaevals, in whom, for example, the victory of an army, which is shared by all the soldiers, differs from something like one's health, which is not shared and so is individual.[8] Something is *sumpheron* under certain circumstances, not under others; it is *sumpheron* for some entity, not for others. The *sumpheron* is contrasted with the harmful, the necessary, and the just, though it might coincide with any of them in some cases, and it differs for different cities and for different parts of the same city. One formula for the *sumpheron* does not work in every place, and it can be spoken of as plural. Given its diversity, it is almost certain to be an occasion of disagreement; and while

---

7. Newman, *The Politics of Aristotle*, 4: 384 ad loc.

8. See now Kempshall, *The Common Good in Late Medieval Political Thought*.

disagreement of one city with another is to be expected, disagreement within a household or a city over the *sumpheron* was, for the Greeks, a cause of *stasis*. Thus, while perhaps not everything can be *sumpheron*, the range of things that can be is extensive, and the question is how the *sumpheron* so described, which is not some one thing in which everyone can share, could be common—*koinēi*.

As to *koinēi*: Of the twenty-five occurrences of this inflection in the *Politics*, the following may be especially instructive: "[They believe that] some *politeiai* are maintained by strength (*tōi kratein*) and not for the *koinēi sumpheron*" (1276a13, trans. Robinson modified).[9] This passage, whose translation Robinson, following Jowett and Barker, forces by translating with "common good," occurs in an aporia about those who share in the regime after a change has taken place, as Cleisthenes made after the expulsion of the Peisistratids. As is clear from the account in *Politeia of the Athenians* 19–21, Aristotle has in mind here one of the *staseis* in which Athens and the other cities found themselves from time to time—conflicts that often were resolved, even if only temporarily, not, as in the case of Solon, by agreement about what to do but by the strength of one party.

1278b21:

Because of this, even when they need no help from each other, [men] none the less want to live together. Not but that the *koinēi sumpheron* also brings them together (following Newman).[10]

This passage occurs in an inquiry into why the city is established and how many kinds of rule there are. It says that even when people are not in need of help from one another, they desire to live together no less. That is to say, their living together may not depend upon choice. This living together above all then is the end, both for all together and for all separately. It is striking that Aristotle views men here as not needing help from one another, since his view elsewhere is that they do need help from one another. He probably is speaking here of those who already live in a city, since it is only in a city that men can enjoy something like *autarkeia*,

---

9. (. . . ὡς ἐνίας τῶν πολιτειῶν τῷ
κρατεῖν οὔσας, ἀλλὰ οὐ διὰ τὸ κοινῇ συμφέρον)

10. διὸ καὶ μηδὲν δεόμενοι τῆς παρὰ ἀλλήλων βοηθείας οὐκ (20)
ἔλαττον ὀρέγονται τοῦ συζῆν· οὐ μὴν ἀλλὰ καὶ τὸ κοινῇ
συμφέρον συνάγει,

and he probably is suggesting that the *koinēi sumpheron* is a matter for them, especially perhaps in respect of the kinds of rule (1278b16), which he will go on to consider.

> 1279a17:[11]
>
> It is clear then that as many *politeiai* as look to (*skopousin*) the *koinēi sumpheron* ["common good" in Sinclair-Saunders] happen to be right with respect to the just simply [speaking], while as many as look only to the advantage of the rulers, all are wrong and deviations from the right *politeiai*.[12]

This passage comes where Aristotle observes that it is easy to distinguish the mentioned ways of rule. It says that as many regimes as look to the *koinēi sumpheron* happen to be right according to the just simply speaking—that is, without qualification. *Koinēi* here includes both the rulers and those ruled. The ruler is to aim at his own advantage, as Aristotle makes clear, but not at that only, as he says at line 19. The *koinēi sumpheron* apparently is the *sumpheron* on which they can agree.

> 1282b14–20:
>
> Since . . . the good related to the citizen is the just, and this is the *koinēi sumpheron*, it seems to all that the just is a certain equal, and so far they agree (*homologousi*) with the arguments of philosophy in which a determination has been made about the things related to character.[13]

In this passage, with its reference to the *ēthika*, Aristotle is considering different claims to rule. He identifies the agreed advantage—that is, the

---

11. Mentioned by Cooper, "Political Animals and Civic Friendship," 278, along with 1279a28–29.

12. φανερὸν τοίνυν ὡς ὅσαι μὲν πολιτεῖαι τὸ κοινῇ συμφέρον
σκοποῦσιν, αὗται μὲν ὀρθαὶ τυγχάνουσιν οὖσαι κατὰ τὸ
ἁπλῶς δίκαιον, ὅσαι δὲ τὸ σφέτερον μόνον τῶν ἀρχόντων,
ἡμαρτημέναι πᾶσαι καὶ παρεκβάσεις τῶν ὀρθῶν πολιτειῶν·

13. Ἐπεὶ . . . ἔστι δὲ
πολιτικὸν ἀγαθὸν τὸ δίκαιον, τοῦτο δ' ἐστὶ τὸ κοινῇ συμφέρον, δοκεῖ δὲ πᾶσιν ἴσον τι τὸ δίκαιον εἶναι, καὶ μέχρι
γέ τινος ὁμολογοῦσι τοῖς κατὰ φιλοσοφίαν λόγοις, ἐν οἷς
διώρισται περὶ τῶν ἠθικῶν

advantage as agreed by both the ruler and the ruled, as the just. He apparently has in mind *EN* 5, where the difference over the equal is discussed most thoroughly.

1283b42:

> Citizens, in the common sense of that term, are all who share in the civic life of ruling and being ruled in turn.[14] (Trans. Barker)

Barker has changed *politēs* from singular to plural, and he has translated as if Aristotle had said that the sharing was by turns (*kata meros*) as a little later in 1285b39, though Aristotle doesn't say that here. But his "in the common sense of that term" probably is more to the point in suggesting agreement than Jowett's declining to translate *koinēi* at all or Rackham's giving "in general" (also Sinclair-Saunders), Robinson's "everywhere," or Simpson's "generally." Aristotle goes on immediately to say that [the citizen] is different in each *politeia*. The contrast appears to be that of what the citizen is from who is a citizen. So, for example, in a democracy, the citizens might rule and be ruled in turn, and also in an oligarchy the citizens might rule and be ruled in turn, even though the pool of those counting as citizens probably would be smaller in the oligarchy. Aristotle would be suggesting then that in Greece there was more agreement on what a citizen was than on who was a citizen.

While these passages of the *Politics* are indicative rather than dispositive concerning Aristotle's use of *koinēi*, there is further important information in the *Nicomachean Ethics*. In 5.1134b35–1135a1—a sentence that receives little attention—Aristotle uses *kata sunthēkēn* and [*kata*] *to sumpheron* together in addressing what is just in a market situation. He says that "the things that are just by agreement and advantage are like measures" (trans. Ostwald).[15] And he immediately goes on, "for wine and corn measures are not everywhere equal, but larger in wholesale and smaller in retail markets."[16] Given the market context, it is preferable

---

14. πολίτης δὲ κοινῇ μὲν ὁ μετέχων τοῦ ἄρχειν καὶ ἄρ-
(1284a) χεσθαί ἐστι,

15. M. Ostwald, *Aristotle, Nicomachean Ethics* (Indianapolis: Bobbs-Merrill, 1962).

16. τὰ δὲ κατὰ συνθήκην καὶ τὸ συμφέρον τῶν (35)
(1135a) δικαίων ὅμοιά ἐστι τοῖς μέτροις· οὐ γὰρ πανταχοῦ ἴσα τὰ
οἰνηρὰ καὶ σιτηρὰ μέτρα, ἀλλ' οὗ μὲν ὠνοῦνται, μείζω, οὗ
δὲ πωλοῦσιν, ἐλάττω.

to render this way with Ostwald rather than with Ross's "by virtue of convention and expediency" (followed by Brown), because the measures have to be agreed to be advantageous (not merely to be advantageous) for the market to function. In fact, in using *kata sunthēkēn* and [*kata*] *to sumpheron* together, Aristotle may be using *kata sunthēkēn* as he would use *koinēi* in the *Politics*.

A similar sentiment appears in 9.1167a22–b2, where Aristotle addresses *homonoia* in the course of his analysis of *philia*:

> It is not identity of opinion; for that might occur even with people who do not know each other; nor do we say that people who have the same views on any and every subject are likeminded; e.g., those who agree about the heavenly bodies (for likemindedness about these is not a friendly relation), but we do say that a city is likeminded when men agree about what is to their advantage (*peri tōn sumpherontōn homognōmonōsi*), and choose the same actions, and do things that seem right to them *koinēi*. It is about things to be done (*peri tōn praktōn*), therefore, that people are said to be likeminded, and, among these, about matters of consequence and in which it is possible for both or all parties to get what they want; e.g., a city is likeminded when all its citizens think that the offices in it should be elective, or that they should form an alliance with Sparta, or that Pittacus should be their ruler—at a time when (*hote*) he himself also wished to rule. But when each of two people wishes himself to have the thing in question, like the captains in the *Phoenissai*, they are in a state of *stasis*; for it is not likeness of mind when each of two parties thinks of the same thing, whatever that may be, but when they think of the same thing in relation to the same person, e.g., when both the common people and those of the better class wish the best men to rule; for thus do all get what they aim at. (Trans. Ross-Urmson revised)[17]

---

17. διόπερ οὐκ ἔστιν
   ὁμοδοξία· τοῦτο μὲν γὰρ καὶ ἀγνοοῦσιν ἀλλήλους ὑπάρξειεν
   ἄν· οὐδὲ τοὺς περὶ ὁτουοῦν ὁμογνωμονοῦντας ὁμονοεῖν φασίν, οἷον τοὺς περὶ τῶν οὐρανίων (οὐ γὰρ φιλικὸν τὸ περὶ (25)
   τούτων ὁμονοεῖν), ἀλλὰ τὰς πόλεις ὁμονοεῖν φασίν, ὅταν

In this passage, Aristotle expands on what might be summarized in the phrase *koinēi sumpheron* in the *Politics*: the citizens must agree at the same time about what things are advantageous, and they must choose these and must act on the things that seem advantageous to them by agreement, achieving what they pursue. Thus, as is clear in the case of *homonoia*, where and if it can be achieved, the *koinēi sumpheron* is the advantage in things to be done on which the citizens agree—the agreed advantage. Aristotle may be echoing or foreshadowing here the account in the *Laws* of the uneven record of the Greeks in their combat with Persia—a situation saved ultimately by the *koinēi dianoēma* (692E6) or agreed purpose of the Athenians and the Lacedaemonians.[18]

Aristotle does not take the view that those who agree always will be correct in their agreement, which will be about *prakta*, and thus relatively short range. Many of those who agree will lack both the virtues of character and practical wisdom. They will pursue what seems advantageous to them, but it might not be advantageous after all or in the long haul. It might turn out to be either *sumpheron* or *blaberon*. It might be hypothetically necessary—necessary because of some unfavorable event out of their control with which they must deal or because of some mistake that they have made in the past that requires correction or because they need it to get what they want. It might be just, but it might not be, as may appear on further consideration. It might be advantageous for their city, as in the case of an alliance, but not for the city with which they are allied. It might be advantageous for the defense of their city, but it might not be. It might be advantageous for the assembly but not for a council in the same city. Compared to *stasis*, their agreement about their advantage still can be valuable, even if events show that it needs to be

περὶ τῶν συμφερόντων ὁμογνωμονῶσι καὶ ταὐτὰ προαι-
ρῶνται καὶ πράττωσι τὰ κοινῇ δόξαντα. περὶ τὰ πρακτὰ
δὴ ὁμονοοῦσιν, καὶ τούτων περὶ τὰ ἐν μεγέθει καὶ ἐνδε-
χόμενα ἀμφοῖν ὑπάρχειν ἢ πᾶσιν, οἷον αἱ πόλεις, ὅταν
πᾶσι δοκῇ τὰς ἀρχὰς αἱρετὰς εἶναι, ἢ συμμαχεῖν Λακε-
δαιμονίοις, ἢ ἄρχειν Πιττακὸν ὅτε καὶ αὐτὸς ἤθελεν. ὅταν
δ' ἑκάτερος ἑαυτὸν βούληται, ὥσπερ οἱ ἐν ταῖς Φοινίσσαις,
στασιάζουσιν· οὐ γάρ ἐστιν ὁμονοεῖν τὸ αὐτὸ ἑκάτερον ἐννοεῖν
ὁδήποτε, ἀλλὰ τὸ ἐν τῷ αὐτῷ, οἷον ὅταν καὶ ὁ δῆμος
καὶ οἱ ἐπιεικεῖς τοὺς ἀρίστους ἄρχειν· οὕτω γὰρ πᾶσι γίνεται οὗ ἐφίενται.

18. J. Burnet, *Platonis Opera*, vol. 5 (Oxford: Clarendon Press, 1907).

revised subsequently, since it buys time in a situation in which permanent stability is too much to be hoped for. Aristotle apparently had learned the ameliorist lesson that Plutarch attributes to Solon who, when asked whether he had given the Athenians the best laws, replied that he had given them the best they would accept[19]—a sentence that sums up the account in the Peripatetic *Politeia of the Athenians* of the agreement Solon achieved; that achievement was the agreed advantage and was welcome at the time, and Aristotle apparently admired Solon for having brought it off, even though it shortly fell apart.

This interpretation can be strengthened by looking further at what Aristotle has to say about agreement. Of the dozen or so Greek words that might be used to designate agreeing, Aristotle favors *homologeō* and its cognates. In a striking passage at 5.1301a25–39 that uses *homologeō*, for example, Aristotle says: "It is necessary first to take the starting point, as many *politeiai* come to be with all agreeing (*homologountōn*) on the just in the sense of the equal by proportion, but they are mistaken about what this [proportional equality] is, as has also been said before . . . and for this reason, when they do not share in the *politeia* according to the judgment that they separately happen to have, they engage in *stasis*."[20] So here they agree on the definition of justice, which Aristotle sometimes tells us is *sumpheron*, but they are mistaken about what is just, and the result is *stasis*. Newman identified the passages to which Aristotle refers as 1280a7 sqq. and 1282b14 sqq.,[21] the latter of which, as previously noted, makes the connection with the *koinēi sumpheron* expressly.

To sum up: Little is said by Aristotle of what might be construed as the common good, for which it was left to later writers to attempt an ontology. The *koinēi sumpheron*, about which Aristotle has more to say, is not a matter of ontology, and so it is not helpful to render it by 'common good', even if doing so gives the appearance of making it fit with some

---

19. *Solon*, 15.2.

20. δεῖ δὲ πρῶτον ὑπολαβεῖν (25)
    τὴν ἀρχήν, ὅτι πολλαὶ γεγένηνται πολιτεῖαι πάντων μὲν
    ὁμολογούντων τὸ δίκαιον καὶ τὸ κατ' ἀναλογίαν ἴσον, τούτου
    δ' ἁμαρτανόντων, ὥσπερ εἴρηται καὶ πρότερον. , , ,
    καὶ διὰ ταύτην τὴν αἰτίαν, ὅταν μὴ κατὰ τὴν ὑπόληψιν
    ἣν ἑκάτεροι τυγχάνουσιν ἔχοντες μετέχωσι τῆς πολιτείας,
    στασιάζουσιν.

21. Newman, *The Politics of Aristotle*, 4: 283, *ad* 28.

otherwise attractive historical narrative. Perhaps more importantly, doing so tends to obscure an important point that Aristotle is at pains to bring out—the political salience of agreement and disagreement, especially where a democratic ideology is influential, even in matters in which certainty and accuracy may be unobtainable. As he makes clear, *stasis* arises out of conflicts,[22] often reflecting the cleavage of the poor from the wealthy along with other cleavages, and these conflicts are over differing notions, perhaps inchoate, of the just, the equal, and so on. As in markets so in cities, reaching a modicum of agreement about what is acceptably advantageous to different parties who have different and conflicting interests and views is required for partnerships to be carried on, even if the agreement is short-lived and must be renegotiated frequently. This shared agreement of parties whose interests typically conflict, even including the *despotēs* and the *doulos*, who, despite their different interests, may find the same thing beneficial (*tauto sumpherei*, 1252a34), may well be what Aristotle had in mind by the *koinēi sumpheron*.

The preceding chapters all address Aristotle's language in considering things related to the citizen—the development of the citizen, the growth of households and villages into cities, those mature individuals who live in households or cities but are not citizens themselves, the things that citizens possess, the contributions that citizens will make to the city and how they are measured, the conflicts that cities and citizens may have with one another, the advantages in which citizens might share even when their interests differ. As the next chapter will show, considering Aristotle's language in detail sheds some light on how he thought of the citizen.

---

22. For one twentieth-century treatment based on this axiom, see E. C. Banfield and J. Q. Wilson, *City Politics* (Cambridge: Harvard University Press, 1965), 7.

Chapter 7

The Citizen Without Qualification
(*Ton Haplōs Politēn, Pol.* 3.1275a19)

In book 3 of the *Politics*, Aristotle attempts to clarify earlier discussions
of the *politeia*, including those of Herodotus, the Pseudo-Xenophon, Thucydides, Xenophon, Plato, and perhaps others,[1] by working back from the
politeia to the *polis* and then to the *politēs*. Looking to his definition of
the *politēs*, he defines a city as a *politōn ti plēthos* (1274b41)—a certain
multiplicity of citizens—and only then goes on to deal with the *politeia*.
The treatment of the *politēs* thus arguably provides the foundation for the
rest of what Aristotle has to say on the subject of the *politeia*.

In his supplementary essay to Richard Robinson's Clarendon Aristotle
translation of *Politics* 3 and 4,[2] David Keyt follows Robinson (4) in rendering *ton haplōs politēn* (τὸν ἁπλῶς πολίτην) by "citizen proper" (1275a19,
130) (which may be equivalent to Robinson's "citizen most properly so
called"; see *legetai malista*, 1278a35–36, and Robinson ad loc., 18); slides
without explanation to "full citizen" (131); and then goes on to adopt the
language of "first-class citizens" and "second-class citizens" (132). Thus,
beginning from Robinson's understandable translation of the adverb *haplōs*
by "proper," from which, however, the adverbial form has disappeared, Keyt
constructs an interpretation according to which Aristotle in this part of
the *Politics* has a theory of first-class citizens and second-class citizens—an
interpretation that diverges from the interpretation in Keyt's own essay

---

1. J. Bordes, *POLITEIA dans la pensée grecque jusqu'à Aristote* (Paris: Les Belles
Lettres, 1982).

2. Robinson, *Aristotle Politics: Books III and IV*, supplementary essay.

"Aristotle's Theory of Distributive Justice" on which the supplementary essay ostensibly is based.[3]

One crippling difficulty with this interpretation is that Aristotle does not use expressions here—presumably combinations of ordinal adjectives and nouns—that we might translate by 'first class' or 'second class' or any 'nth class'; we have no *prōton telos* or *deuteron telos*. Nor does Aristotle incorporate a corresponding value ranking of citizens. Indeed, there is no suggestion here that he is opposing one class of citizens to others or is evaluating classes of citizens. Aristotle may recognize what we might consider ordinal classes of citizens, of course, in *Politics* 2 (1274a20–22) and in *Ath.* 7.3, as noted earlier, where he reports that Solon divided the citizens by assessment (*timēmati*) into four *telē*, if this is an ordinal division; but these do not correspond to Keyt's supposed first-class and second-class citizens in any obvious way.

In this chapter, I propose to show, in part by a lexical analysis, that Aristotle in the *Politics* expects us to understand *haplōs*, which occurs fifty-five times, as an adverb that modifies verb forms indicating speech such as *kalein* (1275a1), *phateon* (1275a16), *horizetai* (1275a21), *eipein* (1275b21), whether stated or understood, rather than as expressions that modify nouns for citizens or for classes of citizens. Aristotle is not concerned here with classes in either the Boolean or the Marxian sense. He is concerned, however, with method, and his method includes definition. At this point, his concern is to define the citizen in such a way as to unravel confusions in thinking and speaking about the citizen. These points come out as one works through the texts.

Haplōs in 1275a19–20

"For we are seeking the citizen *haplōs* and not one having a challenge against him such that it requires straightening out."[4] In this text, Aristotle explains that he is searching for a definition of the citizen. Defining the citizen is important to him because people do not agree on who is a citizen or what it is to be a citizen, and of course those for whom the

---

3. In D. Keyt and Fred D. Miller, Jr., *A Companion to Aristotle's Politics* (Oxford: Blackwell, 1991).

4. ζητοῦμεν γὰρ τὸν ἁπλῶς πολίτην καὶ μηδὲν ἔχοντα
   τοιοῦτον ἔγκλημα διορθώσεως δεόμενον,

Politics was written had an interest in knowing who is a citizen and who is not. Aristotle begins by dismissing the cases of adoption, domicile, legal standing, and patronage in their relation to citizen status; and then he comes to the cases of children and elders who must be said to be citizens in a way (*phateon . . . pōs*), though they are not said to be citizens *haplōs* (1275a16). He then goes on to explain what he means by 'in a way'. He means that they are said to be citizens by something's being added (*prostithentas*, 1275a17), presumably to the definiendum. But what would be added?

In considering what is added, Aristotle uses here the expression *enklēma*—an expression that sometimes is translated by 'charge' or 'indictment' or 'accusation' or 'claim'. In any case, an *enklēma* is a linguistic entity. Perhaps he has in mind a challenge to those who are too young or too old to serve and yet are presenting themselves for recognition.[5] He might be drawing on legal language again as he does in adopting *katēgoria* into his logical vocabulary. The things that are added here are the adjectives 'premature' and 'superannuated' (*ateleis* and *parēkmakotas*, 1275a17). Aristotle shortly adds the dishonored and the exiles (the *atimoi* and the *phugades*, 1275a20–21) to the examples of those who are not citizens *haplōs*, although they may have exercised citizenship once upon a time and might do so again.[6] But there is little reason to believe that an *enklēma* in the legal sense must precipitate every case in which something is added.

The notion of something's being added clearly is important for understanding Aristotle's use of *haplōs*, and Aristotle addresses it at the end of book 2 of the *Topics* (115b29–35) using exactly the language of the *Politics*. He says there that the *haplōs* is that to which nothing is added or *mēdenos prostethentos* (29–30), and he goes on in the same passage to use the same technical language twice more—*ouden prostitheis* (33) and *mēdenos prostithemenou* (34)—to explain his use of *haplōs*.

It should be noted, of course, that Aristotle gives *eidos* in combination with ordinal adjectives in a new aporia starting at 1275a35 and leading up to the statement that there must be a different citizen for each *politeia* (1275b4–5). The *lusis* for this aporia lies in a straightening out or *diorthōsis*, which he begins to explain in 1275b13. Here an *eidos* clearly is not a class, and Aristotle still is talking about definition.

---

5. See, for example, *Ath.* 42.

6. Newman thought that ἔγκλημα had the sense of 'defect'. See Newman, *The Politics of Aristotle*, 3: 135.

At the end of the *diorthōsis*, Aristotle gives a parallel definition of the *polis* that he indicates by the phrase 'to speak *haplōs*' (1275b21). He then contrasts this definition with another definition with respect to use (*pros tēn chrēsin*, 1275b22). He characterizes the latter definition as quick (*tacheōs*, 1275b25), perhaps in the way we might use 'quick and dirty'.

To summarize: In this passage Aristotle is concerned with definition; he suggests that what is said *haplōs* involves no addition to the definiendum; and he does not combine ordinal adjectives with class words.

Aristotle often brings out the sense of *haplōs* by contrasting it with other expressions. One of these expressions is *ex hupotheseōs*, and this one may be especially important for understanding the present text given other occurrences of *ex hupotheseōs* that are to be found in the *Politics*.

Ex hupotheseōs in the *Politics*

Three of the six occurrences in the *Politics* may be of special interest:

1278a5:

These [are citizens] *haplōs*, the others [are citizens] *ex hupotheseōs*; for they are citizens, but they are immature.[7]

In this text, Aristotle still is addressing an offshoot of the same *aporia* about the citizen that occupied him at 1275a19. If the citizen is someone who shares or might share in the *archē* or rule, what is to be done with those who do not share in it but are spoken of as citizens nonetheless? Aristotle often deals with this sort of question, which arises because common speech sometimes is reliable only in part. In this case, the issue has to do with age, since sharing in the *archē*, which at Athens means deliberating in the assembly and sitting in the jury court, at a minimum, or at least being entitled to do so, was reserved to citizens who met lower and upper age limitations. So the same citizen might share in the *archē* at one time but not at others. Aristotle dealt with this issue by noting that a child or cadet was on the way to sharing in the *archē* and that an elder was someone who had shared in it. The child or cadet is a citizen in such a way that, *if* he matures, he will share, or will be eligible to share, in the *archē*; and the elder is a citizen in such a way that, *if* he has aged,

---

7. οἱ μὲν ἁπλῶς οἱ δ' ἐξ ὑποθέσεως· πολῖται μὲν γάρ εἰσιν, (5) ἀλλ' ἀτελεῖς.

he has shared, or has been eligible to share, in the *archē*, even if he is not sharing in it at present. Of course the child or cadet might not survive to maturity, and the mature citizen might not survive into old age. The question here includes both identity and current activity, and the two are linked by if clauses, or *ex hupotheseōs*.

> 1288b28:

> It belongs to the same science . . . to consider . . . in the third place the [*politeia*] *ex hupotheseōs*.[8]

In this passage, Aristotle has moved beyond the citizen and the *politeiai* and is attempting to deal with four ways of discussing the *aristē politeia*, which ways can be confused with one another, yielding deleterious results in practice. An ordinal adjective does occur here, but it has nothing to do with classes of citizens.

This text has to do not only with *politeiai* themselves but also with how a certain one might be established, preserved, and so on. Thus Aristotle begins with the one that is said to be (1) the best or perhaps most enduring *haplōs* (1288b25–26), which may come to be where nothing external [to its normal growth] obstructs (*mēdenos empodizontos tōn ektos*, 23–24), though it is impossible for many to achieve; next comes (2) the best from the subjects (*tēn ek tōn hupokeimenōn aristēn*, 26); then (3) the best from an assumption (*ex hupotheseōs*, 28); and finally (4) the one that is suitable most of all to all the cities (*malista pasais tais polesin harmottousan*, 34–35).

The *haplōs* and the *ek tōn hupokeimenōn* are distinguished from one another by recourse to two different frameworks—the categorial and the circumstantial. The *haplōs* is explained by the categorial *tis esti kai poia tis* (23),[9] or the definition and the quality, while the *ek tōn hupokeimenōn* is explained by the circumstantial *tisin* (24), or the with what or to what or for what, or the with whom or to whom or for whom.[10] The former thus is a matter of definition while the latter is a matter of circumstance, and especially of the circumstance who, the who being the subjects of the *politeia*. Aristotle is recognizing here that, while one may deal with a definition of the *politeia* without thinking of the people to whom it is

---

8. τῆς αὐτῆς ἐστιν ἐπιστήμης . . . θεωρῆσαι . . . ἔτι δὲ τρίτην τὴν ἐξ ὑποθέσεως

9. *Cat.* cc. 4–5.

10. *EN* 1111a3–5.

appropriate, one also may speak realistically of the best *politeia* in the sense of that which is most appropriate for a certain people.[11]

In the third way, a *politeia* can be explained assumptively. Sir Ernest Barker explained *ex hupotheseōs* here in terms of the assumption of a lower standard of civic attainment than the absolute or even the relative [circumstantial] best. It is an assumption which, in the sphere of politics, corresponds to that made in the sphere of training by the man who "does not want to attain the standard . . . needed for competition."[12] The sense of Aristotle's extended analogy about athletic training seems to be that one might describe a certain regimen as 'the best one' and add to it 'if one does not want to attain the standard needed for competition'. That regimen would be the best *ex hupotheseōs* but not the best in the other two senses. The assumption should change the way one reasons about what is to be done even if one retains a definition and considers the circumstances. So, for example, while the best standard in the first case might be training for a marathon and the best standard in the second case might be training for a half-marathon, the best standard in the third case might be preparing for a daily run that raises one's heart rate. Obviously, one would train differently for each of the three.

The last way in which a *politeia* can be said to be the best is the way most people (*hoi pleistoi*, 35) speak; Aristotle says that even if they say the other things well most people miss the useful things (1288b35–37).[13] Since Aristotle is concerned with what is useful to the statesman, this last way of speaking does not commend itself to him except, presumably, as a starting point. Indeed, when the *pleistoi* speak, they may do so without an explicit analytic framework.

I conclude from this catalogue that *ex hupotheseōs* provides a promising avenue for clarifying the meaning of *haplōs* in the *Politics*. But is it possible to get a still clearer view of what Aristotle means by *ex hupotheseōs*? Other texts may be helpful, for example:

1332a10–11:

I mean *ex hupotheseōs* with respect to the necessary things, *haplōs* with respect to [what is done] nobly.[14]

---

11. See P. Pellegrin, *Les Politiques* (Paris: Flammarion, 1990), 39.

12. Barker, *The Politics of Aristotle*, 181, n. 2.

13. *Top.* 100b22.

14. λέγω δ' ἐξ ὑποθέσεως τἀναγκαῖα, τὸ δ' ἁπλῶς τὸ καλῶς

Here Aristotle is explaining his use of *ex hupotheseōs* and of *haplōs* in the course of discussing what and what sort of *politeia* will make the city happy. He refers to what he has defined in the *Ethics*—perhaps, but not surely, referring to what we know as *EN* 1098a16 or 1176b4; and he goes on to say what he means by happiness and to distinguish what is called happiness *ex hupotheseōs* from what is called happiness *haplōs*.

His argument is that happiness involves virtue and that Ath the virtue of the city depends upon the virtue of the citizens, all of whom, by definition, share in the citizenship or *politeia*. But what counts as virtuous action for the citizen may be conditional or *ex hupotheseōs*. Inflicting punishment, for example, can be just and so virtuous; but the act of punishment is said to be just only *if* some offense has been committed that warrants the punishment, and it would be better had the offense not been committed and the punishment not been necessary. So also with other actions. While some actions may be said to be just or virtuous only if necessity warrants them, the actions that are said to be virtuous *haplōs* are virtuous without any such necessity. These are the ones associated with leisure and peace (1333a35–36).

I conclude so far that, in the *Politics*, Aristotle uses *haplōs* not mainly as an expression that modifies *politēs* and describes a certain kind of citizen but as an adverb that modifies certain verbs. Sometimes *haplōs* is explained by contrast with the prepositional phrase *ex hupotheseōs*, which is on its way to becoming an adverb and functions somewhat as our adverb 'hypothetically', since Aristotle does not use *hupothetikōs*, which doesn't occur until later, in Demetrius and especially in commentaries on Aristotle and in scholia. *Haplōs* and *ex hupotheseōs* are not unique in being used this way as modifiers of certain verbs; and in these cases, the verb sometimes is understood rather than being stated explicitly.[15] Other passages in the *Politics* thus can help us understand 1275a19.[16]

Classes of Citizens in *Politics* 1274a20–22 and in *Ath.* 7.3

Where Aristotle does talk about classes of citizens, he does not have in mind the immature or the superannuated or any other such group. Instead,

---

15. See my " 'Universally', 'Quniversal', 'The Universal'," *Teorema* 5 (1975): 277–284; and "ΤΑ ΚΑΘ ΕΚΑΣΤΑ ΓΝΩΡΙΖΕΙΝ (*EN* 1141b14–21)," *Classical Philology* 70 (1975): 124–125.

16. Also enlightening may be *EE* 1238b6, where Aristotle uses ἁπλῶς to modify βούλομαι and contrasts it with both ἐξ ὑποθέσεως and τοῦ ἕνεκα, reprising, perhaps, the earlier contrast with πρὸς τὴν προαίρεσιν (1238a39–b1); and *EN* 1149a24 and 1151b2.

he has in mind a division of citizens according to their productive output. In *Politics* 1274a19–21, for example, he says that Solon instituted all the offices "from those with five hundred *medimnoi* and the ox drivers and a third (*tritou*) class called cavalry. But the fourth, the laborers, shared in no *archē*."[17] The ordinal here clearly shows that he has in mind a list of classes whose members achieve different levels of output.

In *Ath.* 7.3, Aristotle gives a fuller account of Solon's action in language whose syntax is slightly different: "He divided it [the citizen body] by assessment into four classes, as it also had been divided before: the five hundred–*medimnos* class, the cavalry, the ox drivers, and the laborers."[18] Here are all four of the classes, and it has been customary to see in this passage a division of households. These households would include both the immature and the superannuated, not to mention those who once were without honor or exiled or who might become so, as well as those actively taking part in the city's deliberation and judgment. So there is here a quite different principle for dividing citizens into classes. Further, the division here clearly is a description in the object language. Aristotle here is not talking about definition; and there is no occurrence here of *haplōs* or *ex hupotheseōs* or the like modifying the usual verbs.

Conclusion

I have argued in this chapter that, in book 3 of the *Politics* where Aristotle is engaged in defining the citizen, he is not adverting to classes of citizens in the sense in which some people speak of first-class citizens and second-class citizens. Instead, he is dealing with an *aporia* about who is a citizen and who is not, what it is to be a citizen and what it is not. He uses a technical language here in developing his *lusis* and, as in some other signal cases, his technical language involves adverbs or prepositional phrases that work the way adverbs work to modify verbs of saying. Sometimes the status of these adverbs is not obvious right away because Aristotle, in his terse way, leaves the verbs to be understood. But it would be a mistake in these cases to treat these adverbs as if they modified nouns just because

---

17. ἐκ τῶν πεντακοσιομεδίμνων καὶ ζευγιτῶν καὶ τρίτου τέλους τῆς καλουμένης ἱππάδος· τὸ δὲ τέταρτον τὸ θητικόν, οἷς οὐδεμιᾶς ἀρχῆς μετῆν.

18. τιμήματι διεῖλεν εἰς τέτταρα τέλη, καθάπερ διήρητο καὶ πρότερον, εἰς πεντακοσιομέδιμνον καὶ ἱπ[πέα] καὶ ζευγίτην καὶ θῆτα.

we have to supply the verbs; and, in fact, when one attempts to treat them this way, the results typically are obscure or worse.

The insertion of 'first-class' and 'second-class' into the translation or discussion of this passage is inappropriate for three reasons. The first is that there is nothing to support it in the Greek. The second is that expressions of this kind—ordinal adjectives combined with a noun that we might render by 'class'—already have been spoken for; they are used by Aristotle in treating the classification of citizens by output as the result of assessment. The third reason is that they tend to mislead because they introduce an emotive meaning into a passage that is far from emotive. If one wants to convey the meaning of Aristotle's Greek in English, it is best to translate with words that match both the descriptive and emotive meanings of the Greek. Where doing so exceeds one's ingenuity, a note can call attention to the difficulty.

With the citizen simply speaking clarified, Aristotle was in a position to consider the question of the *politeia* in its original sense of citizenship and in the other senses it had acquired over time. The senses of *politeia* in Aristotle are discussed in the next chapter.

Chapter 8

Citizenship, Citizen Body, Constitution, and Regime (*Politeia*)[1]

Politeia occurs only very occasionally in the *Eudemian Ethics* (six times), *Virtues and Vices* (once), and *Magna Moralia* (thrice); but it is more frequent in the *Politeia of the Athenians* (sixty-two occurrences), the *Nicomachean Ethics* (18 actual occurrences and one often understood), and the *Politics* (522 occurrences). In this chapter I shall address its occurrences in the latter three works. For other occurrences in Greek literature and occurrences in inscriptions, the reader is referred to the opening pages of an earlier treatment of the *Politics*.[2] For more on the understood occurrence in the *Nicomachean Ethics*, see chapter 9 in the present volume.

Translators often use 'constitution', or latterly 'regime', to render these occurrences. There are difficulties with this approach, however. For one, the ancient city did not have anything that quite answers to the English 'constitution', which acquired its current sense, more or less, only in the eighteenth century, according to the *OED*. Further, Aristotle gives different senses for it in book 3 of the *Politics*. Also, sometimes he seems to be

---

1. I wish to acknowledge assistance on several key points from the late Martin Ostwald. Portions of this chapter appeared in my "*Politeia* in Greek Literature and Inscriptions and in Aristotle's *Politics*: Reflections on Translation and Interpretation," in *Aristotle's Politics: A Critical Guide*, ed. Thornton Lockwood and Thanassis Samaras (Cambridge: Cambridge University Press, 2015), 84–102, © published by Cambridge University Press, reproduced with permission, and in my "Πολιτεία in Aristotle's *Nicomachean Ethics*," in *Studies in Ancient Greek Philosophy in Honor of Professor Anthony Preus* (London: Routledge, 2023), 230–241, © published by Routledge, reproduced with permission.

2. See my "*Politeia* in Greek Literature and Inscriptions and in Aristotle's *Politics*."

designedly inexplicit. And sometimes he uses it for the combination of what he calls democracy and oligarchy, where he seems to be speaking mainly of those who rule rather than of an arrangement or ordering of offices or officers—ordering as making one ruling authority superior to others or making its judgment final. In the face of these circumstances, prudence dictates looking carefully at each occurrence in its context to determine what Aristotle may have in mind, if possible.

In all three works with relatively many occurrences, *politeia* has a range of senses. The author apparently intended by this expression some-times citizenship (a condition in which citizens share), sometimes the citizenry (the body of citizens), sometimes the arrangement or ordering of offices (arguably closest to the constitution in approximately the British or American sense), and sometimes those who actually are in charge (the regime). Further, sometimes the author's precise intention is difficult to divine, and sometimes he may intend more than one sense. Conscientious English translators have tried to deal with this complexity by using differ-ent translations in different places, though usually favoring 'constitution'.

The author himself gives the reader some help in discerning his meaning. He sometimes will use *politeia* in an idiom with a Greek expres-sion for sharing, in which citizenship apparently is meant; citizenship is a condition in which the Greeks thought one can give a share or have a share.[3] Again, he sometimes will embed his use of *politeia* in a discussion of members of the citizen body. Also, in some cases he might signal that he has in mind the arrangement or ordering of people or offices by using *taxis* or *tattō*. Finally, he sometimes will use *politeia* in contexts in which he is considering those who actually occupy the offices—the regime. Another help is associated with the tags in what Professor Keaney, writing on the *Politeia of the Athenians*, identified as part of the author's use of ring composition.[4] These formulaic tags indicate where a discussion begins and where it leaves off. After using these helps to isolate the meanings, the reader will find that there are some occurrences in which no one meaning can be isolated or in which two or more might be intended, even if one meaning may be dominant.

---

3. This likely is the meaning Aristotle has in mind when he uses *bios tis*—a certain life—in 1295b1, since sharing in the citizenship is sharing in the life of the city.

4. J. J. Keaney, *The Composition of Aristotle's Athenaion Politeia: Observation and Explanation* (New York: Oxford University Press, 1992).

The Aristotelian *Politeia of the Athenians*

Whether Aristotle wrote this work or not, it remains of interest.[5] If it was written by someone else, it is an independent testimony to the language in use in Aristotle's time in the Lyceum. Readers will note that its title is in the form of the titles apparently used by Critias and Xenophon, with *politeia* and the name of the people concerned—a form that still may have seemed appropriate late in the fourth century. If it was written by Aristotle, it provides a look into how he developed the material one finds in the *Nicomachean Ethics*, where he refers to the collections of *nomoi* and *politeiai*, and in the *Politics*. He would have been wise, of course, to have his students put together reports on their own cities in a conventional format, even if he touched them up before they went into the library at the Lyceum.

When Kenyon, after identifying this lost work in papyri in the British Museum, issued his edition in 1891 under the title *Aristotle on the Constitution of Athens*,[6] he may have contributed to the belief that the ancient *politeia* was continuous with what people in his own time thought of as a constitution, whether a document or a system of conventions formed by accretion, and to the expectation that 'constitution' should be used regularly in translating all the occurrences of *politeia* in the work, fifty-nine of which are in the historical section (chapters 1–41) and three in the section on the author's own time (chapters 42–69).[7]

The history of Athens as recounted here is not a legal or constitutional history in any modern sense, however, but rather a record of

---

5. For an earlier treatment of this work, see J. J. Mulhern, "*Politeia* as Citizenship in Aristotle," *Society for Ancient Greek Philosophy Newsletter* 12, no. 2 (2012): 41–47, https://orb.binghamton.edu/sagp/458.

6. Aristotle, *On the Constitution of Athens*, 2nd ed., ed. F. G. Kenyon (Oxford: Clarendon Press, 1891).

7. Some German scholars pointed out, perhaps in reaction, that the Greeks did not have *Verfassungen* of the modern sort, which was correct, so that 'constitution' was misleading as a translation. This insight may have helped to prompt Professor Strauss to adopt 'regime' as a translation in lectures that he delivered in Jerusalem in 1954 and 1955, in which he interpreted *politeia* very broadly so that it might cover most or all of the senses presented here. He apparently did not intend 'regime' in Aristotle's exact sense of *politeuma*, as it is used here; nor does it appear from the published version of the lectures that he was proposing to render *politeia* in every place in Aristotle and in other authors by 'regime'.

conflict from archaic times forward, including eleven shifts in who was to be dominant, often reflecting temporary changes in the relative positions of the more numerous worse off and the fewer better off, typically with other adjustments, up until around 330, and a description of the situation at that time—the offices and officers and matters of procedure. Several features stand out in the historical section—the unsettled situation of the seventh century, Solon's ultimately unsuccessful attempt at a compromise early in the sixth century, Peisistratus' illegal takeover and the failure of his dynasty later in that century, several externally driven reorganizations at the end of the Peloponnesian War late in the fifth century, including that in which the Thirty ruled. Many of the failures came from the inability of participants to understand that their claims to exclusive rule were not justifiable, as Aristotle would point out in the *Politics*, and that their conflicting alignments made them susceptible to control by those notables who came to power through enlisting the demos against other notables.

Here I transliterate the title rather than following Kenyon's example because I shall consider the different senses of *politeia* in this work, comparing my results mainly with those in the instructive Penguin translation of the late P. J. Rhodes.[8] My results agree with his translation in twenty-seven of the sixty-two occurrences. In the other instances they differ from his, especially in choosing 'citizenship' more frequently than he does (seventeen to two, where we agree on the two), but in other ways also. In his Oxford commentary, in which he considered thirteen of the occurrences, Rhodes also distinguished four senses—constitution, control of state, citizenship, and body of citizens.[9] Once these are rearranged into citizenship, body of citizens, constitution, and control of state, it should be clear that these four senses correspond closely to the four senses distinguished here, despite the preference for 'constitution' in his translation.

What the author intends is clearer in some occurrences than in others, and many of the sixty-two will be considered in this chapter. The occurrences in which the sense most clearly is citizenship, since they use verbs of sharing or giving a share, are the following:

---

8. P. J. Rhodes, *Aristotle: The Athenian Constitution* (Harmondsworth: Penguin, 1984).

9. P. J. Rhodes, *A Commentary on the Aristotelian Athenaion Politeia* (Oxford: Clarendon Press, 1981), 786. He says also (89–90) that *politeia* "in *A.P.* most commonly means 'régime,' 'constitution,' 'government of the state.' . . . Sometimes the word means 'control of the government,' and so 'citizenship' . . . , and in three passages in *A.P.* it refers to the body of those possessing citizenship."

In 4.2, he observes with reference to Draco that the *politeia* had been granted (*apedidoto*) to those who furnished their own weapons. Although the *meta-* prefix is not used here, it seems clear that a share was being given, not the whole citizenship. Rhodes renders by "political rights," though it certainly is arguable that the Greeks of this period did not use a language of rights that works the way the modern one does (see chapter 5 in this volume). 'Citizenship' fits, since the author goes on to discuss different groups of citizens based on their output and on their shares in the *archai*.

In 13.5, the author reports on the situation after Solon left Athens and looks ahead to the period after the overthrow of the Peisistratids, when questions were raised about those who did not have two Athenian parents; the Athenians held a vote on claims of registration of citizenship, since many were sharing in the *politeia* for whom it was not proper. Here Rhodes uses "political rights," though the author seems to have in mind sharing in the citizenship, since he uses "sharing," or perhaps "partnering" (*koinōnein*), and so one of the traditional idioms recognized by Ostwald and Bordes[10] for being a citizen.

In 20.1, the author describes the sequel to the fall of the Peisistratids. There was another contest, and Cleisthenes succeeded by granting (*apodidous*) the *politeia* to the demos. Rhodes offers "political power" as a translation. It seems, though, that the demos was getting participation in the citizenship and so eligibility to share in the regime. Of course this participation would have brought some measure of what we might call political power with it.

In 21.2, the author is discussing the revisions of Cleisthenes. Rhodes renders "so that more men should have a share (*metaschōsi*) in the running of the state." The use of *metechein* is decisive here. The author has in mind that Cleisthenes was making a change in the citizenship, which had been associated with families, since he then says that hence came the saying 'Don't judge by tribes' with respect to those who wished to search out heredity. Here, then, 'citizenship' seems to be in order, though of course having more people share in the citizenship might well lead to having more share in the running of the city and so in the regime.

---

10. M. Ostwald, *Language and History in Ancient Greek Culture* (Philadelphia: University of Pennsylvania Press, 2009), 17–19; Bordes, *POLITEIA dans la pensée grecque jusqu'à Aristote*, 491–492.

In 36.1–2, the Thirty are in the ascendant but are under pressure, especially from Theramenes, who complains that, while wishing to give a share in citizenship to the better people, they gave it to only three thousand. Here the author twice uses the same verb that Herodotus had used in book 9 in recounting the gift of citizenship to Tisamenus (*metadounai, metadidoasi*). Rhodes gives "control of the state." Perhaps control of the state would come nearer with citizenship, though it is not the same thing as citizenship.

In 37.1, the author tells how the Thirty proposed to get rid of people by preventing them from sharing (*koinōnein*) in the present *politeia* because they were not included in the Three Thousand or if they had helped to destroy the fort of Eetionea in the Peiraeus or had opposed the Four Hundred. Not being included in the Three Thousand would put one outside the citizen body and so outside the condition of citizenship. The meaning seems to be that people who had been citizens before were not included in the Three Thousand and so in effect lost their citizenship and their place in the citizen body. Rhodes uses "citizen body" here.

In 40.2, Rhodes uses 'citizenship'. This is the first of only two such instances in which he uses 'citizenship'. Here the author mentions the prosecution of Thrasybulus for the psephism which gave a share (*metedidou*) in the citizenship to all returning from the Peiraeus, of whom some clearly were *douloi*. This is a case of an abstract noun's denoting a condition, which is something that can be shared.

Rhodes uses 'citizenship' again in 54.3, where the author is noting that the prytany secretary is recorded on *stēlai* in connection with alliances, proxenies, and citizenships. Rhodes gives "alliances, appointments of *proxeni* and grants of citizenship." The author, however, was following the lapidary convention. No appointments and grants are mentioned here, only the alliances and the proxenies and the citizenships themselves, as on the stones. In any case, citizenship clearly is intended.

Two occurrences in which the sense apparently is citizen body, since the author uses the appropriate prepositions, are these:

> In 4.3, where the preposition is *ek*, the author says that the council was four hundred and one selected by lot from the *politeia*. Rhodes here renders "appointed by lot from (*ek*) the men possessing political rights," which says a good deal more than the Greek. Perhaps the newer and controvertible language of rights can be avoided. Moore had used "selected by lot from

the citizen body."[11] The latter translation is supported by the author's going on immediately to describe the drawing of lots by those who were eligible because of age.

In 37.1, the author explains that Theramenes became outside (*exō*) the *politeia* so that the Thirty were authorized to kill him. Rhodes uses "excluded from the citizen body," which Theramenes surely was. The further argument for this view is that the Three Thousand at this point were the citizen body except where some member of the Three Thousand had committed some other disqualifying act.

As for examples in which the sense is arrangement or ordering of offices, or constitution, looking ahead to the *Politics*, the clearest indicator might be expected to be the use of *taxis* and *tattō*, which occur respectively seven and nine times, but caution is called for in interpreting these cases.

In 3.1, the author introduces the *taxis* of the ancient *politeia* before Draco. After a sentence on appointments, he goes on to explain what the offices were and which were more important than others. In 3.6 he treats the council of the Areopagus, whose *taxis* was to pay attention to the laws. This account is continued in 4.2, where the author describes the *taxis* of the citizens and the officials. It finishes in 5.1; the author mentions the *taxis* of the citizen body, in which the many were *douloi* to the few, when the demos rose up against the notables. All four of these might be rendered by 'arrangement', though what is arranged may not be quite the same thing in all four cases.

In 11.2, the author is describing the discontent produced by Solon's reforms, because the notables thought that Solon would give them back the same *taxis* as before, which he didn't. In 41.2, a summary of the historical part of the work is underway, and the author mentions the *taxis* of the *politeia* that came to be after Theseus, who accomplished the synoecism of Athens. Presumably he is using *taxis* somewhat loosely here for any arrangement. Then, in 42.4, in the second part of the book, he is describing the pass in review that occurs in the second year of a cadet's training; there is a gathering in the theater, and the cadets demonstrate to the people the *taxeis*, probably the military formations, that soldiers

---

11. J. M. Moore, *Aristotle and Xenophon on Democracy and Oligarchy* (Berkeley: University of California Press, 1975), reprinted in S. Everson, ed., *Aristotle: The Politics and The Constitution of Athens* (Cambridge: Cambridge University Press, 1996), 213.

had to learn for fighting together. All in all, *taxis* covers more items here than the *taxis tōn archōn*, which one finds in the *Politics* (1278b9) and which regularly is taken for the constitution.

The first occurrence of *tattō* is at 8.3, where the author is discussing the laws of Solon, when the tribes were divided into twelve naucrariae or divisions each, with an authority assigned (*tetagmenē*) to collections and disbursements.

In the second (8.4), the author reports that Solon ordered (*etaxen*) the council of the Areopagites to guard the laws. This is a case of putting certain people in charge rather than of arranging the offices.

In 13.4, the author is describing the situation after Solon in the time of the three factions, the third of which was organized (*tetagmenos*) by Peisistratus. Here the sense may depend on the way *tattō* was used in a military context.

In describing the place of Aristides in the middle of the fifth century (23.5), the author says that he was the one who was ordering (*taxas*) the first tributes from the [Ionian] cities. This action clearly is not an arrangement of offices.

In 39.3, the context is the reconciliation after the overthrow of the Thirty. Athenians who had taken a house at Eleusis were required to negotiate an agreement with its possessor; if they were not able to agree with one another, each was to choose three assessors, and to accept whatever value they set (*taxōsin*). Here the putting in order clearly is not arranging the offices.

The author begins his account of the *politeia* in his own day in 42; it begins with registration of young men in the demes. After the first year of cadet training, there is an assembly in the theater of Dionysus at which the cadets demonstrate to the demos the formations (*taxeis*) they have learned, as noted earlier.

In 51.3 the author describes market regulation at Athens with the magistrates involved. They take care that the bakers sell loaves of bread based on the prices of wheat and that the loaves weigh as much as the magistrates require (*taxōsin*). For the law directs that they arrange (*tattein*) these things. These are the last two occurrences of *tattō* in the work. It appears that the author was using *tattō* only occasionally in connection with an arrangement of the offices. In short, while the author's use of *taxis* and *tattō* may suggest that he has in mind the *taxis tōn archōn*—the ordering of offices or constitution—in this work, he uses them regularly with other things in mind.

The author seems to have the fourth sense most clearly in mind—regime, or government—in his treatment of the Peloponnesian War and its aftermath, when there were bitter controversies at Athens over who would rule. These controversies also affected the ordering of offices and the citizen body. The citizenship by this time was corrupted, and it does not seem to have been much on anyone's mind until the reconciliation. The demos with its leaders had demonstrated its shortcomings in drifting into a war that it would lose, alienating its generals, undertaking unwise military expeditions, and ceding control to unprincipled men.

In chapters 24 to 28, the author recounts the growth of the empire and the growth of lawlessness as the Areopagus declined. In 24.2, the author reports that, while the Athenians became more domineering with most of their allies, they allowed the Chians, Lesbians, and Samians their regimes (*politeias*) and their ruling over those they happened to rule. The reference to those ruling (*archontes*) is an argument in favor of regime as what is intended here, though there may have been some effect as well on the ordering of offices. In 25.1 he observes that the regime (*politeia*) of the Areopagites remained mainly in charge, though diminished bit by bit, for seventeen years after the Persian wars, when Ephialtes began attacking its members, persisting with others until he had taken away its ability to function. Chapter 26 nearly finishes the demise of the council of the Areopagites; there is a line on it in 27. In 28.1, it is said that while Pericles was leader of the demos the things related to the *politeia* were better, but when Pericles died much worse. Here the sense seems to be regime, since who rules is the main consideration. The author goes on in 28.5 to say that there was disagreement on the judgment of Theramenes, since in his time the regimes (*politeias*) were disordered, and that he did not undermine all the regimes.

Chapters 29–33 cover the Four Hundred and the Five Thousand. After the Sicilian expedition failed, the Athenians were influenced to give up the democracy and to set up the regime (*politeia*) of the Four Hundred (29.1) in the belief that a regime (*politeia*) of the few would attract the support of the Persian king against Sparta. The outcome was the regime of the Five Thousand. In chapter 30, the Five Thousand select a committee of one hundred men to draw up a regime (30.1) who will occupy the offices and thus rule. But that is only for the future. Chapter 31 gives the outline for the present, which established the rule of the Four Hundred. In 32.1, the author observes that this regime (*politeian*) was confirmed by the multitude; and in 32.3 he notes that, when this regime was in place, the Five Thousand were selected in name only while the Four Hundred with the ten generals entered the council house and ruled the city. The preoccupation with who rules continues into chapter 33, where the Four Hundred are overthrown and the initiative shifts back to the Five Thousand.

Chapter 34 recounts the overthrow of the regime (*politeian*, 34.1; Rhodes gives "control of the state") of the Five Thousand by the demos and the serial errors of the demos, following which Lysander set up the Thirty. In the next three chapters, the author explains how the Thirty attempted to cement their position, only to be defeated themselves.

In chapter 38 the Thirty are replaced successively by two groups of ten until a peace under Spartan control is established and a reconciliation of the warring parties begins. In 38.2, the author mentions that those in the regime (*politeiai*), where Rhodes gives "citizen body," were fearful of losing their control and wished to intimidate the others. When the reconciliation was finished, according to the author, the demos set up the present regime (*politeian*, 41.1), "constitution" in Rhodes, seeming to take the regime (*politeian*, 41.1.5) [to themselves] justly, "political power" in Rhodes.

The author is sensitive to the complexity of the events he describes, in which an action undertaken with some outcome in mind may have other outcomes as well. So, for example, an attack on the members of the council of the Areopagites may not only change those who rule but also may alter the position of the council itself and thus the ordering of the offices. Or a change in the citizen body may change the regime, since the barrier that separates these two is permeable. His use of *politeia* is consistent with what will be found in the *Nicomachean Ethics* and the *Politics*.

The *Nicomachean Ethics*

In the *Nicomachean Ethics*, there are occurrences in books 2 (2), 3 (1), 5 (2 actual and 1 understood), 6 (1), 8 (7), and 10 (5). A complete table of occurrences in the *Nicomachean Ethics* is now available.[12] It shows the following:

'Citizenship' appears to be the appropriate rendering in three places. At 1130b32, Aristotle is speaking of justice according to the part (*kata meros*)—the distribution of honor or money or the other divisible things

---

12. Mulhern, "Πολιτεία in Aristotle's *Nicomachean Ethics*," 231.

(*merista*) to those partnering in the citizenship (*tois koinōnousi tēs polite-ias*), that is, the citizens. Here the sense is made clear by the idiom with the participle. In 1142a10, Aristotle is finishing his discussion of practical wisdom, and he has noticed that some people think of practical wisdom as seeking the good for themselves; but then he observes that it may not be the good for themselves without household rule and *politeia*. Here he is contrasting life outside the household and the citizenship with life within these institutional arrangements, both of which require a measure of practical wisdom, especially in deliberation and judging. The sense here appears to be citizenship. In 1181b7, Aristotle is coming to the end of the work and suggesting what the budding *politikos* or *nomothetēs* should study, and he refers to his collections of *nomoi* and *politeiai*. Here he continues to have in mind the importance of institutions as they had developed in Greece, rather than situations in which each, as he had said on the page before, lives as he wishes, like a cyclops, quoting *Odyssey* 9.114 (1180a27–28). This is the same place in the *Odyssey* that he will quote again on the first page of his next set of lectures—the *Politics*—adding the reference to the past in Greece, when people lived apart (1252b22–24). Considering that he was addressing an audience that was drawn from different cities, one might suppose that he had in mind more than a regime or government or group of officials, which could change quickly, or an arrangement of offices or a citizen body, which might differ from city to city; he doubtless was concerned in the first place with the complex condition that was the citizenship, with its ways of producing or trying to produce the citizens it needed—citizens who would be excellent. Hence his concern for the Spartan *trophē* and *epitēdeumata*. 'Citizenship' is the preferred sense here.

In four occurrences the sense appears to be citizen body. The first two are in the same line at 1103b6, where, early in book 2, Aristotle is explaining how the lawgiver makes the citizens good by habituating them. And then he says that by this the good citizen body differs from the bad citizen body. In 1135a4, Aristotle divides justice related to the citizen into justice related to *phusis* and justice related to *nomos*, which pair then is replaced by justice related to *phusis* and justice related to men (*anthrōpina*) after a comparison of justice related to men with grain measures. Ostwald explains the passage this way: "What Aristotle seems to mean is that in states where the citizens are buyers rather than sellers of a given commodity, e.g., grain, the official measures tend to be on the large side, since evidently buyers in Greece wanted to make their units of purchase as large as possible; while in states where grain was sold rather than bought, the measures would tend to be smaller."[13] The citizen bodies are the same way: The *anthrōpina* are not simply matters of *phusis* but of the different kinds or stages of *phusis* found in different places and in different situations, as human beings, who are beings that develop conventions, develop different conventions in different circumstances. In 1163b5, Aristotle is comparing reciprocity among unequal citizens with reciprocity among friends who are not able to contribute to the friendship equally, as each may have different things to contribute. It is similar in the citizen body, where, as he points out, citizens receive honor, or official responsibilities, if they contribute to the city overall (the *koinon*), even if doing so imposes costs on them, from those who cannot contribute, while those who cannot contribute receive assistance; and so a kind of proportional equality is maintained. Thus Aristotle says that the reciprocity observed in friendship is apparent also in citizen bodies.

Six of the remaining occurrences are rendered best by regime or government, meaning those who rule. In 1113a8, where Aristotle is talking about deliberation and choice, he uses Homer's portrayal of the ancient regimes as an example: for the kings, he says, announced to the people what they had chosen. The *basileis* are those who rule, and the *politeiai* are the regimes. In 1160a31 and 32, Aristotle again is discussing those who rule—the regimes, rather than arrangements or orderings of offices, despite the tendency of translators and others to use 'constitution'. The kingship, the aristocracy (rule of the best born or otherwise best), and the timocracy (rule of those who are selected on the basis of an assessment, as Aristotle explains; see chapter 4 in this volume)—the kings, the aristocrats, and the timocrats—are in a position to arrange or order the offices however they want. They all could order the offices in exactly the same way, if they wished, or in different ways. In b21 he still has in mind the regimes, where he is considering the change of regimes, especially from timocracy to democracy. So also in 1161a10: Aristotle says that friendship appears in all of these regimes so far as justice does, as for a king in relation to the subjects based on an excess of benefit, and so on. Again, he is considering those who rule. In none of these cases is he focusing on the arrangement or ordering of offices.

The remaining six actual occurrences are not identified readily with any of the four senses. In 1160a34 and 1160b20, Aristotle has in mind the mixture, as some translators have rendered. In the last four, all in 1181b

---

13. M. Ostwald, *Aristotle: Nicomachean Ethics*, 132, n. 46.

at the end of the work (lines 14, 17, 19, and 21), the sense is inexplicit, apparently because Aristotle is pointing ahead to the *Politics*, where all four senses will appear. All of these senses appeared also in the *Politeia of the Athenians*, which very likely was written before the *Nicomachean Ethics* achieved its current form, since, as already noted, Aristotle mentions the collections of *politeiai* in 1181b7.

The *Politics*

In what follows, examples have been drawn from the text of Ross and often from the useful volume of Sinclair-Saunders. Sinclair-Saunders opts for 'constitution' most of the time, though not without second thoughts on occasion, as the examples will show. What I believe to be Aristotle's meaning in each place where it can be discerned has been compared with the Sinclair-Saunders translation and with other translations, mostly from the late nineteenth century forward. My argument will rely in part on an annotated catalogue of the 522 occurrences of *politeia* in the *Politics*.[14]

In the *Politics*, as elsewhere, identifying the senses from line to line or even within a line sometimes is helped by Aristotle's reliance on idiom. A special case is the use of *en* with the title of a literary work—the *Politeia* of Plato. And where *kaloumenē* or *onomazomenē* or *prosagoreuomenē* is used as a modifier, in the sense of 'so-called', the equivalent is 'polity', for the mixture of oligarchy and democracy, though what is being mixed might be the *politeia* in one or more of the four senses and though 'polity' is little more than a transliteration, recalling Moerbeke's *politia*.

In book 1, *politeia* occurs four times, all in the last Bekker column, in a discussion that leads from Aristotle's treatment of the household to that of the city. In 1260b20, which is the third occurrence, Aristotle says that from the children come those who will become partners in the citizenship (*koinōnoi tēs politeias*). In the first two occurrences also the sense seems to be citizenship, while in the fourth the text is inexplicit; the fourth is the first occurrence of *aristē politeia* in the *Politics*.

Book 2 contains eighty-five occurrences. Not all of these occurrences are very informative about Aristotle's intention, since they represent the

---

14. J. J. Mulhern, "*Politeia* in Aristotle's *Politica*: An Annotated Catalogue," University of Pennsylvania Library Scholarly Commons: Departmental Papers (Classical Studies), http://repository.upenn.edu/classics_papers/31/. 2014.

language and views of others. Further, some of the occurrences in this book simply say, for example, that this is the *politeia* of the so and so, which leaves open what may be intended. These formulaic occurrences are part of the frame rather than part of the content, and little can be gotten from them. They occur at 1266a29, for example, where Aristotle says, "Thus the things about the *politeia* in the *Laws* are this way (*touton ton tropon*)"; also at 1271b18 ("Let so much be said about the *politeia* of the Lacedaemonians"), 1272b23 ("Let so much be said about this *politeia*"), 1273b25 ("Thus about the *politeia* of the Lacedaemonians and the Cretan one and the one of the Carthaginians, which are justly well thought of, it is this way"), and 1274b26 ("So then, about the *politeiai*, those in force and those spoken about by some, let it be completed this way [*ton tropon touton*]"). The text is inexplicit. In three of the occurrences in this book, Aristotle is referring to Plato's *Politeia*. Thus some of the occurrences here can be set aside when it comes to investigating Aristotle's meaning.

Still, some items are informative. Where Aristotle begins his critique of the division of the citizens in Hippodamus, he uses both *koinōnousi tēs politeias* (1268a18) and *metechein tēs politeias* (a participle at 24 and then an infinitive at 27). Sinclair-Saunders gives "constitution" in all three places but also refers to the same footnote in all three places: "That is to say, enjoy citizenship, the right to hold office under the constitution." The reason for the footnote is clear: it makes little sense to say "share in the constitution." In fact, the note would be more appropriate if it were to end at "citizenship."

On book 3: Barker thought that, in the first five chapters, Aristotle was addressing citizenship.[15] And that may be so, though *politeia* in these chapters appears to mean citizenship in six cases, citizen body in five, constitution in five, and regime in four. I find the text inexplicit in three cases. At the same time, as the discussion has been going on, Aristotle has been giving successive definitions of *politeia* as he iterates his way toward a measure of clarity about two senses—the *taxis* or ordering of offices and the *politeuma* or regime, as I have shown elsewhere.[16] Having added some precision to the language here, Aristotle might be expected to use *politeia* only or chiefly for the *taxis* and the regime in what follows. And while he does come back to these senses, he continues to use it in other senses as well.

---

15. Barker, *The Politics of Aristotle*, 105–126.

16. Mulhern, "The *Aristē Politeia* and Aristotle's Intended Audience in the *Politica*," 285.

In book 4 (following the traditional order of the books), the focus often is on mixture, since that is what Aristotle's hearers, in his view, would be well advised to attempt, if circumstances allow it, in order to preserve their *politeiai*. There are 154 occurrences here. The book includes multiple occurrences in each of the four senses and is inexplicit in many cases. *Politeia* as mixture appears here not as a fifth sense alongside the four; it might be viewed as a second-order use—for a mixture of the citizen bodies, or a mixture of the arrangements of offices, for example. And of course it might be used for a mixture of more than one of these.

Newman observed that "the broad object which Aristotle has in view" in this book "is to uproot the general impression that there are but two or three constitutions—monarchy, oligarchy, and democracy . . . or at the outside four—these three and aristocracy . . . and that oligarchy and democracy have each of them only one form."[17] Newman's observation here looks at first glance as if he has *politeia* in mind throughout as an arrangement or ordering of offices. And this appearance continues where, in discussing the mixture, he notes that Aristotle "describes in detail the way in which it is instituted and organized. The framer of a polity must effect a fusion of oligarchy and democracy. Sometimes he will adopt an institution from both, sometimes he will steer a midway course between them, sometimes he will borrow partly from the one, partly from the other. He may count himself successful, if the constitution framed by him can be called both a democracy and an oligarchy."[18] Newman's position, like the text, actually is more complex, as can be seen, for example, in his note on 1292a32, which includes the occurrence of *politeia* in 1292a34. Aristotle here argues that it is necessary for the law to rule over all and for the officials and the *politeia* to rule in each case. Newman refers to Bonitz and to Liddell and Scott on the *politeia* in this passage as the *universitas civium*—the "citizen-body."[19] In this case, the *politeia* seems most likely, as Newman suggests, to be the citizen body. So Newman sometimes sees more than the *taxis* here.

But then again, on 1297b1: It is necessary, says Aristotle, that the *politeia* be from those who possess arms only. In Sinclair-Saunders we find a paraphrase: "Citizenship [very unusual in Sinclair-Saunders] ought to be reserved for those who carry arms." This paraphrase has the advantage of

---

17. Newman, *The Politics of Aristotle*, 1: 498.

18. Newman, *The Politics of Aristotle*, 1: 498–499.

19. Newman, *The Politics of Aristotle*, 4: 182.

being coherent; we can understand it. It may even be what Aristotle believed, more or less. It is not quite what he says here. Although citizenship is intended in some places, it apparently is not intended here. The translators dig themselves in deeper in a footnote: "Literally, 'the *politeia*, constitution, should be made up exclusively of those who carry arms,' i.e., they alone should be *politai*." There is little that is literal about this. It doesn't explain the translation; it offers a different and conflicting translation; it doesn't mirror the Greek. And then a third alternative: "By *politeia* Aristotle may however mean polity"—the alternative accepted by Reeve. This is another acknowledgment that the text sometimes is inexplicit. Newman renders: "'but the constitution [of the polity] should indeed be composed of' (or in other words 'should give political rights to') 'the possessors of heavy arms and none others. . . .'" This is not the clarity that we expect and usually get from Newman. So the translations on offer so far are citizenship, constitution, polity, and political rights. Jowett gives "government," Simpson gives "regime," and Robinson adds "political community." So what is the student to think? There is a wonderful history of confusion here. It seems that, while Aristotle has the citizen body in a mixture in mind, he intends the citizen body. In that case the translation would be that it is necessary that the citizen body be from those who possess arms only, as Bonitz thought, though Newman ad loc. disagreed, opting for constitution.

Book 5 is the longest book in the surviving text at thirty-two Bekker columns, and it contains 133 occurrences—the second highest total, second only to book 4. This book is marked by continuous discussions where the meaning of *politeia* seems to be mostly the same (allowing for exceptions) from one end to the other—constitution from early in 1301b to early in 1302a, regime from the middle of 1303a to the middle of 1306a, constitution from that point to the end of 1308a, citizen body often from the end of 1309a to the beginning of 1310b, and regime from that point to the end of the book in 1316b. Again, Aristotle frequently in this book uses *politeia* for the mixture of democracy and oligarchy, or polity. Polity seems to be the subject from early in 1306b to the end of 1307a and again from the end of 1308a into the beginning of 1308b. Also, there are cases in which the text is inexplicit.

Because the mixture may be intended both where it is not clear what is being mixed and where one or more of the four items usually intended is being mixed, a special challenge in reading this book is to determine, where one can, what Aristotle has in mind as being mixed. In 1306a26, Aristotle is talking about how oligarchies change in war. He says that they give a share of the *politeia* to the multitude because they are compelled to use the demos [as warriors]. Here the traditional idiom with *metadidoasi* is helpful and probably indicates that the oligarchs are giving a share in the citizenship.

In 1306b11, he observes that if there were an output assessment for office fixed at a certain level, which would include some but not others, it would determine who participated in the *politeia* in each case—the citizenship here (see chapter 4). But if then there were a widespread rise in output so that many more met the assessment, and everyone were to share (*metechein*, b14), then there would be a change in the citizen body, even though it might be gradual. The result would be a mixture in the citizen body and in the regime, assuming that the ordering of offices remained the same, though that might become mixed as well over time, with new offices established for the new group or some old offices disestablished or weakened or strengthened.

Book 6 is a short book, at only twelve Bekker columns, and it has been thought to repeat material from the prior two books. It contains thirty-six occurrences. The text is inexplicit in eleven instances and has mostly the first three senses and polity up through 1318a9; but after this there are eight cases where the sense is regime. In 1320b22, the polity appears to be a mixture of regimes. Here Aristotle is dealing with oligarchies in a chapter that often is considered to be about the preservation of oligarchies, though he doesn't say that exactly until the end of the chapter—the very last word (1321a4). In any case, the idiom here is that of the so-called *politeia*, and so he has in mind the mixture, as he explains. The mixture is a mixture of assessments first of all, which permits people of different assessments to share in different offices. As a result, people of low assessments hold some offices and people of high assessments hold other offices. So here the so-called *politeia* is identified as a mixture of regimes, though the citizenship and the citizen body doubtless would change as well with the mixture of regimes. There is no suggestion that the arrangement or ordering of offices will change.

Book 7 runs to twenty-eight Bekker columns and contains thirty-five occurrences. The text is inexplicit in thirteen cases. The sense is structural—arrangement or ordering of offices, or constitution—in two cases. For the rest, the sense is citizenship in twelve cases, citizen body in five cases, and regime in four cases. Polity has disappeared. Sinclair-Saunders gives constitution in all but one case (1329a41), in which no translation is given.

One case of citizenship can be found in 1326b21. Here Aristotle is finishing up with the big city, and he observes that it is easy for foreigners and metics to share in the *politeia*, here citizenship, in the big city. For it is not difficult not to be noticed (or to evade notice) because of the excess of the multitude. Here the verb for sharing is *metalambanein*. Bonitz also takes *politeia* as citizenship here. Sinclair-Saunders actually renders "to become possessed of citizenship" but then inserts a note, "Literally, 'get a share in the constitution,'"[20] followed verbatim by Reeve. No reason is given for the note; certainly there is nothing literal here, unless one simply assumes that *politeia* always should be rendered by 'constitution.'

In 1329b37, Aristotle reminds us that it has been said before that it is necessary for the land to be of those possessing arms and of those sharing in the *politeia*. The idiom leaves no doubt that he intends the citizenship. The verb is the participle *metechontōn*, and Bonitz again seems to understand *politeia* as citizenship here.

To the extent that historians of political thought have supposed based in part on book 7 of the *Politics* that Aristotle proposed something or other as the best constitution consistent with their view that book 7 should follow book 3, these results suggest that one might take another look. The historians' proposal presupposes that Aristotle is using *politeia* throughout in the sense of constitution or arrangement of offices in book 7, following one definition of *politeia* along these lines in book 3; but that view is made more difficult to accept by the examples just cited in which the sense clearly is citizenship. Here also the inadvisability of attempting to attract Aristotle into the history of constitutions, which are quite modern artifacts, as the history of the word in English shows, reveals itself with especial clarity. We cannot know that Aristotle was talking about the best constitution throughout this book, since he mostly was talking about other things that we can identify except when he was inexplicit, as he sometimes was.

Book 8, with twelve Bekker columns and only five occurrences, has little to tell us. The last occurrence is for Plato's *Politeia*. One occurrence might have the sense of citizen body but is not entirely explicit. There again is no trace of polity in this book. Aristotle begins this book by linking education to the *politeia*; the first four occurrences are in 1337a. After this, *politeia* does not occur again until the end with the allusion to the *Republic*. Aristotle's focus has shifted to something else related to

---

20. Sinclair-Saunders, *Aristotle: The Politics*, 405.

the citizen—his education. From a causal standpoint, the first thing that education is intended to affect is the character of the citizens, and so the citizen body would seem to be what he is most likely to have in mind when he uses *politeia* at the outset here.

Up to the present, this chapter has been concerned mainly with ascertaining what Aristotle's words seem to tell us about what he had in mind. Because of Aristotle's pivotal position in the history of thought and culture, both Eastern and Western, there may be some value in considering what an exact understanding of Aristotle's teaching on the *politeia* tells us in a substantive way that differs from what we might expect.

An exact understanding leads away from treating Aristotle's argument as focused on constitutions or forms of government in every case. Indeed, despite what is suggested by some translators, the expression that 'forms of government' might be expected to render—*eidos/ē tēs politeias*—is very rare in the *Politics*. And when it does occur, it does not appear always to have the sense of form of government (see chapter 9 in this volume). Translators who render this way when only *politeia* occurs in the text, especially in the plural, are likely to distract their readers from Aristotle's argument. Rackham's Loeb translation in particular is in need of revision here.[21] 'Form' introduces the notion of something visual, whereas not every use of *politeia* is visual for Aristotle. And so it could prejudice the translation and interpretation in an unfortunate way. Or it may suggest that Aristotle has in mind something like a logical genus-species relation, which does not seem to be the case either; *politeia* is not a logical genus. Rather, the democracy might be a genus, as also the oligarchy, since, although there are different kinds of them, all the democracies have the same *horos*, as do all the oligarchies and aristocracies (1294a10–11; see also a20 and chapter 9).

The form-of-government line of argument seems to have propelled some writers to suppose that Aristotle must have been suggesting that there was some best form of government without regard to circumstances. But, while Aristotle uses the expression *aristē politeia*, he does not use the expression *ariston eidos tēs politeias*. Much has been written on the related notion of the ideal constitution in Aristotle, though Aristotle has no word quite corresponding to 'ideal'; 'ideal' comes from other sources. Nor is the city of God in question since, for Aristotle, cities are for things that are neither beasts nor gods (1253a26–29); of course a measure of divine

---

21. Rackham, *Aristotle: Politics.*

direction would help, though there is little reason to believe that it would make everything work out quite as everyone might like.

Malcolm Schofield has suggested that "the core meaning of *politeia* is 'citizenship,' 'the condition of being a citizen.' "[22] Citizenship may be regarded as primary in a historical sense. It is the earliest sense of which we have a record in literature (Herodotus 9); it is well represented in inscriptions for grants of citizenship, which are of great institutional importance, over an extended period; and it endures as a readily identifiable meaning into later Greek literature. But language develops, and words acquire new senses which encroach on the old ones. Words are especially subject to perversion and abuse in political discourse, as users appropriate words with favorable emotive meanings to their own advantage, changing their descriptive meanings, as the author of the *Republic* clearly understood and as Stevenson has shown in detail.[23] Aristotle appeared at a critical time in the history of this word, and, drawing on his extensive knowledge of Greek literature and material culture, he seems to have devoted considerable attention to sorting out its senses and uses. Perhaps his attention contributed to the continued use of *politeia* for citizenship in later authors, especially where the traditional idioms were preserved.

Aristotle does not give a categorial analysis of *politeia* in the *Politics*, nor is *politeia* known to the *Categories*. Citizenship is not primary in the logical sense in which the definition of citizenship would be required for the definition of citizen body, arrangement of offices, or regime. If Aristotle had wanted to suggest this kind of logical relation, he could have done as he does in book 3, where he requires that the citizen be defined before the city, since the city is the multitude of the citizens (1274b41). In the framework of the *Categories*, it seems, *politeia* would be a homonym, since only the name is the same for the four senses.

This chapter has presented some examples of the use of the word *politeia* in the Aristotelian political works. These examples suggest that the word had a variety of senses and uses which were available to Aristotle when he set out to write these works. For him, the four senses—citizenship, citizen body, arrangement or ordering of offices, or constitution, and regime—would not have been entirely independent of one another, since they were related to one another by historical development as well as by idiom, where, for instance, the abstract could be used for the concrete

---

22. M. Schofield, *Plato: Political Philosophy* (Oxford: Oxford University Press, 2006), 33.

23. Stevenson, *Ethics and Language*, 206–226.

(citizenship and citizen body). Perhaps more importantly, they were related as well because achieving or preserving stability required attention to the condition of citizenship in which the citizens partook, to the citizen body or men, to the constitution or ordering of citizens and offices, and to the regime that occupied these offices. Some translators and others have tended to make this complexity more difficult to perceive by using mainly one expression to render *politeia*, typically 'constitution' or 'regime' or *Verfassung*, perhaps in the belief that structure was the key variable, in policymaking parlance, in setting up a government; and that, once a structure was offered, behavior would change to conform to it. Aristotle, as the evidence suggests, took a different and more comprehensive view, about which he and some of the older scholars have much to tell us.

Before it was made clear that *politeia* was used by Aristotle in these different ways, it was not unusual to find scholars focusing on just one of them—arrangement or ordering of offices (constitution)—and supposing that Aristotle must have been suggesting that the fundamental questions in respect to constitutions were how many kinds there were and which one of these kinds was best, or even ideal, though what any of this meant was not made very clear. Aristotle's language, however, suggests something else, in all three works discussed in this chapter. The next chapter will address the language of kinds in this context, and the following two chapters will consider the language of best and ideal, which are distinct.

Chapter 9

Lineage and Recognizable Configuration
(*Genos* and *Eidos*)

It is supposed sometimes, as suggested in the last chapter, that, in the
Politics, Aristotle is using the language of *genos* and *eidos* in the way the
traditional Porphyrian logic uses genus and species,[1] so that the *politeia* is
the genus and the democracy or the oligarchy or whatever is the species.[2]

---

1. On the Porphyrian origin of species as a predicable, see W. Kneale and M. Kneale,
The Development of Logic (Oxford: Clarendon Press, 1962), 187.

2. Examples can be found in Richard Robinson and others. Robinson writes in his
comments on 4.12, for example:

> It is a doubtful question whether Aristotle in the second half of this
> chapter means 'constitution' in the generic or the specific sense. Newman
> I 501 thought he meant it specifically: "We look for the mention of a
> definite form of constitution in this passage, for not only are democracy
> and oligarchy mentioned in the corresponding sentences, 1296b26, 32, but
> the question under consideration is what constitution suits what people.
> This is a strong reason. And another is that the word 'this' in 1297a3
> looks much like a reference to the specific 'constitution.'"

See *Aristotle's Politics: Books III and IV*, 106. For more recent discussion, see C. A.
Bates Jr., *Aristotle's "Best Regime": Kingship, Democracy, and the Rule of Law* (Baton
Rouge: Louisiana State University Press, 2003) and the review of Bates by J. Lewis
in *Bryn Mawr Classical Review* (July 2003). Bates writes: "The second use of *politeia*,
as a specific regime type, is another source of contention. Scholars such as Lord and
Nichols—as well as Barker—translate *politeia*, in this instance, differently when it
is used to refer to the generic understanding of *politeia*, i.e., regime. In the use of

The text of the *Politics*, however, provides little or no support for this view. In the *Politics*, *genos* is used most often to indicate a hereditary connection (continuous coming to be of things having the same *eidos*)—the first sense given in *Metaphysica* Δ (1024a29–31);[3] and its other uses in the *Politics* do not suggest the logical genus. *Eidos* is used for a recognizable kind rather than for the logical species. As will be seen, many of the occurrences of *eidos* in connection with the *politeia* occur in phrases that must be rendered as 'kind of democracy' or 'kind of oligarchy' or the like. And, in the few instances in which expressions that might be rendered by 'kind of constitution' or 'form of government'—common renderings—do occur, they sometimes mean something else when read in context. 'Form of government' is especially inappropriate, since Aristotle uses *morphē* only four times in the *Politics*, *schema* five times, and *tupos* only six, and never in a phrase about government. *Genos* and *eidos* sometimes occur in the same sentence or in close proximity to one another; and these instances are revealing, since they fail to suggest genus and species, though their use together as genus and species would be required to show that *politeia* is a genus that has several species. This issue is important for the interpretation of the *Politics*, especially because it has been argued in the course of a long-standing controversy that the putative best *politeia* in the *Politics* is a genus that has multiple species.[4] As will be seen, this way of thinking is foreign to the *Politics*. The following account of Aristotle's use of *genos*

---

politeia to refer to a particular form of regime, they translate it as 'polity,' thus agreeing with traditional usage" (104). And Lewis writes: "Here the genus-species framework is assumed. This follows from recognizing that *politeia* here is not a specific regime type, but refers rather to regimes in general."

Also, perhaps, P. L. P. Simpson, *A Philosophical Commentary on the Politics of Aristotle* (Chapel Hill: University of North Carolina Press, 1998), xxvi: "Aristotle also uses *politeia* to mean a particular species or kind of regime."

3. "We call something a kind (1) if there is continuous generation of things which have the same form, e.g., 'while mankind lasts' means 'while the generation of them goes on continuously.'" J. Barnes, *The Complete Works of Aristotle* (Princeton: Princeton University Press, 1984), 2: 1617.

4. Keyt suggests that " 'the one constitution that is best' is a genus whose species are absolute kingship and true aristocracy." See D. Keyt, "Aristotle's Theory of Distributive Justice," in *A Companion to Aristotle's Politics*, ed. D. Keyt and F. D. Miller Jr. (Oxford: Blackwell, 1991), 240.

and *eidos* in the *Politics* is consistent in the main with what D. M. Balme found in the biological works.[5]

My project in this chapter is to clarify Aristotle's use of this language in the *Politics* by surveying the 153 occurrences of *genos* and *eidos* in this work—fifty-eight of *genos*[6] and ninety-five of *eidos*. I begin by addressing the main concentration of occurrences of both expressions in an extended connected discourse, which may be found in the first twelve chapters of book 4. Then I go on to consider separately the remaining occurrences of *genos* and of *eidos*, which are scattered through the work and so do not make up into extended connected discourses. At the end I draw a few conclusions, including that the putative best *politeia* is not a genus, in the sense of the traditional logic, which has multiple species. In references to *genos* and *eidos* I cite the Bekker line in which these expressions occur as given in Ross's text.

Book 4, Chapters 1–12 (1288b10–1297a13)

The first twelve chapters of book 4, where Aristotle mostly is organizing his treatment of the different kinds of democracies, oligarchies, and so on, contain forty-eight occurrences of *genos* and *eidos* in all, or almost one-third of the total. The occurrences by number and case are of *genē* (2), *genos* (5), *eidei* (2), *eidē* (19), and *eidos* (20).

---

5. D. M. Balme, "GENOS and EIDOS in Aristotle's Biology," *Classical Quarterly* 12 (1962): 81–98. Balme notes on 87: "If they differ in meaning, the difference is not that of higher and lower rungs on the same ladder. They belong to different ladders, and the original difference sometimes shows through, *genos* being a statement about kinship and *eidos* a statement about shape or form." It might be objected that the occurrences of διαφορά in *PA* 1.2–3 suggest a genus-species distinction as some have claimed to find it in the *Politics*. Balme's comments rule that objection out. See further Balme, "Aristotle's Use of Differentiae in Zoology," in *Aristote et les problèmes de méthode*, ed. S. Mansion (Louvain: Publications Universitaires, 1961), 195–212. In *de re publica* 1.64, Cicero uses *genus . . . rei publicae* for the kingship rather than *species* or *forma*; so Cicero apparently is not an authority for the interpretation that πολιτεία (=*res publica*) is the genus while kingship, say, is the species.

6. A lemma search of the TLG gives sixty-two instead of fifty-eight because it includes four occurrences of γένεσιν as the accusative singular of γένεσις.

Aristotle begins chapter 1 by using *genos* twice (1288b11, 12) in arguing that arts and sciences that are complete with respect to a *genos* should address what is suitable to the *genos*; and then he gives the example of bodily training for different kinds of trainees. Bodily training will be the analogate for his remarks on the *politeia* through the remainder of Aristotle's chapter. Further on in the chapter, Aristotle notes the importance of knowing how many *eidē* of *politeia* there are (1289a8). This is one of seven places in the *Politics* in which *politeias eidos/eidē* occurs, though translations often suggest that there are many other occurrences of this phrase, as will be seen in this chapter. It is clear that Aristotle is concerned here not with *politeia* as genus and democracy or oligarchy as species but with people who mistakenly think that there is one democracy and that there is one oligarchy (a8–10); he will show that there are many configurations of democracy and many of oligarchy.

Chapter 2 begins with a more characteristic way of speaking for Aristotle, since he typically does not use *politeias eidos/eidē* as he does in chapter 1.[7] Instead he uses just the plural *politeiai*; that is to say, he

---

7. In some cases, the language of the dialogues, which may reflect the language of the Academy, seems to be compatible with the genus-species tradition. In *Resp.* 427A2, for example, *eidos* is used in the phrase 'such a kind' followed by a prepositional phrase with πέρι (τὸ τοιοῦτον εἶδος νόμων πέρι καὶ πολιτείας). On closer examination, though, this is not a case of πολιτείας εἶδος from a grammatical standpoint. In 544C8–D1, one finds "Do you have some other kind of *politeia*, which also is laid down in a certain clear shape?" (ἤ τινα ἄλλην ἔχεις ἰδέαν πολιτείας, ἥτις καὶ ἐν εἴδει διαφανεῖ τινι κεῖται; Shorey renders εἴδει by 'species' here rather than by 'shape'. See Shorey, *Plato: The Republic*, 2: 239. The new Loeb of C. Emlyn-Jones and W. Preddy (Cambridge: Harvard University Press, 2013) gives "character" and splits διαφανεῖ into two words. But διαφανεῖ suggests something visible at least as much as something logical. In *Legg.* 735A5, although we find πολιτείας εἴδη, the situation is quite different, since πολιτεία seems to mean constitution making here, and constitution making seems to have two functions—"the institutions of ἀρχαί, and the laws' being assigned to these several ἀρχαί" (ἐστὸν γὰρ δὴ δύο πολιτείας εἴδη, τὸ μὲν ἀρχῶν καταστάσεις (5) ἑκάστοις, τὸ δὲ νόμοι ταῖς ἀρχαῖς ἀποδοθέντες). If there were species here, they would have to be species of activities rather than of things. In translating this sentence, I follow Morrow's suggested rearrangement of the text. According to Morrow, ἑκάστοις "has lost its original position and gender; clearly it must go with ἀρχαῖς." G. R. Morrow, *Plato's Cretan City: A Historical Interpretation of the Laws* (Princeton: Princeton University Press, 1960), 197, n. 101. On this reading, πολιτεία here means not just the citizenship but the work of setting up the citizenship, which is visible especially in the ἀρχαί. In the note just cited, Morrow justifies his rearrangement by comparison with 751A4–B2, which he renders: "There are two aspects of constitution making: first,

typically uses not what might be rendered 'species' or 'kinds' or 'forms' or 'varieties' with the genitive singular *politeias* but instead uses the plural of *politeia* in the appropriate case (1289a26, 27, 30) without *eidos*. English-language translators sometimes used to preserve Aristotle's plurals. The Scottish scholar John Gillies, for example, the third edition of whose translation appeared in 1813, based on a text that preceded Bekker's, gives "the general division of *governments* into monarchies, aristocracies, and republics" in his rendering of the beginning of chapter 4.[8] (The italics in this passage are mine.) But, at least since the appearance of Jowett's translation in 1885, there has been a tendency among English translators to interpolate 'forms' or the like in these passages and to substitute the singular for the plural of *politeia*. Jowett exhibits the first feature of this tendency in rendering the first five lines of this chapter: "In our original discussions about governments we divided them into three true *forms* [my italics]: kingly rule, aristocracy, and constitutional government, and three corresponding perversions—tyranny, oligarchy, and democracy."[9] Rackham illustrates both features of this tendency in his Loeb translation, which appeared originally in 1932 and still is in print: "And inasmuch as in our first inquiry about the *forms* of the *constitution* [my italics] we classified the right constitutions as three, kingship, aristocracy, and constitutional government, and the deviations from these as three, tyranny from kingship, oligarchy from aristocracy and democracy from constitutional government." [10] And Barker, writing in the war years, reveals this tendency, too, though using 'varieties' instead of 'forms'.[11] In fact, however, there is no occurrence of *eidē* here, only the genitive plural *politeiōn*. Some later translators, including Robinson, Sinclair-Saunders, and Simpson, give a

---

the determination of offices, how many there are to be, and how they are to be filled; and then the assigning of laws to them, determining what they are to be, and how many and what sort would be appropriate for each office." The parallel of the Greek vocabulary of this passage with that of 735A5 is very close. Morrow refers also to 768D[7]–E[3], where the Athenian Stranger makes a transition from the determining of offices to the assigning of laws to these offices. The Stranger's line of thought is strikingly similar to Aristotle's in the *Politics*, for which see Mulhern, "The *Aristē Politeia* and Aristotle's Intended Audience in the *Politica*."

8. Gillies, *Aristotle's Ethics and Politics*, 325.

9. Barnes, *The Complete Works of Aristotle*, 2: 2046.

10. Rackham, *Aristotle: Politics*, 281–283.

11. Barker, *The Politics of Aristotle*, 184.

more accurate rendering of this passage, avoiding the interpolation of 'forms' and preserving the plural of *politeia*.

As Aristotle gets into his discussion, he notes that his project is to find out how many differences (*diaphorai*) of *politeiai* there are, "since there are many *eidē* of the democracy and of the oligarchy" (1289b13). This way of speaking, as previously noted, is Aristotle's characteristic way. And so he shortly speaks of "how someone wishing to do so should set up these *politeiai*, that is to say, democracies of each form and again oligarchies" (1289b22, trans. Robinson modified). These lines illustrate well how his typical use of the appropriate case of the plural *politeiai* and his typical use of *eidos* or *eidē* with the genitive singular of the Greek for democracy or oligarchy or whatever contrast with his less frequent use of *eidos* or *eidē* with the genitive singular *politeias*.

Chapter 3 begins with Aristotle's explaining why there are many *politeiai*, not "many forms of government" (Jowett) or "several forms of constitution" (Rackham). Gillies gives Aristotle's plural ("the wide variety in governments").[12] Aristotle's explanation is that the parts of every city are many in number. He notes that these parts include parts distinguished by wealth but that there are also hereditary distinctions and distinctions in virtue (1289b40–1290a1). Here 'hereditary' renders *kata genos* (by family). This prepositional phrase used as a modifier occurs ten times in the *Politics* among the total of fifty-eight occurrences of *genos* and its inflections, as will be noted later.

Aristotle recaps his argument that there must be many *politeiai* differing in kind (*eidei*) from one another in 1290a6 and 7 (two occurrences). There are twelve occurrences in the *Politics* of the dative singular *eidei*, and ten of these, including the present two, are instances of the idiom *diapherein eidei*—to differ in kind. These other occurrences will be noted in due course. As the chapter goes on, Aristotle again employs his usual way of speaking—the plural *politeiai* and its inflections along with *eidos* and the genitive singular of the Greek for oligarchy or whatever (1290a17).

A few lines further on, Aristotle uses *eidē* in speaking of musical modes, in this case the Dorian and Phrygian (1290a21). He is using this language in comparing the ways people speak about winds and harmonies. People tend to divide phenomena into twos even though there are more than two; so they speak of all winds as north or south and of all modes

---

12. Gillies, *Aristotle's Ethics and Politics*, 325.

as Dorian or Phrygian and of all *politeiai* as democracies or oligarchies. In Aristotle's view, this approach is mistaken in politics, as elsewhere, because it doesn't pay sufficient attention to the different ways in which the parts of an entity may be arranged.

Chapter 4 develops further the rationale for there being kinds of democracy. Again Aristotle goes back to the importance of the parts and their arrangement, and here he uses the illustration of animals and how they will be taken as *eidē* (1290b25), which depends on the parts that every one must have. These include many *genē* of organs that will be combined into many *genē* of animals (1290b30, 33). The result will be different *eidē* of animal (1290b36, two occurrences). The *politeiai* already mentioned, Aristotle says, will work the same way (1290b37–38), and so he begins to list each *genos* (1291a7) of occupation or function that he finds in the city. These apparently are the organs of the city. This chapter includes occurrences of *genos* and *eidos* in close proximity; they do not seem to have the systematic relation to one another of genus and species in the traditional logic.

After this preliminary discussion, Aristotle addresses the *eidē* of democracy (1291b15) in detail, beginning with the many *eidē* of the demos (1291b17, 18) or another *eidos* of the crowd (1291b28). He mentions each *eidos* of democracy in turn (1291b39, 1292a1, 1292a2–3, 1292a4) and summarizes that he has covered the *eidē* of democracy in 1292a38.

Since chapter 4 provides so much in the way of rationale with its discussion of parts and organs, the other chapters can be shorter—only about half as long. Chapter 5 addresses the *eidē* of oligarchy (1292a39) and goes through them severally (as at 1292b4) before summarizing in 1292b11. Then chapter 6 rehearses what has been said about both democracy and oligarchy. Their *eidē* are mentioned in 1292b22 and 1293a11, and each *eidos* is mentioned severally in 1292b33, 34, 38, and 41 and in 1293a14, 22, and 33. In 1292b36, *genos* occurs in the expression *kata to genos*, where Aristotle is talking about a kind of democracy in which there is no objection to a young man's being admitted to citizenship on hereditary grounds but in which such people may not serve regularly in the assembly because they lack the leisure to do so. Thus *kata to genos* here apparently has the same sense (by family) as *kata genos* earlier on.

Chapter 7 goes into new ground, since it takes up subjects other than democracy and oligarchy. Jowett's translation of the opening lines is revealing: "There are still two forms besides democracy and oligarchy;

one of them is universally recognized and included among the four principal forms of government."[13] The Greek, however, says that there are two *politeiai*—the usual plural—besides democracy and oligarchy, and that of these all talk about the other, and it is said that it is one *eidos* (1293a37) of the four *politeiai*. So there are not "two forms [of *politeia*]" here, nor are there "forms of government." *Eidos* does not occur in the plural in this passage, nor does *politeia* occur in the singular here. The language is quite different and is rendered more accurately in respect of number by Sinclair-Saunders: "There are besides democracy and oligarchy two constitutions, one of which is generally recognized and has been included as one type in the list of four."[14] Aristotle continues his enumeration and comes to the fifth *politeia*, which, he says, is forgotten by those who try to count the *eidē* of *politeiai* (1293a42). Here the genitive plural *politeiōn* occurs, but Jowett insists on rendering it with the singular—"the kinds of government."[15] And he is followed by Rackham, who gives "forms of constitution."[16] Sinclair-Saunders is correct here in giving the plural. The chapter ends with mention of two *eidē* of aristocracy (1293b19) and also a third.

Chapter 8 goes off in another new direction to describe a mixed arrangement called *politeia*, which is to be distinguished from those that are mentioned when Aristotle speaks of *politeiai*. Where the expression *to tēs politeias eidos* occurs in 1294a15, Aristotle has this mixed arrangement in mind. And so this occurrence is parallel with *eidos* of democracy or of oligarchy or of whatever rather than suggesting a putative logical genus for all of them. Then the discussion of *eidē* begins to recede. The expression *politeias eidē* occurs at the end of the chapter in 1294a25–26, where Aristotle is summarizing his views about *politeiai* besides monarchy and democracy and oligarchy, what sorts they are, and how the aristocracies differ from one another and the mixed arrangement from aristocracy. *Politeia* is not identified as a *genos* here.

Chapter 9 addresses how to achieve this mixed arrangement; there is no occurrence of either *genos* or *eidos* here. Chapter 10 begins to round out the connected discussion by addressing the *eidē* of tyranny (1295a8). Aristotle goes through his enumeration and mentions a third *eidos* of tyranny in 1295a17. He finishes his discussion of the *eidē* of tyranny in 1295a24.

---

13. Barnes, *The Complete Works of Aristotle*, 2: 2053.

14. Sinclair-Saunders, *Aristotle: The Politics*, 257.

15. Barnes, *The Complete Works of Aristotle*, 2: 2053.

16. Rackham, *Aristotle: Politics*, 313.

After a lull, Aristotle mentions each *eidos* of democracy (1296b27) and each *eidos* of oligarchy (1296b34) in chapter 12, but here the continuous discussion ends.

To summarize Aristotle's language in these chapters: Aristotle uses *genos* and *eidos* in approximately the same sense as one another in comparing the *politeiai* with physical training in chapter 1, and he goes on to mention the *eidē* of democracy and oligarchy in chapter 2. Chapter 3 features two idioms—*kata genos* for 'hereditary' and *diapherein eidei* for 'to differ in kind', where kind is not able to be construed as the traditional logical species. And he uses *eidē* also for musical modes. In methodological observations in chapter 4, he explains that there are different *eidē* (configurations) of animals because they have different *genē* of organs, and then he mentions the different *genē* of occupations in a city that will produce different *politeiai*. There follow the many occurrences of *eidos* and *eidē* with democracy and oligarchy in chapters 4, 5, and 6. In chapter 6, *kata to genos* occurs again with the sense of 'hereditary'. Chapters 7 and 8 also contain occurrences of *eidos* and *eidē* that are used in Aristotle's characteristic way; and while there is no occurrence in chapter 9, both occur in chapter 10 in the discussion of tyranny; and after another hiatus, the *eidos* of oligarchy occurs in chapter 12.

There are in this connected discussion three occurrences of *politeias eidos/eidē*—one in chapter 1 and two in chapter 8. But there is no suggestion of genus and species in any of them. Instead, in chapter 1 (*eidē*, 1289a8), Aristotle immediately goes on to explain that his concern is with people who think that there is only one democracy or one oligarchy, while he wants to point out that there are many *eidē* of democracy and oligarchy, which he goes on to do. In chapter 8, *politeia* in its first occurrence (with *eidos*, 1294a15) is being used for the distinctive combination of oligarchy and democracy rather than for the putative genus. And in the second occurrence in this chapter (with *eidē*, 26), Aristotle is addressing several different situations in a summary way without identifying anything as a genus.

Four of the seven uses of *genos* in these chapters are for hereditary relations, while the uses of *eidos* are varied. If one wanted to argue that genus and species are at work in the *Politics* based on these chapters, it would be most plausible to argue that the genus is democracy or oligarchy or one of the others, which are said repeatedly to have different *eidē*. But even this approach is blocked, since neither democracy nor oligarchy is said to be a *genos* in these chapters. *Genos* is used of democracies and oligarchies in a later passage (1306b19, discussed further on).

Outside Book 4, Chapters 1–12

In reviewing the occurrences outside these chapters, it will be convenient to consider *genos* and *eidos* separately.

Genos

Since the first twelve chapters of book 4 contain seven of the fifty-eight occurrences of *genos* and its inflections, fifty-one remain to be accounted for. Of this number, nine are additional occurrences of *kata genos* in the sense of 'hereditary'; there remain forty-two. Again, in twenty-seven of these other occurrences, Aristotle has in mind some hereditary relation such as membership in a family or some larger group.[17] Modern English translators use a range of expressions—'birth', 'family', 'race', 'nation', 'clan', and so on, where Aristotle has only the one expression *genos*. Once these occurrences are brought into the account, there remain fifteen other occurrences to be dealt with.

Of these, five are in book 1. They are included in phrases that indicate kind of service (1255b27),[18] kind of art (1256a18),[19] kind of men (1256a39), kind of acquisitive art (1256b40),[20] and kinds of mining (1258b32).[21] Of the rest, two more are in book 3 in discussions of kinds

---

17. Γένει 1259b15, 1277b8, 1284a12, 1300a17, 1317b39, 1332b36; γένεσι 1280b34; γένος 1272b39, 1274a32, 1276a35, 1281a6, 1286b24, 1288a9, 1288a10, 1288a13, 1288a15, 1288a18, 1288a35, 1325a8, 1327b29, 1329b22; γένους 1283a37, 1285b24, 1310b12; γενῶν 1269b26, 1272a34, 1280b40.

18. The text at 1255b27 offers an example in which 'kind' is a good rendering, where Aristotle is discussing knowledge and household service, such as the service of a chef. There are different γένη of household service, and each of them has to be learned separately.

19. In 1256a18, Aristotle poses the question whether agriculture is a part of χρηματιστική (moneymaking) or of some other γένος [of discipline], and he goes on to speak of many εἴδη of nourishment. Both of these expressions come over well as 'kind' in English.

20. The text at 1256b40 is part of a discussion of the arts that someone like Aristotle might teach. In this case, the focus is on the art of getting things.

21. Again, in 1258b32, which also occurs in the discussion of χρηματιστική, Aristotle observes that the art of mining has many γένη, since there are many εἴδη of things mined from the earth. Here there does not seem to be any special technical use of these expressions; both can be rendered by 'kind'.

of kingship (1284b41 and 1285a2).[22] Late in book 4 there is a reference to kinds of offices (1299b21), and in book 5 Aristotle uses an expression that may be translated by 'of the same kind' in speaking of democracies and oligarchies (1306b19); this is a passage in which *genos* is used of both democracies and oligarchies.[23] In book 6 *genos* is used for people who might not have any hereditary relation but still are recognizable as a kind—the kind of people who attend the assembly (1319a30). In book 7 there are several occurrences. The first (at 1328a25) is obscure. Then there is a reference to some class that would be like the banausics (1329a20), then to the class of the priests (1329a27), and then to different groups into which the city is divided—warriors and agricultural workers (1329a41). And at last there is the use of *genos* for a musical mode in book 8 (1342a27). None of these appears to be the logical genus of traditional logic.

In short, forty of the fifty-eight occurrences of *genos* in the *Politics* are used to indicate heredity or approximately that; the rest are miscellaneous but not susceptible to being construed as the traditional logical genus. The fifty-eight occurrences thus can be summarized as in table 9.1.

---

22. The text at 1285a2 observes that there are many γένη of kingship and that the manner of rule is not the same in all. This passage goes on to consider the Spartan kingship as an example, which is followed immediately by an allusion to Homer's Agamemnon (1285a16), where Aristotle notes that Homer's Agamemnon illustrates "one *eidos* of kingship, generalship for life, of which some [kinds of kingship] are κατὰ γένος and others are elective. Besides this another *eidos* of monarchy, as are kingships among some of the barbarians." Here the prepositional phrase κατὰ γένος has its usual sense indicating heredity, and *eidos* is used in saying that kingship has several εἴδη or kinds. It appears that γένος and *eidos* in this passage do not have the systematic relation to one another of the logical genus and species.

23. A discussion of μεταβολαὶ τῶν πολιτειῶν is the context for 1306b19, where Aristotle is pointing out that the change sometimes is not to the contrary πολιτεῖαι but to something in the same γένος, as from law-abiding democracies and oligarchies into domineering ones and back again. Here γένος is used not of πολιτεία itself, though, but of the democracies and oligarchies, of which there are different kinds. Further, the kinds that Aristotle has in mind here are not identified as ones with obviously different τάξεις but as ones that exhibit behavioral differences.

Table 9.1. Distribution of Occurrences of *Genos*.

4, 1–12			7
	Heredity	4	
	Other	3	
Elsewhere			51
	Heredity	36	
	Other	15	
Total			**58**

Source: The author.

Eidos

Besides the forty-one occurrences of *eidos* and its inflections in the first twelve chapters of book 4, there are fifty-four occurrences elsewhere in the *Politics*. The sense that runs through them all is that of something noticeable and so distinctive, sometimes but not always distinguishable from somewhat similar things.

Of these fifty-four other occurrences, ten address the kinds of democracy (2),[24] of monarchy (3),[25] of kingship (4),[26] and of royal rule (1).[27] These are unproblematic; they simply indicate that there are *eidē* of each. Presumably, the different kinds of democracy differ in important or notable ways, although they have something in common, which might be, as Newman suggests, "the attribute, or group of attributes, to which it awards power," such as freedom in the case of the democracy.[28] Once these ten occurrences are put aside, forty-four remain to be dealt with.

Of these forty-four, ten are occurrences in the dative singular, eight of which are instances of the idiom *diapherein eidei*—to differ in kind—which was mentioned earlier; these eight are in addition to the two occurrences in the first twelve chapters of book 4. In these eight, the items that differ in kind include the rule of the prince and the rule of

---

24. 1316b36, 1317a21

25. 1285a17, 1285a29, 1285b4

26. 1285a15, 1285b20, 1285b29, 1285b34

27. 1259b12

28. Newman, *The Politics of Aristotle*, 1: 220.

the householder, which are not different simply in ruling over different numbers (1252a10); also making and doing (1254a5), ruling and being ruled (1259b37), the differing people who make up a city (1261a23, 30), the first and second or prior and posterior *politeiai* (1275a36, 39), and the *politeia* that becomes different in kind (1276b2). The other examples of the dative singular are an assistant in the arts who is in kind a tool (1253b30) and a league whose cities are the same in kind (1261a26). After this, thirty-four remain.

There is one occurrence in the dative plural (1314a15), where Aristotle is talking about kinds of tyrannical behavior and is about to give an enumeration. And so he says, looking forward, "They are all included under three *eidē*, so to speak." And there is one occurrence in the genitive plural (1277a10), where Aristotle is dealing with the different kinds of people who make up a city; he says that a city consists "of all these and in addition to these of other dissimilar *eidē*." The rest of the occurrences all are nominatives or accusatives, either singular or plural—thirty-two in all. Four of these thirty-two examples have *politeias eidos/eidē*, and these are the ones that call for attention here (the rest are listed in table 9.3 at the end of this chapter):

1276b31: *Politeias eidē*

This line occurs in book 4, chapter 4—"a chapter," Robinson notes, "more aporetic even than usual in the *Politics*."[29] And so this chapter may benefit from a fresh look.

Aristotle begins the chapter with a question: "Are we to say that the goodness of a good man and a good citizen are the same, or not?" (1276b17–18, trans. Robinson). As noted in the introduction, Develin has pointed out that the English 'good' is being used here for two distinct words in Greek, which throws the translation off. Worse still, the use of 'goodness' for *aretē* complicates the situation further. In any case, Aristotle then goes on, approximately as Robinson renders it but with modifications that accommodate Develin:

> If this ought to be examined, we must first get some outline
> of the virtue of the citizen. We say, then, that the citizen, like
> the sailor, is one of the partners. Sailors are unlike each other

---

29. Robinson, *Aristotle's Politics: Books III and IV*, 14.

in capacity[, and citizens are, too]: one is an oarsman, another a helmsman, another a bowman, and others have other such names; but it is clear that, while the most precise account of each one's virtue will be peculiar to himself, there will also be some common account fitting them all alike. T[his common account derives from the fact that t]he safety of the voyage is the business (*ergon*) of them all, for each of the sailors aims at that. Similarly the citizens, though unlike each other, have the safety of the partnership (*koinōnia*) as their business; and their *koinōnia* is the *politeia*. Hence the virtue of the citizen must be relative to the *politeia* [just as the virtue of the sailor must be relative to the voyage or *nautilia*]; and since there are more [than one] kinds of *politeia* [as of *nautilia*; here the implied comparison might be with 'seamanship'], there clearly cannot be one single virtue of the effective citizen, namely perfect [virtue, any more than there is one single virtue of the effective sailor]. (1276b19–34, trans. Robinson modified and expanded, with the Greek inserted occasionally for his English)

Here the analogy is close, though *plōtēr* for sailor is not cognate with *nautilia*. Aristotle might have used *nautēs* here to make the parallel closer, except that, for him, *nautēs* seems to be somewhat dyslogistic (see 1327b13). Also, *nautilia* covers a range of things that might be designated differently in English, including seamanship, the voyage itself, and so on. Still, citizens and sailors both are partners in something; each citizen and each sailor differs from the others in capacity or ability and so in work or assignment (the assumption being, perhaps, that ability and assignment might be matched); each has his own virtue connected with what he must do, but there will be a common account of virtue fitting them all, since their work, or what they are trying to do, is the same at some point: the safety of the *koinōnia* or what they are trying to achieve in common is their work, whether what they are trying to achieve together is a successful voyage or a successful citizenship. A sailor has a part in saving the voyage, and a citizen has a part in saving the citizenship. Here one *koinōnia* is the community of citizens in the thing in which they are partners, which is the citizenship. If the analogy is as close as I have represented it, the translation of lines 27–34 might be: "Similarly the citizens, though unlike each other, have the safety of the partnership as their business; and their partnership is the citizenship. Hence the virtue of the citizen must be relative to the citizenship; and since there are more [than one] kinds of citizenship, there clearly cannot be one single virtue of the effective citizen, namely complete [virtue]." More kinds of citizenship? Yes. Aristotle goes on to explain what the kinds of citizenship are, and these different kinds of citizenship turn out to be ruling and being ruled rather than being different kinds of rule or regime, as one might think them to be if one rendered *politeia* by 'constitution' as Robinson does here. The citizen who is being ruled does not require the intellectual virtue of the one who is ruling, so the virtue of the one who is being ruled is not complete.[30] Indeed, the citizen who rules and is ruled in turn requires different virtues at different times, so being no more than an effective ruled citizen makes him less than a good man, who always would have the intellectual virtue that the ruling citizen requires when he is ruling. There is none of this discussion of ruling and being ruled in Robinson's comment, which overlooks Aristotle's statements here on ruling and being ruled entirely and so can go off in a completely different, and I believe mistaken, direction.

In short, in this passage, Aristotle is using *politeia* in the sense of 'citizenship' rather than of 'constitution', and the different kinds of citizenship are ruling and being ruled. Once this use is made clear, Aristotle's concluding statement makes perfect sense: "The above makes clear whether or not the virtue of a good man is the same as that of an effective citizen, and in what respect they are the same and in what respect different" (1277b30–32, trans. Robinson modified). Here, then, there is no suggestion that there are species of constitution, since the discussion is not about constitutions or arrangements of offices but about citizenship.

1286a6: *Politeias eidos*

This occurrence is in book 3, chapter 15, where Aristotle is about to finish up his discussion of kingship. He has just considered four kinds of kingship, concluding with the Spartan kingship, and then introduced a fifth kind. At the beginning of chapter 15, he notes that the fourth and fifth kinds are most in need of consideration since the other three kinds lie between them more or less; and then he comes to this line. Robinson describes this chapter as "intensely aporetic."[31]

---

30. 1277a26–29; 1277b25–26

31. Robinson, *Aristotle's Politics: Books III and IV*, 16.

The whole clause in which this phrase occurs is: "The *tropos* of kingship that's left is an *eidos* of *politeia*." The translators have been less than unanimous about *tropos* and *eidos* in this clause, which is an indicator that there may be a latent issue here. Jowett gives "kind" and "sort," Robinson "sort" and "species," Rackham and Simpson "mode" and "kind," and Sinclair-Saunders "style" and "type." Robinson, with "species," is taking things a bit further than the other translators were comfortable in doing. Perhaps the most important thing about this occurrence is that the *explicandum* is spoken of as a *tropos* and the *explicans* is spoken of as an *eidos*. Since *tropos* is an expression that indicates a direction or turn that something takes, often behavioral, it can be used in a range of ways depending on how the direction or turn is construed. Here, *eidos* is treated as roughly the same in meaning as *tropos*, and so *eidos* cannot have a much clearer outline than *tropos*. Neither corresponds to the logical species.

Perhaps here, however, the emphasis should be on *politeia*. Of its four main meanings in the *Politics*, which is the one most likely to be intended here? Aristotle is quite clear, in what he regards as the starting point, that he is concerned here with what or who rules, and so with what in book 3 he has identified as the regime or the *polite-uma*. The kingship with which he is concerned here might well count as a kind of regime, in fact one of two main kinds of kingship, so one almost might say, as he has just said that it is (1285b33–35). It seems here that the sense is regime; if so, there is no *eidos* of constitution here.

1287a4: *Eidos politeias*

In this line, Aristotle refers back to say more fully what he has said just before (1286a6), that the so-called kingship according to law is not an *eidos* of *politeia*,[32] since the perpetual generalship can belong to all, as in democracy and aristocracy, and many put [some]one in charge to manage things. Here he is recognizing again that the *politeia* in one sense is a matter of who rules and that the same arrangement or ordering of offices is possible no matter who occupies them. Thus he cannot here be using

---

32. The codices and Moerbeke give βασιλείας.

politeia in the sense of arrangement of offices or constitution. And then he goes on again to the king who rules over all according to his wish. This line, in chapter 16, refers back to 1286a6 and can be interpreted accordingly.

1304b19: *Eidos politeias*

In this passage Aristotle considers the causes of revolution in each separate kind of *politeia*. After the opening sentence, Aristotle devotes the rest of the chapter to different kinds of democracies as illustrated in historical examples. It appears here that Aristotle is using 'kind of *politeia*' for 'kind of democracy' as a kind of shorthand. In any case, this is one of a very few unusual cases.

In short, the ninety-five occurrences of *eidos* in the *Politics*, including the fifty-four occurrences outside book 4, chapters 1–12, can be summarized as in table 9.2.

The four residual occurrences of *eidos*, which might appear at first glance to offer some support for the genus-species view of constitutions in Aristotle, actually offer little clear support or none at all. The first is about citizenship rather than constitutions, the second and third are about regimes, and the fourth is focused on democracies exclusively.

Table 9.2. Distribution of Occurrences of *Eidos*

4, 1–12			41
	With *politeias*	3	
	Other	38	
Elsewhere			54
	With *politeias*	4	
	Other	50	
Total			**95**

Source: The author.

Conclusion

I have argued that Aristotle used *genos* and *eidos* frequently in the *Politics* in certain regular ways but not together for genus and species in the traditional logical sense; and it is their use together in this sense that would be required to show that, for example, *politeia* is a genus that has several species or that the *aristē politeia* is a genus that has several species. In the *Politics*, *genos* suggests a hereditary relation (Balme's "kinship") in more than two-thirds of its occurrences, and *eidos* often suggests something that distinguishes the things of which it is said from other things in a detectable or perceptible way (Balme's "shape or form") rather than in a logical way.

Further, *politeia* is not said to be a *genos* in the *Politics*, and democracy and oligarchy and so on are not said to be *eidē* of it. Two features mark Aristotle's vocabulary here: He regularly uses the plural *politeiai* when he wants to talk about democracy and oligarchy and the rest together rather than using anything approximating some translators' 'forms of constitution' or the like; and he regularly speaks of *eidē* of democracy and oligarchy and so on.

There are seven apparent exceptions to this rule out of the total of fifty-eight occurrences of *genos* and ninety-five occurrences of *eidos* where Aristotle uses *politeias eidos/eidē*. One of these seven occurrences refers to the *mixis* or mixture of democracy and oligarchy that Aristotle knows as the so-called *politeia* (1293b33–34). Another refers to the citizenship. The remaining five are the only candidates for the genus-species relation. But Aristotle does not say in any of these places that the *politeia* is a genus that has several species. And so there certainly is no reason here to suppose that, for Aristotle, the best *politeia* is a genus that has multiple species. Still, some scholars, once having thought that Aristotle did think in terms of forms of government or kinds of constitution when he spoke of the *politeia*, have been led to ask, what is the best kind of constitution or form of government, or what is the ideal? That way of proceeding is addressed in the next two chapters.

Table 9.3. Occurrences of *Eidos* in the Nominative and Accusative Singular and Plural Not Otherwise Mentioned

Book 1	1252b26: *eidē* shapes [of the gods] 1254a24: *eidē* many kinds of rulers and of ruled 1256a19: *eidē* many kinds of food 1256a14: *eidos* kind 1256b26: *eidos* kind of the acquisitive art 1257a29: *eidos* kind of moneymaking art 1257b2: *eidos* kind of moneymaking art 1258a6: *eidos* kind of moneymaking art 1258b27: *eidos* kind of moneymaking art 1258b32: *eidē* kinds of mined things
Book 2	1267b37: *eidē* kinds of laws
Book 3	1276b7: *eidos* shape [of composite] 1277a37: *eidē* kinds of δοῦλος 1277b17: *eidos* kind of temperance and justice 1277b19: *eidē* kinds of justice 1278a15: *eidē* kinds of citizen 1278a35: *eidē* kinds of citizen 1278b16: *eidē* kinds of rule 1286a3: *eidos* of investigation
Book 4	1300b11: *eidos* kind of power 1300b17: *eidē* kinds of jury courts 1300b19: *eidē* kinds of jury courts 1300b24: *eidē* kinds of homicide court
Book 6	1322b6: *eidos* class of military officers 1322b18: *eidos* kind of care
Book 7	1326b39: *eidos* appearance of the territory 1328a40: *eidē* kinds of city
Book 8	1338b11: *eidē* shapes and growth of bodies

Source: The author.

Chapter 10

Everywhere and Potency
(*Pantachou* and *Dunamis*)[1]

As previously shown in chapter 8, recognizing Aristotle's use of *politeia* in senses other than arrangement or ordering of offices (constitution) opens up additional ground for interpretation, as does the recognition that Aristotle's concern in the *Politics* is rather that the citizens should be *eudaimones* than that some arrangement of offices should be universalized. How, then, should one interpret the sentence at *EN* 1135a5, on which some scholars have relied for interpreting Aristotle's view of the best *politeia*? In this chapter I take up the interpretation of this line and the adjacent text and its importance for the *Politics*. I shall start with a short review of the occurrences of *politeia* in the *Nicomachean Ethics*. For more detail, see chapter 8 in this volume.

There are eighteen occurrences. The translators favor 'constitution' for the most part, though, as noted earlier, Martin Ostwald used 'political system' in four of the eighteen instances, which might be a way of referring to citizenship, since he notes in his glossary that *politeia* "designates the peculiar bond that unites citizen to citizen to form the state, and, in fact, it is *politeia*, or the nature of this bond, that gives the state its identity."[2] There appear to be good contextual reasons for citizenship in three cases, citizen body in four, regime in five, and a mixture in two; the text is

---

1. Portions of this chapter appeared in my "ΜΙΑ ΜΟΝΟΝ ΠΑΝΤΑΧΟΥ ΚΑΤΑ ΦΥΣΙΝ Η ΑΡΙΣΤΗ (*EN* 1135a5)," *Phronesis* 17 (1972): 260–268, reproduced with permission.

2. Ostwald, *Aristotle: Nicomachean Ethics*, 312.

inexplicit in four cases. In 1103b6 (two occurrences), for example, Aristotle is explaining that lawgivers make the citizens good by habituating them, and he goes on shortly to say that the good *politeia* differs from the foul *politeia* in this. He hardly can mean anything but that the good citizen body differs from the foul citizen body in the way it is habituated. Thus the sense here apparently is citizen body. Again, in 1113a8, Aristotle is mentioning the ancient *politeiai* as Homer portrayed them; for the kings announced what they had chosen to the people. Here Aristotle is talking about the behavior of the kings—the regimes of the day. And in 1130b32, Aristotle has *tois koinōnousi tēs politeias*, where the expression seems to refer to those partnering in the citizenship; he goes on shortly to point out that they can have equal or unequal shares. Thus in what follows, while the scholarship shows many occurrences of 'constitution', the reader should bear in mind that Aristotle may have had something else in mind when he used *politeia*—citizenship, citizen body, regime, or a mixture.

In 1962, Robinson wrote, in comments on *Politics* 3.17: "What he [Aristotle] rejects is the general principle that there is only one right constitution, the same for all peoples at all times, no matter what the peculiarities of their society and culture and circumstances. I wish he had said so here explicitly. But he says it clearly enough in the next book, particularly in IV 12."[3] Robinson took up the question again when he commented on 4.12 1296b24–34, in which Aristotle does say, for example, as Robinson renders him: "Where the number of the needy exceeds the stated proportion, there democracy is natural [*pephuken*], and the particular kind of democracy [*hekaston eidos dēmokratias*] [is natural] that accords with the excess [in quantity] of that particular demos. . . . But where the class of the prosperous and notable exceeds in quality more than it falls behind in quantity, there oligarchy is natural, and, as before, the particular kind of oligarchy [*tēs oligarchias ton auton tropon hekaston eidos*] that accords with the superiority of that oligarchic class."[4] These sentences, while they

---

3. Robinson, *Aristotle's Politics: Books III and IV*, 65.

4. Robinson, *Aristotle's Politics: Books III and IV*, 105. This discussion occurs in a chapter in which Aristotle deals with the incommensurability of categories. His considered view is that, though incommensurable, they must be judged in relation to one another by those in his intended audience, who may have to decide, for example, whether in fact the needy will be numerous enough to carry the day against the prosperous and notable, who may or may not have the vigor to carry the day themselves—a question that recurs in Greek history. Thus Aristotle indicates that it is necessary, presumably for the *politikos*, to judge these things—quality and quantity—in relation to one

do suggest that Aristotle considered that different *politeiai* would develop under different circumstances, barring some external obstacle (see chapter 1 on *pephuka*), fall short of being the clear denial of "the general principle that there is only one right constitution" which Robinson was seeking, and Robinson did not go on to give a broader discussion of the question or any analysis that would help to resolve it. Scholars continued in the established view to which Robinson was objecting, drawing on the *Nicomachean Ethics* for support.

In his 1968 monograph *Aristotle's Ethical Theory*, for example, W. F. R. Hardie made use for this purpose of Ross's translation of the *Nicomachean Ethics*, which ran as follows (beginning from 1135a3): "The things which are just not by nature but by human enactment are not everywhere the same, since constitutions also are not the same, though there is but one which is everywhere by nature the best." Hardie said that the distinction being drawn by Aristotle is that of "principles or rules of justice which would be observed in an ideal community and which accord with the real nature of man and the conditions of human happiness" from "rules observed in some community which falls short of the human ideal."[5] Thus he attributed to Aristotle a theory about an ideal community and the constitution that belongs to it.

Hardie's position was strikingly similar to that of Henry Jackson nearly a century before. Jackson had written, by way of explaining these lines, that "human δίκαια [as opposed to the eternal, natural δίκαιον] differ, inasmuch as the πολιτεῖαι to which they belong are all deviations from the one perfect πολιτεία."[6] He translated thus: "δίκαια which are not natural

---

another (1296b24). And he shortly suggests that one might understand how these categories might be judged in relation to one another if one looks at what he has said about proportion before, which presumably is a reference to *kata tēn analogian* in 1282b39 and throughout. There the *analogia* or proportion expresses the relation of the individual to the individual's performance and of the instrument to its use; the example is that of the relation of the individual who will play the flute exceptionally well to the flute that lends itself to being played exceptionally well. The point is that superior fluting, rather than superiority in wealth or beauty or lineage, warrants the claim to a superior flute; and so there must be a comparison on the basis of an appropriate merit (1282b27). Where it is a matter of making claims to the *archai* (1283a11), the claim must be made on the basis of those things on which the city is set up, such as lineage, freedom, or wealth (1283a14–17).

5. Hardie, *Aristotle's Ethical Theory*, 205.

6. Jackson, *ΠΕΡΙ ΔΙΚΑΙΟΣΥΝΗΣ*, 107. These are Jackson's own square brackets.

but of human appointment are not the same in all places, inasmuch as constitutions are not all the same, though in all places there is only one that is natural, i.e., the perfect constitution."[7] The main thrust of both translations, and of both interpretations, is the same: Aristotle believed that one and the same constitution, since it alone is natural, is the best for every community everywhere. This is the established view.

But which *politeia*, after all, is best? Hardie did not tell us, nor did Jackson. One might look for guidance to 1160a35–36, where Aristotle says that kingship is the best of these *politeiai* (*toutōn* [scil. *tōn politeiōn*] *de beltistē men hē basileia*). As Grant and Burnet noted, however, this statement is not intended to apply to all cases.[8] Burnet concludes by saying that the question "is thoroughly discussed in the Third Book of the Politics."

Now the whole question is thoroughly discussed in *Politics* 3. At the end of that book, however, Aristotle declares, not that one *politeia* is best, but only that, as Jowett gives it: "The best must be that which is administered by the best, and in which there is one man, or a whole family, or many persons, excelling all the others together in virtue, and both rulers and subjects are fitted, the one to rule, the others to be ruled, in such a manner as to attain the most eligible life" (1288a33–37.). So far as this passage goes, Aristotle does not choose one among possible *politeiai*, in the modern sense of constitutions, as the best. He does not say, for instance, that the rule of one, or that the rule of a few (a family), or that the rule of many is best; in fact, he appears to say that these organizational considerations should take second place to considerations of virtue in establishing a *politeia*.

Here then is the difficulty: In 1135a3–5, according to the established view, Aristotle says that one and the same *politeia* is best for every community; in 1288a33–37, he discountenances this thesis.

A fresh approach to resolving this difficulty was offered in 1972.[9] The argument presented was that, although one view of the matter was well established, its proponents seemed not to have noticed that Aristotle's words in 1135a5 are ambiguous. The 1972 essay began with a characterization of the established view, proceeded to an analysis of the ambiguity, offered an interpretation of the text, stated and answered anticipated objections

---

7. Jackson, *ΠΕΡΙ ΔΙΚΑΙΟΣΥΝΗΣ*, 41.

8. A. Grant, *The Ethics of Aristotle*, 2 vols. (London: Longmans, Green, 1885), 2: 270; J. Burnet, *The Ethics of Aristotle* (London: Methuen, 1900), 384.

9. Mulhern, "ΜΙΑ ΜΟΝΟΝ ΠΑΝΤΑΧΟΥ ΚΑΤΑ ΦΥΣΙΝ Η ΑΡΙΣΤΗ (*EN* 1135a5)."

to the proposed interpretation, and then concluded by calling attention to a common misconception about the sense of *dunamis* in 1134b19—a misconception which helped to explain the widespread acceptance of the established view.

The argument began with the ambiguity of 1135a5 itself, which can be traced in large part to the role played in it by *pantachou*. According as we construe the role of this expression one way or the other, and provisionally using 'constitution' for the understood *politeia*, the statement may mean either, but not both, of these two quite different things:

1. There is only one constitution that is best by nature for every place.

2. For every place, there is only one constitution that is best by nature for it.

The difference is this: (1) states that, whatever place you choose, you will find that the best constitution by nature for that place will be the best constitution by nature for every other place as well; (2) states only that, whatever place you choose, one constitution will be best by nature for that place, no matter whether it is best by nature for every other place also or not. In order to make the difference as clear as possible, these two formulae were transcribed into the notation of predicate calculus; in the first the particular quantifier ranging over constitutions came first, and in the second the universal quantifier ranging over places came first.

I take it that (2) is what Aristotle meant to say and actually did say at 1135a5. This view is recommended not only by his remarks in the *Politics* but also by the linguistic evidence. If Aristotle had meant (1), there is no reason why he should not have availed himself of the idiom *mia kai hē autē*[10] or something else of the kind; but he did not. Indeed, *autē* does not occur at all in this line of text.

To this interpretation, however, it may be objected that the construction it places upon *pantachou* in 1135a5 clearly does not accord with the construction called for by its occurrences in 1134b19 and 25, 1135a1 and 4—all of which belong to the same conventional chapter as 1135a5. That is to say, it may be objected that *pantachou* is likely to have a single use in a single chapter and that, since, if the alternative interpretation were

---

10. Cf. *Parmenides* 131B3–4.

correct, the use of *pantachou* would differ from its use in these four other nearby occurrences, the alternative interpretation must be incorrect.

This objection may be countered by pointing out that the sentences that contain the four other occurrences of *pantachou* differ markedly from 1135a5 in their logical grammar. It has been noted already that *autē* does not occur in 1135a5. It does occur, however, in 1134b19 and 25 and 1135a4; and although it does not occur in 1135a1, in its stead an expression indicating a variety of sameness—equality—puts in an appearance. This expression is *isa* (*ou gar pantachou isa ta oinēra ktl*). In logical terms, the matter may be put thus:

The four allegedly similar occurrences of *pantachou* are found in contexts that have to do with sameness and equality—relations that are reflexive, symmetrical, and transitive, whereas 1135a5 does not have to do with any such relation. The text at 1135a5 has to do with a relation at all only in the tenuous sense in which one can assert that, if something is best, then it is better than anything else. Even supposing this tenuous sense, however, the relation in question (—is better than—) is neither reflexive (if anything a is better than everything else b, c, d, . . . , it does not follow that a is better than itself) nor symmetrical (if a is better than b, it does not follow that b is better than a), although it may be transitive (if a is better than b, and b is better than c, it does follow that a is better than c). The point is this: to assert that, for every place, a certain reflexive, symmetrical, and transitive relation obtains, is quite a different thing from asserting that, for every place, a feature (=—is best) obtains that, if it is a relational property (=—is better than—) at all, is neither reflexive nor symmetrical.

Even if this point be won from the objector, however, there will remain the question whether the whole drift of Aristotle's argument does not rule out the alternative interpretation. My reply is that Aristotle's argument, far from ruling it out, rather weighs in its favor.

It probably would be correct to say that the established view has relied for its strength not so much on the supposedly uniform use of *pantachou*, and not so much on the alleged overall drift of the argument, as on a reading of 1134b19 that at least tends to occasion misunderstandings.

We find here: *phusikon men to pantachou tēn autēn echon dunamin*. It will be noted that both *pantachou* and *dunamin* make their weight felt. This sentence tells us in no uncertain terms that the *phusikon* has the same *dunamis* in every place. Whatever place you choose, it tells us, you will find that the *dunamis* that is natural for that place will be the same as the *dunamis* that is natural for every other place. On the strength of this line, scholars have assumed Aristotle to have argued, from the ubiquity of a certain natural *dunamis*, that only one constitution is natural everywhere and that the natural constitution is the best everywhere.

Such a reading, however, depends upon taking *dunamis* in what must be considered a questionable sense. If b19 is to support the established view, it must be taken to say that natural justice everywhere has the same effectiveness or actuality, that what is just in one place actually is just in every other also. It must mean that "natural law has everywhere the same *validity*," as Sir Ernest Barker put it,[11] and thus that it is continuously actual, always in the same way. Perhaps it is symptomatic of this view that Ross, followed by Ostwald, uses 'force' to translate *dunamis* here, though Ross's usual translation is the much less aggressive 'potentiality' or 'faculty' in the *Ethics* or 'potency' in the *Metaphysics*.

To see that *dunamis* in this place does not have the sense required by the established view, it should be sufficient to compare Aristotle's discussion at *de Interpretatione* 22b36–23a4—a passage of which the present one is strikingly reminiscent. In Ackrill's version it proceeds as follows:

> Well now, it is evident that not everything capable of being or of walking is capable of the opposites also. There are cases of which this is not true. Firstly, with things capable non-rationally [*tōn mē kata logon dunatōn*]; fire, for example, can heat [fire also is the example at *EN* 1134b25] and has an irrational capability. While the same rational capabilities [*hai men oun meta logou dunameis hai autai*] are capabilities for more than one thing, for contraries, not all irrational capabilities are like this. Fire, as has been said, is not capable of heating and of not heating, and similarly with everything else that is actualized all the time. Some, indeed, even of the things with irrational capabilities are at the same time capable of opposites.[12]

Aristotle here clearly states the view that, while most irrational capabilities, like that of fire to burn, are capabilities for one actualization only,

---

11. E. Barker, *The Political Thought of Plato and Aristotle* (New York: Russell & Russell, 1959), 327. Rackham also had rendered 'validity' in this place.

12. J. L. Ackrill, *Aristotle's Categories and De Interpretatione* (Oxford: Clarendon Press, 1966), 63–64.

the same rational capability will be a capability for more than one actualization. Thus even where the same capability is to be found, its several actualizations may differ among themselves, especially if the capability is *meta logou*. The point is that, if the natural *dunamis* in b19 were *mē kata logon*, then it could make sense to argue that only one of its actualizations was natural and all the others unnatural, even though there might be exceptions; but since this *dunamis* is *meta logou*, then the argument to a single natural actualization will not hold up at all. That this *dunamis* is thought by Aristotle to be *meta logou* will not, I think, be denied. On the assumption that the *dunamis* in question is *meta logou*, the argument from 1134b18 to 1135a5 may be construed in outline as follows: although the natural everywhere has the same capability, different of its actualizations are natural; but no matter what place you choose, there is only one constitution that is best by nature for it.

It was anticipated at the time that critics would attempt to save the established view by arguing that *pantachou* would have had to be used in the same way throughout chapter 7, that the overall drift of the chapter supported the first formula, and that 1134b19 told in favor of the first formula. All three objections were answered preemptively.

In 1980, Pierre Aubenque argued, also against the established interpretation, that *pantachou* in 1135a5 ought to be interpreted as "distributif, et non pas collectif; autrement dit, il n'y a pas une bonne constitution valable pour tous les pays (et pourrions-nous ajouter, pour tous les temps), mais la meilleure constitution est à chaque fois celle qui est conforme à la nature du pays et de ses habitants" (distributive, and not collective; in other words, there is not one good constitution valid for all people, and, we might add, for all times, but the best constitution is for each time that which is conformed to the nature of the country and of its inhabitants).[13] Aubenque was reflecting here Aristotle's concern that the *politikos* and the *nomothetēs* pay attention to the place and the men. Aubenque explained what he intended by *distributif* (*autrement dit*) though not by *collectif*.

In 1990, Pierre Pellegrin adopted Aubenque's argument, criticizing Gauthier and Jolif for not understanding that *pantachou* here had *un sens distibutif*: "Aristote ne fait pas ici allusion à une quelconque "constitution idéale," partout la même chez tous les peuples, ce qui le mettrait en contradiction avec tout le reste de sa pensée politique et avec l'environnement de ce passage lui-même. Il affirme que dans chaque situation concrète il y a une et une seule forme constitutionnelle qui soit excellente. Excellente

---

13. P. Aubenque, "La loi selon Aristote," *Archives de philosophie du droit* 25 (1980): 154.

c'est-à-dire conforme à la nature, et plus précisément à la nature du groupe humain concerné" (Aristotle is not alluding here to any one ideal constitution, everywhere the same for all people, which would put him at odds with all the rest of his political thought and with the environment of this passage itself. He is affirming that in each concrete situation there is one and only one constitutional form which is excellent. Excellent, that is to say conformed to nature, and more precisely to the nature of the human group concerned).[14] Here Pellegrin, following Aubenque, leaves a place for *phusis* as growth or development, especially the development of the human group concerned, with which the treatment of *phusis* in chapter 1 in this volume is consistent.

In 1991, David Keyt attempted to preserve the established interpretation of 1135a5, that there is only one *politeia* that is best by nature for every place, by claiming that the alternative interpretation was not incompatible with it after all. He used this approach in his essay "Aristotle's Theory of Distributive Justice" in arguing that the unity of Aristotle's political thought, especially in the *Politics*, had its origin in "a single conception of distributive justice."[15] But Aristotle had had little of importance to say about distributive justice in the *Politics* beyond what he had said in book 5 of the *Nicomachean Ethics*, to which Aristotle in fact refers us in 1280a18; and so Keyt had to address that book. Keyt wrote in reference to that book: "The *most* correct (*orthotatê*) constitution is the best constitution, the one that aims at good life and happiness, of which there are two species: absolute kingship and true aristocracy (*Pol.* IV.2.1289a31–3, 8.1293b23–7, VII.2. 1324a23–5). . . . Strictly speaking, the only constitution that is according to nature is the best or most correct. Aristotle says this explicitly in the *Nicomachean Ethics*: 'one [sc. constitution] is in all places according to nature—the best' (V.7.1135a5)." These sentences assert Keyt's own hybrid version of the established interpretation of what Aristotle was saying. He gestures at a defense of his position against the alternative interpretation in a footnote appended to these sentences, saying:

> In a long note on this one line of text J. J. Mulhern considers whether it means (1) "There is only one constitution that is best by nature for every place" or (2) "For every place, there is only one constitution that is best by nature for it." In other

---

14. P. Pellegrin, *Les Politiques* (Paris: Flammarion, 1990), 39.

15. Keyt, "Aristotle's Theory of Distributive Justice," 240.

> words, does the universal quantifier follow or precede the uniqueness quantifier? The first alternative, which is the traditional [or established] rendering, seems incompatible with *Aristotle's view that absolute kingship is best in some places whereas true aristocracy is best in others* [my italics]; and so Mulhern concludes that (2) must be the correct interpretation. See Mulhern, "ΜΙΑ ΜΟΝΟΝ ΠΑΝΤΑΧΟΥ ΚΑΤΑ ΦΥΣΙΝ Η ΑΡΙΣΤΗ (*EN* 1135a5)," *Phronesis* 17 (1972), pp. 260–268. However, the alleged incompatibility vanishes once one notices that "the one constitution that is best" is a genus whose species are absolute kingship and true aristocracy (*Pol.* IV.2.1289a31–3).[16]

The alleged incompatibility does not vanish as easily as Keyt might wish, however. Keyt does not say why anyone should notice that the one constitution that is best is thought by Aristotle to be a genus. Indeed, it would be difficult to notice, since Aristotle does not say that the best constitution is a genus, certainly not in 1289a31–33; and Keyt does not offer any texts from which one reasonably might infer that Aristotle thought that the best constitution is a genus. On the question of genus and species (*genos* and *eidos*) in the *Politics*, see chapter 9 in this volume.

In 1994, Aubenque took a position much like his original one in a paper delivered to a colloquium at the Warburg Institute and published the following year, observing: "We are clearly giving a partitive rather than a collective sense to *pantachou* in line 1135a5: 'everywhere on each occasion there is one constitution which is best according to nature,' and not: there is only one constitution that is everywhere by nature the best."[17] In his reply to Aubenque's essay, Troels Engberg-Pedersen took issue with Aubenque, objecting that "Aubenque reads the *pantachou* (everywhere) *distributively*"; Engberg-Pedersen argued on his reading of the "whole passage" that what is "naturally just is, first, that which everywhere (*pantachou*) has the same

---

16. Keyt, "Aristotle's Theory of Distributive Justice," 257, n. 43. The article cited by Keyt apparently was the first in which both the established interpretation and the alternative interpretation were given exact formulations with the aid of the notation of predicate logic to suggest explicitly that 1135a5 might be construed as either (1) there is only one constitution that is best by nature for every place, or (2) for every place, there is only one constitution that is best by nature for it—or (1'): ($\exists$c) [(p) [Bcp & (d) [Bdp $\supset$ d = c]]] as opposed to (2'): (p) [($\exists$c) [Bcp & (d) [Bdp $\supset$ d = c]]].

17. P. Aubenque, "The Twofold Natural Foundation of Justice According to Aristotle," in *Aristotle and Moral Realism*, ed. R. Heinaman (London: UCL Press, 1995), 44, n. 13.

force,"[18] and he added that 'by nature' "presumably means by birth and in accordance with human (genetic) nature."[19] Here three mutually reinforcing mistakes come together—the misconstrual of *dunamis* as force instead of potency or capacity; the primitivist view of *phusis* as *natura* in the Roman Law tradition,[20] especially in the *Digest*, which *natura* is supposed to be the inborn and so universal (see chapter 1 in this volume); and the universalist interpretation of *pantachou*. These three are mutually reinforcing in the sense that taking *dunamis* as force, that is, actuality, instead of as capacity, may make it easier to believe that the *dunamis* is by nature and that what is by nature is actual everywhere, also that what is natural always will exhibit the same force everywhere instead of having the ability to develop into different actualities under different circumstances, and that what is everywhere the same must be the natural and the actual. See further discussion of Keyt and Destrée later in this chapter.

In 1998, in a chapter addressing the conflict of liberals with communitarians, especially his differences with Alasdair MacIntyre, Aubenque returned to this subject and modified his position, writing: "Au moment même où il reconnaît une certaine diversité naturelle—parce que fondées sur des différences naturelles de caractères et de situations—des formes d'organization de la vie sociale, Aristote maintient l'exigence téléologique d'une excellence unique, qui transcende au moins tendanciellement la diversité de fait" (at the very moment when he recognizes a certain natural diversity—because founded on some natural differences of characters and of situations—of the forms of organization of social life, Aristotle maintains the teleological necessity of an unique excellence, which transcends at least tendentially the diversity of fact).[21] He added, in a note: "Dans ce passage, j'entends désormais 'partout' (*pantachou*) au sens obvie de: en tous lieux" (In this passage, I understand hereafter 'everywhere' (*pantachou*) in the obvious sense of: in all places). And he went on to suggest that he was acceding to Engberg-Pedersen's argument.[22]

---

18. T. Engberg-Pedersen, "Justice at a Distance," 55.

19. Engberg-Pedersen, "Justice at a Distance," 56.

20. J. J. Mulhern, "Φύσις as *Natura* in St. Thomas Aquinas's Commentary on the *Politics* and in *STh* I–II Question 94," *The Thomist* 88 (2024): 599–626.

21. P. Aubenque, "Aristote était-il communautariste?" In *En torno a Aristoteles: Homenage al Profesor Pierre Aubenque* (Santiago de Campostela: University Press of Santiago de Campostela, 1998), 43.

22. Aubenque, "Aristote était-il communautariste?," 43, n. 15.

In 2000, Pierre Destrée directed the burden of his argument against Aubenque's original position, according to which, wrote Destrée, "Il faudrait comprendre cette dernière occurrence de l'adverbe πανταχοῦ non pas en un sens collectif, mais distributif" (This last occurrence of the adverb πανταχοῦ should be understood not in a collective sense, but in a distributive one). Here 'collective' presumably means that a predicate is being said of the aggregate of individuals in view—of a heap of sand, say, rather than of each of the grains of sand in it, while 'distributive' means that the predicate is being said of each of the individuals over which the quantifier ranges—of each grain of sand.[23] It is not easy to see how *pantachou* could suggest a heap of *politeiai*. Destrée also tried to save the established interpretation by suggesting against the alternative

---

23. Destrée apparently is arguing for the presumption that an expression will be used uniformly in any given patch of text. But of course an expression can be used in different ways in the same patch of text if the thought demands it. And so Aristotle actually says *to pantes ditton* in 1261b20, for example, and he says in a connected piece of exposition what the two senses of the expression *pantes* are that he has in mind—*hōs hekastos* (severally or distributively, 1261b21) or *ouch hōs hekastos* (not severally, 1261b26). Thus Aristotle himself provides a counterexample to Destrée's view in his comments on the position of the Socrates of the *Republic*. So there is no reason whatsoever to suppose that adjacent occurrences of the same expression always should be supposed to have the same meaning in Aristotle; it is necessary to look at the sense of the text. If *pantachou* can be understood either way, which way will not be determined as easily as with the adjective *pas*, which may be what Destrée has in mind. How *pas* is understood typically depends on its position. So, in the predicate position (not falling between the noun and its article but coming either before or after them—for example, *pantes hoi politai* or *hoi politai pantes*), *pas* has the sense of every one of the citizens, or the citizens—every one of them; while in the attributive position (occurring between the article and its noun, or immediately after the article if the noun precedes), *pas* has the sense of 'all' regarded as a whole of the sum, or an aggregate (as in *hoi pantes politai*—the whole body of citizens). The example is from Smyth, *Greek Grammar*, 296 (1174). What is true of every one of the citizens of ancient Athens, such as weighing so many pounds (on average), obviously will not be true of the whole body of citizens; so this distinction, which we have seen was known to Aristotle himself, is important. Note also, for example, *ouden gar kōluei pote to plēthos einai beltion tōn oligōn kai plousiōteron, ouch hōs kath' hekaston all' hōs athroous* (for nothing prevents the multitude from being better and wealthier sometimes than the few, not severally but together, 1283b33–35). In any case, it certainly would be possible to use *pas* in two ways in the same chapter, even in the same sentence, if one wanted to and were careful about it. But *pantachou* is an adverb not an adjective and is not being used as if it were an adjective here, and so it does not have a predicate or attributive position to indicate that it is being used one way or the other in the way that *pas* does.

interpretation that, for it to be correct, "Il faut tout d'abord postuler que l'adverbe πανταχοῦ a ici un autre sens que dans les autres occurrences du même texte, ce qui est évidemment très improbable" (It is necessary in the first place to postulate that the adverb πανταχοῦ has here a sense different from that in the other occurrences in the same text, which clearly is highly improbable).[24] But, as shown earlier, it is not improbable at all, since the sentences in which the expression occurs have different logical grammars. Destrée also relied on construing *dunamis* in 1134b19 as force, as is clear not only from his translation[25] but also from his comments here and there. With these points lost, there is little left of his argument.

The alternative interpretation in fact does not rest on distinguishing collective from distributive uses. It rests instead on the position of the quantifier—a point that Destrée seems to have missed, though Keyt saw it. Quantifiers always range over individuals distributively, because, in (first-order) predicate logic, the predicate belongs to the individuals, identified by individual variables, over which the quantifier ranges, not to the aggregate of those individuals. Thus Destrée's discussion of collective and distributive uses of *pantachou* fails to engage the alternative interpretation.

His own suggestion is that the text should be read as a discussion of rights (*droits*) where Aristotle has *dikaia*;[26] but to do this, he must take *dunamis* in 1134b19 again in the sense of force rather than in that of the more usual potentiality or faculty—another tack anticipated and addressed, as previously noted, in 1972. On the question of rights in Aristotle, see chapter 5 in this volume.

---

24. P. Destrée, "Aristote et la question du droit naturel (*Eth. Nic.*, V, 10, 1134b18–1135a5)," *Phronesis* 45 (2000): 226. Destrée notes: "On trouve déjà une defense de cette interpretation par J. J. Mulhern, MIA MONON [ΠΑΝΤΑΧΟΥ] KATA FUSIN H ARISTE [*sic*] (*EN* 1135a5), dans: *Phronesis* 17, 1972, pp. 260–268, mais cette defense n'est pas vraiment plausible sur le terrain proprement philologique, car, comme chez P. Aubenque, les arguments avancés relèvent en fait d'une interprétation philosophique préalable!" (One finds a defense of this interpretation already in J. J. Mulhern, MIA MONON [ΠΑΝΤΑΧΟΥ] KATA FUSIN H ARISTE [*sic*] (*EN* 1135a5), in: *Phronesis* 17, 1972, pp. 260–268, but this defense is not truly plausible on properly philological grounds, for, as with P. Aubenque, the arguments brought forward depend in fact upon a prior philosophical interpretation!) Unfortunately, Destrée does not identify what the "interprétation philosophique préalable" might be, and the article to which he refers does not suggest any philosophical position at all on the part of its author.

25. Destrée, "Aristote et la question du droit naturel," 238.

26. Destrée, "Aristote et la question du droit naturel," 229.

In 2007, the criticisms of Keyt and Destrée were addressed in an article on the *aristē politeia* and Aristotle's intended audience. It was argued here on the basis of the language of advice given in the *Politics* that Aristotle's intended audience included *politikoi* and *nomothetai* who were interested in finding the best *politeiai* and *nomoi* for this or that place, depending especially on how many and what kind of people might be available, and on how large and of what kind each place was, and also probably on other circumstances. It was pointed out that the established interpretation, according to which there is only one *politeia* that is best by nature for every place, runs counter to the concern for circumstances that is built into Aristotle's words to his intended audience, while the alternative interpretation—that, for every place, there is only one *politeia* that is best by nature for it—does allow for Aristotle's concern with the circumstances of his intended audience.[27]

In 2017, Pierre Pellegrin restated his position as follows and went on to qualify it, though not in a substantive way:

> A passage in the *Nicomachean Ethics* has been badly interpreted, even by the best commentators. We read there, "There is just one constitution that is everywhere by nature the best" (5.7, 1135a5). Aristotle does not at all want to say that, notably from the fact of the political nature of human beings, there is for all cities one single form of constitution that would be completely natural, the same for all. The "everywhere" has a distributive sense, and in this passage it means that in each particular case, for a given city at a given moment, there is just one constitutional form that is naturally the best, or, to look at the superlative another way that is *excellent*, and this rule is valid everywhere. (Trans. Preus)[28]

Allowing for the rendering by "constitution" and "form of constitution," for which see chapters 8 and 9 here, and for using "distributive" rather than looking to the position of the quantifier, this position seems sound.

In short, the established interpretation of *EN* 1135a5, which continues to be favored by, for example, Simpson and Destrée, thus is difficult

---

27. Mulhern, "The *Aristē Politeia* and Aristotle's Intended Audience in the *Politica*."

28. Pellegrin, *L'Excellence menacée*, 204; trans. A. Preus as *Endangered Excellence*, 183.

to reconcile with Aristotle's practice in the *Politics*.[29] Aristotle's remarks to his intended audience instead support the alternative interpretation, according to which, for every place, there is only one *politeia* that is best by nature for it, as Pellegrin has recognized.

It still might be argued that Aristotle has the established view in mind when he uses the expression *kat' euchēn*, sometimes rendered by 'ideal'. That expression is discussed in the next chapter.

---

29. Simpson, *A Philosophical Commentary on the Politics of Aristotle*, 27; Destrée, "Aristote et la question du droit naturel," 226.

Chapter 11

According to Prayer or Wish (*Kat' Euchēn*)

Translators who use 'ideal constitution' or the like in their translations and authors who use this expression in writing about Aristotle appear to be suggesting that Aristotle had in mind an ideal city or constitution, whatever that might be; the details typically are not spelled out. A recent Festschrift chapter[1] and a special issue of a journal ostensibly devoted to this question perpetuate the established view.[2] A closer look suggests, however, that none of this may be as clear as it has been thought to be. I consider here the Greek expression that is rendered by 'ideal' or is taken to indicate the ideal. This is the prepositional phrase whose noun—*euchē*—is rendered properly by 'prayer' or 'wish'. The chapter addresses *euchē* and its cognate verb in three places where Aristotle quotes the poetic literature: Homer, an unnamed source for the Midas myth, and Phocylides. The evidence from these places may provide an interpretative control for what Aristotle might mean. It then treats the places in which Aristotle uses these expressions outside quotations or allusions, including nine occurrences of *kat' euchēn*.

Kat' euchēn does not correspond in an obvious way to the English or German 'ideal', and I shall not have much to say about 'ideal', though

---

1. G. Giorgini, "Aristotle on the Best Form of Government," in *Enthousiasmos: Essays in Ancient Philosophy, History, and Literature. Festschrift for Eckart Schütrumpf on His 80th Birthday* (Baden-Baden: Academia Verlag, 2019), 121–145.

2. A. Jaulin, "Aristote: le nécessaire et le beau dans la cité 'selon nos vœux,'" and J. Terrel, "En quel sens la cité décrite au livre VII est-elle κατ' εὐχὴν, conforme au vœu de la science politique?," *Polis* 36, no. 1 (2019): 97–116 and 117–138. This number of the journal carried the subtitle *Aristote Politique VII: La constitution "selon nos vœux."* As will be seen later from a review of the pertinent texts, however, Aristotle never uses the Greek equivalent of 'la cité selon nos vœux' or 'la constitution selon nos vœux' in the *Politics*.

175

its history is not without interest.[3] I shall concentrate instead on showing that these occurrences of *kat' euchēn* point to circumstances for which one might wish or pray, especially the men and the land, since these circumstances might further or retard the opportunity for success in founding or reorganizing a city. I don't find that they point to what a Greek who was founding or reorganizing a city might be aiming at, such as at some putatively best arrangement of offices or officials.

Euchē and Its Cognates

Aristotle uses inflections of both *euchē* and its cognate verb *euchomai*. Other cognates are sparse or lacking. He quotes Homer's *euchōlē* (i.e., prayer, vow, or boast) once in the *Rhetoric* (1363a5), but he does not use the rare diminutive *euchion* or the more common *euchos* (i.e., vow or object of prayer). Most of the occurrences of *euchē* occur in the phrase *kat' euchēn*. As will be seen in this chapter, the first occurrence of this phrase is in 1260b29. Jowett, Rackham, and Barker all used 'ideal' here and rendered later occurrences fairly consistently with this one. Sinclair-Saunders departed from this tradition by using "as we would like" (102); Simpson has departed from this tradition as well by using "according to prayer" (34; in other contexts Simpson uses "one would pray for" or "with our prayer"); and Schütrumpf regularly uses *Wunsch* and *wünschen* rather than *Bitte* and *beten*. The last three have the considerable merit of attempting to save the language, Sinclair-Saunders and Schütrumpf in a terrestrial way and Simpson in a more celestial way that is associated with his view (at one time) that Aristotle had in mind a *civitas Dei* or heavenly city.[4]

It appears that Aristotle is concerned with the objects of *euchē* for his intended audience, namely for the *politikos* and for the *nomothetēs*—for the individual preoccupied with citizen issues and for the lawgiver, at least one of whom he mentions explicitly in three of the nine passages in which *kat' euchēn* occurs. These functionaries are concerned with the circumstances, including the men who are to be citizens and the places that are to be populated or fortified, which are presented by *phusis* or by chance and so which the *politikos* and the *nomothetēs* do not control, though

---

3. Kant speaks of the Ideal der reinen Vernunft in *Kritik der reinen Vernunft* B398 (Hamburg: Felix Meiner, 1956), 370.

4. P. L. P. Simpson in his paper "Aristotle's City of God," Annual Meeting, New York State Political Science Association, New York, April 25, 2009.

they might wish or pray that these circumstances be favorable. The actual circumstances will limit what they can accomplish, and it is their work to produce and preserve the best *politeia* that the circumstances permit.[5] If this interpretation is correct, Aristotle's uses of *euchē* and of *euchomai* are consistent with what he says elsewhere in making the *politikos* and the *nomothetēs* causes of the *politai* (not of the men but of the citizens who are made out of them), the *poleis*, and the *politeiai*; and there are things of which they are not the causes, including the circumstances, because chance and *phusis* are the causes of these.

The *Politics* offers one occurrence of the nominative *euchē*, two of the genitive *euchēs*, nine of the accusative *euchēn* (always in the prepositional phrase *kat' euchēn*), and single occurrences of four inflections of the verb. Two of the occurrences of inflections of the verb are found in passages that also contain occurrences of *kat' euchēn*. Thus while there are sixteen occurrences to be reviewed, they appear in just fourteen sentences or logically related groups of sentences. All of them are considered here. Three of these occurrences are especially revealing, since, in them, Aristotle quotes or alludes to literary sources. They are the following:

Quotations and Allusions

Aristotle quotes part of what he speaks of as the *euchē* of Agamemnon (*Iliad* 2.371–372), where Agamemnon is marveling at the good advice of Nestor. And so this text provides an interpretative control from a context that is well known. The pertinent lines of Aristotle are 3.1287b11–15: "Again, the thing said before is, if the excellent man is just to rule because he is better, still two good ones are better than one. For this is 'When two go together' and the prayer [or wish] of Agamemnon 'would that I had ten such counselors.'"[6] The lines in Homer to which Aristotle is referring in the second quotation are:

---

5. The evidence for these assertions has been presented in Mulhern, "The *Aristē Politeia* and Aristotle's Intended Audience in the *Politica*." Aristotle gives his longest but not exhaustive list of circumstances in *EN* 1111a3–5.

6. ἔτι, ὃ καὶ πρότερον εἰρημένον
  ἐστίν, εἴπερ ὁ ἀνὴρ ὁ σπουδαῖος, διότι βελτίων, ἄρχειν δίκαιος, τοῦ γε ἑνὸς οἱ δύο ἀγαθοὶ βελτίους· τοῦτο γάρ ἐστι τὸ
  "σύν τε δύ' ἐρχομένω" καὶ ἡ εὐχὴ τοῦ Ἀγαμέμνονος "τοιοῦτοι δέκα μοι συμφράδμονες."

> O father Zeus, Athene, Apollo:
> would that among the Achaians I had ten such counselors.[7]

Aristotle quotes the first four words of the second line. Knowing the sense of the passage in Homer may help in building up a picture of what Aristotle had in mind in using *euchē* here.

Agamemnon is addressing Zeus, Athena, and Apollo, and his address is, if a prayer, then a prayer expressed as a wish, indicated by *eien*, and not one that Agamemnon expected to be answered or fulfilled. There is only one Nestor, and there won't be nine more. In fact, Agamemnon doesn't have much cachet with these immortals anyway. Agamemnon is not using a prayer of petition or supplication here; his *euchē* is not for something that even he believes is achievable.[8] And he is proven correct. Nestor remains uniquely the wisest (*sophōtatos*) in the Homeric tradition.[9] Aristotle would have recognized that not every *euchē* is likely to be fulfilled. In any case, how many Nestors Agamemnon has is something that Agamemnon cannot control.

The second text in this group, which includes an occurrence in the genitive singular, is an allusion to the Midas story, which provides more evidence for Aristotle's understanding of *euchē*. Aristotle says in 1.1257b14–17: "Yet it is odd that wealth should be such that someone well supplied with it should die from hunger, as they tell the tale of that Midas, with all things near him turning into gold because of the greed of his prayer [or wish]."[10] Aristotle shows us here that he was aware that in Midas's case, the *euchē* was pernicious, a result of Midas's insatiate

---

7. αἲ γὰρ Ζεῦ τε πάτερ καὶ Ἀθηναίη καὶ Ἄπολλον
   τοιοῦτοι δέκα μοι συμφράδμονες εἶεν Ἀχαιῶν
T. W. Allen, *Homeri Ilias*, vols. 2–3 (Oxford: Clarendon Press, 1931). The translations of Homer 10.224 and 2.371–2 are those of R. Lattimore, *The Iliad of Homer* (Chicago: University of Chicago Press, 1951).

8. Seymour's school *Iliad* contains the note: "This appeal to the three chief divinities is made in the case of ardent wishes. Generally, as here, fulfillment of the wish is not expected." Seymour refers to Cicero *de Senectute* 31. See T. D. Seymour, *The First Six Books of Homer's Iliad: Introduction, Commentary, and Vocabulary*, rev. ed. (Boston: Ginn, 1903), 77.

9. In Plato's *Hippias Minor* 364C6, for example.

10. καίτοι ἄτοπον τοιοῦτον
    εἶναι πλοῦτον οὗ εὐπορῶν λιμῷ ἀπολεῖται, καθάπερ καὶ τὸν (15)
    Μίδαν ἐκεῖνον μυθολογοῦσι διὰ τὴν ἀπληστίαν τῆς εὐχῆς
    πάντων αὐτῷ γιγνομένων τῶν παρατιθεμένων χρυσῶν.

desire for wealth, whose outcome was the turning of Midas's aliments into inedible gold and thus his near starvation. It would be nice to know in what version Aristotle had the legend that he says they tell (*muthologousi*) about Midas—perhaps the same source used by Ovid (*Met.* 11.85–145), who had Midas express his wish or prayer to Bacchus. Newman is silent here, and the ancient authors fail to help us identify a common source for the golden touch. Professor Roller points out that this passage of Aristotle's is "the earliest known reference" to the golden touch and that the modern commentaries on Ovid typically ignore it.[11] Indeed, even if Aristotle and Ovid used the same source, Ovid's account would not decide the issue of the sense of *euchē* as either prayer or wish, since Ovid uses inflections of both *optare* (to wish) and *vovēre* (to pray) in his account. But Aristotle's allusion surely suggests that not every *euchē* is appropriate and that the outcomes may be unintended and harmful. When Midas's prayer or wish is fulfilled, it becomes clear that the outcome is out of his control.

A third passage of the *Politics*, which uses the verb, also quotes an earlier author. In 4.1295b28–39 (first occurrence of *euchomai*):

> And these citizens most of all are preserved in the cities because they do not desire the belongings of others, as the poor do, nor do the others desire theirs, as the poor do of the wealthy. And because of neither being plotted against nor plotting, they pass their time without danger. Because of this Phocylides nobly prayed [or wished] "Many of the best things belong to those in the middle. The middle in the city I wish to be."
>
> It is clear then that the citizen community is best because of the middle people, and it is possible for such cities to be well governed in which the middle is big and stronger than both at best, and if not, than of either part. For when it is added, the middle tips the scale and prevents the contrary extremes from coming to be.[12]

---

11. L. E. Roller, "The Legend of Midas," *Classical Antiquity* 2, no. 2 (1983): 310, especially n. 89.

12. καὶ
σῴζονται δ' ἐν ταῖς πόλεσιν οὗτοι μάλιστα τῶν πολιτῶν. οὔτε
γὰρ αὐτοὶ τῶν ἀλλοτρίων, ὥσπερ οἱ πένητες, ἐπιθυμοῦσιν, οὔτε (30)
τῆς τούτων ἕτεροι, καθάπερ τῆς τῶν πλουσίων οἱ πένητες ἐπι-
θυμοῦσιν· καὶ διὰ τὸ μήτ' ἐπιβουλεύεσθαι μήτ' ἐπιβουλεύειν
ἀκινδύνως διάγουσιν. διὰ τοῦτο καλῶς ηὔξατο Φωκυλίδης

This passage also provides an opportunity for interpretative control because of its use of an author known independently.[13] In this passage, Aristotle quotes the sixth-century poet Phocylides of Miletus approvingly because he wished or prayed nobly (*kalōs ēuxato*), "The middle in the city I wish to be." Here *thelō* in Phocylides almost surely means wish and not pray. Aristotle also quotes the words of Phocylides that precede the wish or prayer proper, "Many of the best things belong to those in the middle." Aristotle then interprets: "It is clear then that the citizen community is best because of the middle people." Those in the middle here are middling in wealth, and if they are sufficiently numerous, they will prevent the contrary extremes of wealth and poverty from becoming dominant. Aristotle describes this situation as *eutuchia megistē* (1295b39–40)—the greatest good fortune, again suggesting that the objects of chance rather than of choice are the objects of *euchē*.

The first two of these passages should remove any predisposition in favor of the view that occurrences of these words in Aristotle regularly suggest anything heavenly. The third should confirm the impression that the men who happen to be available to the *politikos* and the *nomothetēs* are the result of chance or *phusis* and are not matters of choice. So, in each of these three places, the items associated with *euchē* are circumstances rather than the *politeia* or the *polis*.

Outside Quotations or Allusions

The remaining occurrences are not connected with quotations or with literary allusions that are easy to identify, so their sense must be divined from evidence internal to Aristotle's text.

In connection with the second and last occurrence of the genitive, Aristotle says in 7.1331b19–22: "For it is not difficult to think such things, but to make them rather. For while to speak is the work of prayer [or

---

"πολλὰ μέσοισιν ἄριστα· μέσος θέλω ἐν πόλει εἶναι."
    δῆλον (34)
ἄρα ὅτι καὶ ἡ κοινωνία ἡ πολιτικὴ ἀρίστη ἡ διὰ τῶν μέσων, (35)
καὶ τὰς τοιαύτας ἐνδέχεται εὖ πολιτεύεσθαι πόλεις ἐν αἷς
δὴ πολὺ τὸ μέσον καὶ κρεῖττον, μάλιστα μὲν ἀμφοῖν, εἰ
δὲ μή, θατέρου μέρους· προστιθέμενον γὰρ ποιεῖ ῥοπὴν καὶ
κωλύει γίνεσθαι τὰς ἐναντίας ὑπερβολάς.

13. See M. L. West, "Phocylides," *Journal of Hellenic Studies* 98 (1978): 164–167.

wish], coming to pass is of chance."[14] In this occurrence, *euchē* is connected explicitly with *tuchē*. These two words may have sounded somewhat similar in classical Greek; and, if so, Aristotle's message would have come across all the more sharply.[15] Aristotle here is dealing with questions of village planning in the countryside, and he suggests that it is necessary to distribute the things related to the land here also according to the arrangement just described (1331b13–14) in discussing the men and the place for the city. And then he makes the connection in the quoted passage of *euchē* with *tuchē* just before moving on to his new topic, which is the *politeia* itself.

In treating this new topic, however, he refers back to *tuchē*, observing that, while some have the opportunity to attain the good life, others do not, because of chance or *phusis*, since living nobly requires a certain resource, although less for the better disposed than for the worse.[16] As in 1331b19–22, *tuchē* and *euchē* have the same object—*tuchē* as producing or providing it, *euchē* as addressing it in a certain way. *Phusis* is brought into parallel with *tuchē*, since the resource required and available may depend upon either or both of them. Clearly *euchē* is associated here with things of which the *politikos* and the *nomothetēs* are not the causes, since *tuchē* and *phusis* are their causes, though the *politikos* and the *nomothetēs* are the causes of the *politeia*.

Kat' euchēn

The association of *euchē* with things of which men are not the causes is repeated in the nine instances of the accusative singular in the prepositional phrase *kat' euchēn*, which are treated here in the order of their occurrence.

2.1260b27–31:

---

14. οὐ
γὰρ χαλεπόν ἐστι τὰ τοιαῦτα νοῆσαι, ἀλλὰ ποιῆσαι μᾶλ- (20)
λον· τὸ μὲν γὰρ λέγειν εὐχῆς ἔργον ἐστί, τὸ δὲ συμβῆναι
τύχης.

15. Newman makes this point in his comments on 1331b20 and 21. See Newman, *The Politics of Aristotle*, 3: 420–421. See also Aristotle's quotation of Agathon in *EN* 1140a19–20.

16. ἀλλὰ τούτων τοῖς μὲν ἐξουσία τυγχάνει τοῖς δὲ οὔ, διά τινα τύχην ἢ φύσιν (δεῖται γὰρ καὶ χορηγίας τινὸς τὸ ζῆν καλῶς, τούτου δὲ ἐλάττονος μὲν τοῖς ἄμεινον διακειμένοις, πλείονος δὲ τοῖς χεῖρον), 1331b40–1332a2.

> Since we choose to consider the citizen community [lit. the community related to the citizen, rather than to, say, the member of an household] which is the strongest of all for those who are able most of all to live *kat' euchēn*, it is necessary to consider the other *politeiai* which some of the cities use which are said to be well regulated.[17]

This occurrence appears at the very beginning of book 2, just after Aristotle has finished his apparent preliminaries. Here Aristotle refers to his method of considering what others have thought and said on the subject. Clearly many people have some idea of how they would prefer to live, although they may be vague about it. They may pray or wish that they will live in a community of a certain kind. Some are able to and some are not, no matter how hard they try and even though they may make some progress. The reason is that some things are out of their control. Indeed, this is why these things are objects of prayers or wishes rather than of their own actions and choices. And so Aristotle suggests that they look to other arrangements—other than those for which they pray or wish—that have been said to work well, especially by his predecessors. Here *kat' euchēn* apparently modifies 'live' (*zēn*).

2.1265a17–20:

> It is necessary then to assume *kat' euchēn*, but not the impossible. And it is said that the lawmaker must make the laws with an eye to two things, the land and the men.[18]

In this second occurrence of *kat' euchēn*, Aristotle is objecting against the tendency of some, such as Socrates in the *Republic*, to assume circumstances that not only are *kat' euchēn* in his sense but actually are

---

17. Ἐπεὶ δὲ προαιρούμεθα θεωρῆσαι περὶ τῆς κοινωνίας τῆς (27) πολιτικῆς, τίς κρατίστη πασῶν τοῖς δυναμένοις ζῆν ὅτι μάλιστα κατ' εὐχήν, δεῖ καὶ τὰς ἄλλας ἐπισκέψασθαι πολιτείας, αἷς τε χρῶνταί τινες τῶν πόλεων τῶν εὐνομεῖσθαι (30) λεγομένων,

18. δεῖ μὲν οὖν ὑποτίθεσθαι κατ' εὐχήν, μηδὲν μέντοι ἀδύνατον. λέγεται δ' ὡς δεῖ τὸν νομοθέτην πρὸς δύο βλέποντα τιθέναι τοὺς νόμους, πρός τε τὴν χώραν καὶ τοὺς ἀνθρώπους.

impossible (*adunaton*). Here Aristotle is pointing out that the *kat' euchēn* differs from the impossible. His auditors are advised (*dei*) to assume one but not the other. And what are the assumptions about? They are about land and men—two things that usually are not within the legislator's control. *Kat' euchēn* modifies 'assume' (*hupotithesthai*).

4.1288b21–27:

So that it is clear in the case of the *politeia* also that it is for the same science to look at what is very good [or best] and at what sort would be most of all according to prayer [or wish], there being no external obstacle, and at what is agreeable to whom (since for many it is perhaps impossible to hit the best, so that the good lawmaker and the individual who truly is concerned with the citizen must not let the strongest strictly speaking and the best considering the subjects go unnoticed).[19]

Here again Aristotle distinguishes the *kat' euchēn* from the impossible, and he focuses on the exogenous causes that the political actor cannot control but with which he must deal when he explains *kat' euchēn* by there being no external obstacle. *Kat' euchēn* modifies 'would be' (*eiē*).

4.1295a25–31:

But what is the best *politeia* and what is the best life for most cities and for most men, if they do not judge in relation to virtue that is beyond individuals in households, nor in relation to education that is in need of *phusis* and of fortune's resources, nor in relation to a *politeia* that has come to be *kat' euchēn*, but a life able to be shared by most and a *politeia* that it is

---

19. ὥστε δῆλον ὅτι
καὶ πολιτείαν τῆς αὐτῆς ἐστιν ἐπιστήμης τὴν ἀρίστην θεωρῆσαι
τίς ἐστι καὶ ποία τις ἂν οὖσα μάλιστ' εἴη κατ' εὐχὴν μηδε-
νὸς ἐμποδίζοντος τῶν ἐκτός, καὶ τίς τίσιν ἁρμόττουσα (πολ-
λοῖς γὰρ τῆς ἀρίστης τυχεῖν ἴσως ἀδύνατον, ὥστε τὴν κρατί- (25)
στην τε ἁπλῶς καὶ τὴν ἐκ τῶν ὑποκειμένων ἀρίστην οὐ δεῖ
λεληθέναι τὸν ἀγαθὸν νομοθέτην καὶ τὸν ὡς ἀληθῶς πολιτικόν),

possible for most cities to share?[20]

In this passage, Aristotle reopens discussion of the excellent or best (*aristē*) *politeia*. He asks what is best for most cities and for most men if they do not judge in relation to a *politeia* that has come to be *kat' euchēn*, among other things. The Sinclair-Saunders translation gives "ideally perfect constitution" here (265), but that seems to be more than Aristotle had in mind and to depart from their view of what is appropriate elsewhere. Again one sees that Aristotle is focused on the circumstances that his auditors do not control but with which they must work as objects of *euchē*, and here these are most explicitly the men. *Kat' euchēn* apparently modifies 'has come to be' (*ginomenēn*).

7.1325b35–40 (second occurrence of *euchomai*):

The start of the remaining things is first to say what sort the assumptions must be concerning the city about to be established *kat' euchēn*. For the *aristē politeia* does not come to be without commensurate resource. It is necessary therefore to assume in advance many things even as if praying [or wishing] (*kathaper euchomenous*), though none of these being impossible. I am talking, for example, about the number of citizens and about the land.[21]

This is the first of the three passages that contain inflections of both

---

20. Τίς δ' ἀρίστη πολιτεία καὶ τίς ἄριστος βίος ταῖς πλεί- (25)
σταις πόλεσι καὶ τοῖς πλείστοις τῶν ἀνθρώπων, μήτε πρὸς
ἀρετὴν συγκρίνουσι τὴν ὑπὲρ τοὺς ἰδιώτας, μήτε πρὸς παιδείαν
ἢ φύσεως δεῖται καὶ χορηγίας τυχηρᾶς, μήτε πρὸς πολιτείαν τὴν κατ' εὐχὴν γινομένην, ἀλλὰ βίον τε τὸν τοῖς
πλείστοις κοινωνῆσαι δυνατὸν καὶ πολιτείαν ἧς τὰς πλείστας (30)
πόλεις ἐνδέχεται μετασχεῖν;

21. ἀρχὴ τῶν λοιπῶν εἰπεῖν πρῶτον ποίας τινὰς δεῖ τὰς ὑπο- (35)
θέσεις εἶναι περὶ τῆς μελλούσης κατ' εὐχὴν συνεστάναι πόλεως.
οὐ γὰρ οἷόν τε πολιτείαν γενέσθαι τὴν ἀρίστην ἄνευ συμ-
μέτρου χορηγίας. διὸ δεῖ πολλὰ προϋποτεθεῖσθαι καθάπερ
εὐχομένους, εἶναι μέντοι μηθὲν τούτων ἀδύνατον· λέγω δὲ
οἷον περί τε πλήθους πολιτῶν καὶ χώρας.

euchē and *euchomai*. Here Aristotle makes quite clear what the *politikos* and the *nomothetēs* might assume as preliminary as if they were praying or wishing. Perhaps even more clearly than some others, it interprets the prepositional phrase to show what is prayed for or wished for—not a certain *polis* or *politeia* but the circumstances in which the *aristē politeia* under the circumstances might be brought about, including suitable people and territory. *Kat' euchēn* modifies 'to be established' (*sunestanai*).

7.1327a3–5:

If it is necessary to make the position of the city *kat' euchēn*, it is appropriate to place it well in relation to the sea and in relation to the land.[22]

Here again, it is not the city that is *kat' euchēn* but rather its position or *thesis*—a circumstance, surely. Of course it is up to the *politikos* to select such a position if he has the option, but he may not have the option. Having it is not something of which he is the cause. He may have to work in less favorable circumstances. *Kat' euchēn* modifies *poiein*.

7.1330a25–30:

If it is necessary *kat' euchēn* for the farmworkers most of all to be *douloi*, neither all of them from the same tribe nor spirited (for thus they would be useful in relation to the occupation and safe in relation to not revolting), still as a second they should be barbarian neighbors resembling the crop in the previous remarks.[23]

---

22. τῆς δὲ πόλεως τὴν θέσιν
   εἰ χρὴ ποιεῖν κατ' εὐχήν, πρός τε τὴν θάλατταν προσήκει
   κεῖσθαι καλῶς πρός τε τὴν χώραν.

23. τοὺς δὲ γεωργήσοντας μάλιστα μέν, εἰ δεῖ κατ' (25)
   εὐχήν, δούλους εἶναι, μήτε ὁμοφύλων πάντων <ὄντων> μήτε
   θυμοειδῶν (οὕτω γὰρ ἂν πρός τε τὴν ἐργασίαν εἶεν χρήσιμοι
   καὶ πρὸς τὸ μηδὲν νεωτερίζειν ἀσφαλεῖς), δεύτερον δὲ
   βαρβάρους περιοίκους παραπλησίους τοῖς εἰρημένοις τὴν φύσιν,

This is another text in which Aristotle is giving advice about the men who are products of *phusis* and of chance, though Aristotle is advising his auditors to select among them. Samaras has embraced an emerging interpretation that this text apparently addresses the situation in new colonies in Asia Minor rather than the situation in mainland Greece.[24] *Kat' euchēn* modifies 'it is necessary' (*dei*).

> 7.1330a34–38 (third occurrence of *euchomai*):

> That it is necessary for the city to communicate with the mainland and the sea and all the land in the same way as far as possible has been said before. It is necessary to pray with a prayer [or wish with a wish] that the position be uphill, in relation to four considerations.[25]

This is the second passage that includes both *kat' euchēn* and an inflection of *euchomai*, the first in which the prepositional phrase modifies this verb. Ross's text here is different from the received text and goes a step further than Immisch. Neither Bekker nor Newman has *kat' euchēn*.[26] On almost any reading, however, Aristotle is making abundantly clear what he means by considering the land. The city should be on a healthy site with respect to air quality and water quality, as we should say. Further, it should work well for military and political purposes, as he goes on to detail. The circumstance of position, however, is not in the control of the *politikos* or the *nomothetēs*, though both might make the most of what they find.

> 7.1332a28–32 (fourth occurrence of *euchomai*):

> It is necessary further from what has been said that while some things spring up, the lawmaker should provide others. Therefore

---

24. A. Samaras, "Aristotle's *Politics*: The City of Book Seven and the Question of Ideology," *Classical Quarterly* 57 (2007): 88–89.

25. Τὴν δὲ πόλιν ὅτι μὲν δεῖ κοινὴν εἶναι τῆς ἠπείρου τε
καὶ τῆς θαλάττης καὶ τῆς χώρας ἁπάσης ὁμοίως ἐκ τῶν
ἐνδεχομένων, εἴρηται πρότερον· αὐτῆς δὲ προσάντη εἶναι
τὴν θέσιν εὔχεσθαι δεῖ κατ' εὐχήν, πρὸς τέτταρα βλέ-
ποντας·

26. Both have κατατυγχάνειν. Dreizehnter, *Aristoteles' Politik*, gives κατὰ τύχην. Newman, *The Politics of Aristotle*, 3: 395–397, discusses the passage in detail.

we pray with a prayer [or wish with a wish] for the city's being composed of the things over which fortune is dominant (for we propose that it is dominant). But the city's being effective is no longer the work of fortune but of knowledge and of choice.[27]

In this third occurrence of the noun and the verb together we have the second occasion on which the prepositional phrase may modify this verb. Newman notes: "Either we may take κατ' εὐχήν adverbial to εὐχόμεθα and translate with Sepulv. 'precibus optamus' (so Vict. and Lamb.), or we may supply εἶναι and translate 'hence in respect of those things over which fortune is supreme we pray that the composition of the State may be all that can be wished.' "[28] While Newman has some preference for the latter, he does not appear to have compared this occurrence systematically with the others in which *kat' euchēn* regularly modifies a verb. These other occurrences certainly make it easier to see an adverbial use here. And Aristotle used other prepositional phrases as adverbs to modify verbs.[29]

Either way, this text perhaps makes clearer than any other the line that Aristotle draws to separate the things that the *politikos* and the *nomothetēs* cause and the things that are beyond their control and for which they can only wish or pray, especially the men and the land with which they will have to work. The contrast of the work of *tuchē* with that of *prohairesis* reflects Aristotle's technical language for discussing human causality in book 6 of the *Ethics*, where Aristotle says that the origin of action is *prohairesis* (1139a31).[30]

Finally, what about the expression itself *kat' euchēn*? How should it be translated? Sepulveda's *precibus* perhaps is echoed in Simpson's "according to prayer." Whatever the translation, it should preserve the sense of the Greek, eschewing 'ideal' and 'best' and the like; and it should be used in a way that shows clearly that the objects of *euchē* are things provided by chance and *phusis* in contrast with the *poleis* and the *politeiai*, which are caused by men through their choices.

---

27. ἀναγκαῖον τοίνυν ἐκ τῶν εἰρημένων τὰ μὲν ὑπάρχειν, τὰ
   δὲ παρασκευάσαι τὸν νομοθέτην. διὸ κατ' εὐχὴν εὐχόμεθα
   τῇ τῆς πόλεως συστάσει ὧν ἡ τύχη κυρία (κυρίαν γὰρ (30)
   ὑπάρχειν τίθεμεν)·τὸ δὲ σπουδαίαν εἶναι τὴν πόλιν
   οὐκέτι τύχης ἔργον ἀλλ' ἐπιστήμης καὶ προαιρέσεως.

28. Newman, *The Politics of Aristotle*, 3: 429.

29. See Mulhern, " 'Universally', 'Universal', 'The Universal'," 277–284.

30. Joachim, *Aristotle: The Nicomachean Ethics*, 100–103.

Summary

It seems likely that Aristotle, who was addressing those who would establish and maintain, or fail to establish and maintain, the best *polis* or *politeia* that they could in the circumstances, recognized that his students were to be efficient causes, if in different ways. Alexander, for example, was to be an efficient cause on a larger scale, and Demetrius of Phalerum was to be an efficient cause on a smaller but still important scale. These men were likely to be more successful if they appreciated correctly the circumstances in which they were operating, which, however, mainly were out of their control. One might pray for or wish for favorable circumstances, as mariners still pray for or wish for fair winds and following seas, for themselves and for their friends. But of course the mariners are not in the position of causing the winds to be fair or the seas to follow. Rather, it is the work of the captain, the officer of the deck, and the navigator as causes to save the ship—to do as well as they can in the circumstances—whether or not the winds are fair and the seas follow. Circumstances were things, though, that it made sense to pray for or wish for, if they weren't impossible, since success depended in part on their being favorable. It would make little sense for Aristotle's students and friends to pray for a *civitas Dei* or for the heavenly city of the eighteenth-century philosophers—two kinds of things that they did not have very clearly in focus. Note that St. Augustine himself did not believe that he or any other human being could cause the *civitas Dei* to come about. It remained for the *philosophes* and their followers, who didn't believe in heaven anyway, to suggest that they were up to establishing the heavenly city, whatever the circumstances.[31]

In short, being *kat' euchēn* is not a feature of the *polis* or the *politeia* in the *Politics*. *Kat' euchēn* is rather a qualification of the circumstances for which one might pray or wish.

---

31. C. L. Becker, *The Heavenly City of the Eighteenth-Century Philosophers* (New Haven: Yale University Press, 1932).

Epilogue

The preceding chapters have been focused on Aristotle's political terminology as a step in clarifying what has come to be known as his political thought, especially as that is found in the *Politics* but elsewhere as well. Until comparatively recently, scholars have had to rely on their own memories, sometimes with help from Bonitz, to assess the way Aristotle was using the language; now, with the TLG, it is possible to search comprehensively and to compare Aristotle's use of the same expression and its cognates in different idioms and contexts. This possibility offers some promise of taking individual scholars beyond their backgrounds, which may have emphasized one point of view or another based on a less complete survey of the texts, to consider all the available occurrences in a given universe.

There has been a tendency to seek the one translation that will render Aristotle's Greek expression everywhere, even though Aristotle himself says occasionally that an expression is said in two ways or in many ways. Some translators of the *Politics* appear to prefer one rendering of a Greek expression throughout, sometimes adding a note to explain any differences in sense. The more direct approach is to give the sense of an expression in a passage and to add a note when, as can happen, the sense has not been able to be determined. Canvassing all the occurrences in a defined universe sometimes throws light on otherwise obscure passages.

As the interpretative tradition has developed, scholars have come to use expressions that correspond to words rarely used by Aristotle or words that are used by him in contexts or ways quite different from the ways the corresponding words are used in the interpreter's language. A prominent example is 'form of government', which came into use in English by Locke's time but whose corresponding Greek is not a common Aristotelian expression. Indeed, where the scholarly tradition may have come to emphasize an item far more than Aristotle did, a comprehensive examination can show that he did not have much to say about it after all, which could suggest that some additional interpretative effort might be in order. More on 'form of government' to come.

While different scholars may interpret the evidence in different ways, one plausible view of some features of Aristotle's political thought that emerges from his terminology as outlined in the preceding chapters is the following:

Phusis appears from the beginning to the end of life, most clearly when coming to be, or growth, is complete, and not so clearly when the object is immature or in decline, since it is only mature individuals who can do whatever they will ever be able to do. That is when *phusis* is most obvious. Further, it is not clear at the outset how any individual human being or other animal will turn out, though it is to be hoped that the individual who receives the appropriate prenatal care will be able to be guided to maturity so that the individual's growth will not be stunted. Even with appropriate prenatal care and guidance, the individual may not turn out to be excellent or as good as other individuals who receive similar prenatal care and guidance.

This insight appears to lie behind Aristotle's attempt to clarify the discussion of *douleia* that was going on in his day. His treatment is descriptive: He argues that those who lack foresight but can work with their bodies, as would be required of dependents in the ancient agricultural subsistence economy, are *phusei douloi*—mature dependents. Aristotle indicates that he has the subsistence farm in mind when he cites *Works and Days* early in the *Politics*. One who has foresight will not be a dependent ordinarily, unless compelled to be by the accident of war or some other force, or perhaps chance or deceit, rather than as a matter of normal growth; and one who cannot work with the body will be unlikely to be a dependent, since a subsistence household will be hard-pressed to keep such an individual.

The *doulos* is often a *ktēma* or possession of the household, though some *douloi* can be possessions of the city, in the sense that the *doulos* has been acquired by the household or city. A *ktēma* held by the household is *idion*, though it can be shared outside the household; *idios* is not used in this context as is the modern English 'property'. Aristotle is careful to distinguish possessions—whatever are possessed, regardless of their status, from *ousia*, or substance, meaning wealth, as in the English phrase 'an individual of substance'. The household may be subject to a *timēma* or assessment of its output, typically conceived in terms of measures of farming output rather than of wealth. These assessments may be more or less frequent, even annual, to assess the household's current condition; farm output is not constant from plot to plot or from year to year, even with hard work. Citizens whose farms showed more output at a given assessment would be expected to contribute more to the city's life, including something analogous to public service; citizen farmers who were in a worse condition should be expected to contribute less or nothing at all so that they might spend their time improving the condition of their households and become able to contribute more after a subsequent assessment.

Citizens sometimes would damage one another and so provoke claims against one another; claims also could be made unjustly, when there was no damage. The courts were active, but the claims were argued on grounds other than appeals to rights. *Dikaion* was not used by Aristotle in the sense of 'right'. Arguments on other grounds were used also in intercity disputes.

Although even excellent citizens can have different interests, under some circumstances it is advantageous for them to work together despite their different interests, and they may agree on what is to their advantage under these circumstances. This agreed advantage need not have the ontology of the common good as that is known to some mediaeval thinkers. The language of agreed advantage is more frequent in Aristotle than the language of common good, and there is little if any reason to suppose that the traditional notion of the common good plays a substantive role in Aristotle's thought.

The citizen simply speaking is one who can be called a citizen without any qualification such as immature or superannuated, or even ostracized, which would indicate that the citizen cannot yet exercise the functions of a citizen or cannot still exercise the functions of a citizen. Knowing what the citizen is comes before knowing who is a citizen.

Over an extended period from Herodotus on, Greek literature and inscriptions show some change in the way the abstract noun cognate with the Greek for citizen, in English 'citizenship', is used. The interlocutors in Plato's *Laws* gave some consideration to its different senses. Aristotle uses it in four main senses, recognizing that the same word can be used for the condition citizens enjoy and for the citizen body which enjoys it, just as in modern English. Because only those who can be engaged in ruling qualify as citizens, it is not surprising that the same word came to be used by him and others for those who actually rule—the regime or government—and for the arrangement or ordering of the ruling offices that the regime occupies—the constitution, which the *Oxford English Dictionary* defines in one place as "the mode in which a state is constituted or organized; especially, as to the location of the sovereign power, as a monarchical, oligarchical, or democratic constitution"; 'government' is used both for the arrangement of offices and for those who occupy the offices also in modern English. Because there are four main distinct senses for the Greek, four different translations are called for when the word is rendered into a modern language. Thus when one reads *politeia* or a translation of it, in the *Politics* or elsewhere, one is well advised to look carefully at the context to discern, if possible, what is intended rather than supposing that it must be the constitution in some modern sense.

There are very few places in which Aristotle uses an expression that can be rendered well by 'form of government' or 'forms of government', because *morphē*, *schēma*, and *tupos* are largely absent from his political vocabulary. When he wants to convey the plural, he regularly uses just *politeiai*. He does use *eidos* with democracy, oligarchy, and the like, however, perhaps because all democracies, for example, ostensibly share the same aim—the welfare of the poor, whereas not all the *politeiai*, as regimes, share their aims with one another.

The multiple senses of *politeia* complicate somewhat the interpretation of *EN* 1135a5 and the surrounding text, where Aristotle speaks of the excellent or the best and scholars typically supply *politeia* and understand it in the sense of constitution or arrangement of offices, thus arriving at the best or ideal constitution or, in Jackson's case, "the perfect constitution,"[1] although, if *politeia* is to be understood here, it could have a sense other than constitution. It appears not to be used for 'constitution' in any of the eighteen places in which it actually occurs in the *Nicomachean Ethics*. Again, translators and interpreters sometimes show a tendency to attribute views about an ideal constitution or ideal state to Aristotle where he uses the phrase 'according to wish' or 'according to prayer' (*kat' euchēn*). Where he is addressing his audience of legislators and others in positions of initiative and command, he is concerned mainly with matters of deliberation rather than with matters of wish or prayer, which matters are not under the legislators' immediate control. Legislators might reasonably wish or pray, however, to have people who can be encouraged to be excellent citizens relatively easily and land that can support them because it is expansive enough and is fertile or has other sustaining resources.

---

1. Jackson, *ΠΕΡΙ ΔΙΚΑΙΟΣΥΝΗΣ*, 41.

In short, Aristotle's political terminology, when viewed as described in the preceding chapters, suggests a way of thinking that differs in many respects from the way of thinking that has been attributed to him on multiple points of importance. It is because Aristotle's thought may differ from our own that it may be especially instructive and therefore worth our attention.

Bibliography

Ackrill, J. L. *Aristotle's Categories and De Interpretatione*. Oxford: Clarendon Press, 1966.

Albini, U. *Lisia: I discorsi*. Florence: Sansoni, 1955.

Allen, T. W. *Homeri Ilias*. Vols. 2–3. Oxford: Clarendon Press, 1931.

Ast, D. F. *Lexicon Platonicum*. 3 vols. Leipzig: Weidmann, 1835–1838.

Aubenque, P. "La loi selon Aristote." *Archives de philosophie du droit* 25 (1980): 147–157.

Aubenque, P. "The Twofold Natural Foundation of Justice According to Aristotle." In *Aristotle and Moral Realism*, edited by R. Heinaman, 35–47. London: UCL Press, 1995.

Aubenque, P. "Aristote était-il communautariste?" In *En torno a Aristoteles: Homenaje al Profesor Pierre Aubenque*, 31–43. Santiago de Campostela: University Press of Santiago de Campostela, 1998.

Balme, D. M. "ΓΕΝΟΣ and ΕΙΔΟΣ in Aristotle's Biology." *Classical Quarterly* 12 (1962): 81–98.

Balme, D. M. "Aristotle's Use of Differentiae in Zoology." In *Aristote et les problèmes de méthode*, ed. S. Mansion, 195–212. Louvain: Publications Universitaires, 1961.

Banfield, E. C. *Political Influence*. Glencoe: Free Press, 1961.

Banfield, E. C., and J. Q. Wilson. *City Politics*. Cambridge: Harvard University Press, 1965.

Barker, E. *The Politics of Aristotle*. Oxford: Clarendon Press, 1948.

Barker, E. *The Political Thought of Plato and Aristotle*. New York: Russell & Russell, 1959.

Barnes, J. *The Complete Works of Aristotle*. 2 vols. Princeton: Princeton University Press, 1984.

Bates, C. A., Jr. *Aristotle's "Best Regime": Kingship, Democracy, and the Rule of Law*. Baton Rouge: Louisiana State University Press, 2003.

Becker, C. L. *The Heavenly City of the Eighteenth-Century Philosophers*. New Haven: Yale University Press, 1932.

Blok, J. "Retracing Steps: Finding Ways into Archaic Greek Citizenship." In *Defining Citizenship in Archaic Greece*, edited by A. Duplouy and R. Brock, 79–101. Oxford: Oxford University Press, 2018.

Bonitz, H. *Index Aristotelicus*. Berlin: Walter de Gruyter, 1870.

Bordes, J. "La place d'Aristote dans l'évolution de la notion de *politeia*." *Ktema* 5 (1980): 249–256.

Bordes, J. *POLITEIA dans la pensée grecque jusqu'à Aristote*. Paris: Les Belles Lettres, 1982.

Brémond, É., and G. Mathieu. *Isocrate: Discours*. Vol. 1. Paris: Les Belles Lettres, 1929.

Brown, L. *Aristotle: The Nicomachean Ethics*. Oxford: Oxford University Press, 2009.

Burnet, J. *The Ethics of Aristotle*. London: Methuen, 1900.

Burnet, J. *Platonis Opera*. Oxford: Clarendon Press, 1900–1907.

Burnet, J. *Early Greek Philosophy*. 4th ed. London: Macmillan, 1930.

Bywater, I. *Aristotelis ethica Nicomachea*. Oxford: Clarendon Press, 1894.

Carey, C. *Lysiae orationes cum fragmentis*. Oxford: Oxford University Press, 2007.

Chamberlain, C. "The Meaning of *Prohairesis* in Aristotle's Ethics." *Transactions of the American Philological Association* 114 (1984): 147–157.

Chambers, M. *Aristoteles Athenaion Politeia*. 2nd ed. Leipzig: Teubner, 1994.

Christ, M. R. "The Evolution of the *Eisphora* in Classical Athens." *Classical Quarterly* 57 (2007): 53–69.

Clinton, K. "The Nature of the Late Fifth-Century Revision of the Athenian Law Code." *Hesperia Supplements* 19 (1982): 27–37.

Cohen, E. E. *Athenian Economy and Society: A Banking Perspective*. Princeton: Princeton University Press, 1992.

Cohen, E. E. *The Athenian Nation*. Princeton: Princeton University Press, 2003.

Collingwood, R. G. *The Idea of Nature*. Oxford: Clarendon Press, 1945.

Cooper, J. M. "Political Animals and Civic Friendship." In *Aristoteles' Politik*, Akten des XI. Symposium Aristotelicum, edited by G. Patzig, 220–241. Göttingen: Vandenhoeck & Ruprecht, 1990.

Denniston, J. D. *Greek Prose Style*. Oxford: Clarendon Press, 1952.

Destrée, P. "Aristote et la question du droit naturel (*Eth. Nic.*, V, 10, 1134 b 18–1135 a 5)." *Phronesis* 45 (2000): 220–239.

Develin, R. "The Good Man and the Good Citizen in Aristotle's 'Politics'." *Phronesis* 18 (1973): 71–79.

Dreizehnter, A. *Aristoteles' Politik*. Munich: Wilhelm Fink, 1970.

Elazar, D. J. *The American Mosaic: The Impact of Space, Time, and Culture on American Politics*. Boulder: Westview Press, 1993.

Emlyn-Jones, C., and W. Preddy. *Plato: The Republic*. Cambridge: Harvard University Press, 2013.

Engberg-Pedersen, T. "Justice at a Distance: Less Foundational, More Naturalistic: A Reply to Pierre Aubenque." In *Aristotle and Moral Realism*, edited by R. Heinaman, 48–60. London: UCL Press, 1995.

Fischer, K. T., and F. Vogel. *Diodorus Siculus Bibliotheca Historica.* 5 vols. Leipzig: Teubner, 1888–1906.

Foxhall, L. "Female Inheritance in Athenian Law." https://classics-at.chs.harvard. edu/wp-content/uploads/2021/05/ca1.2-foxhall.pdf.

Foxhall, L. "Household, Gender, and Property in Classical Athens." *Classical Quarterly* 39 (1989): 22–44.

Fuerth, L. S. "Foresight and Anticipatory Governance." *Foresight* 11, no. 4 (2009): 14–32.

Gagarin, M. *Early Greek Law.* Berkeley: University of California Press, 1986.

Gillies, J. *Aristotle's Ethics and Politics.* 3rd ed. London: Cadell and Davies, 1813.

Giorgini, G. "Aristotle on the Best Form of Government." In *Enthousiasmos: Essays in Ancient Philosophy, History, and Literature. Festschrift for Eckart Schütrumpf on His 80th Birthday*, 121–145. Baden-Baden: Academia Verlag, 2019.

Glotz, G. *Le Travail dans la Grèce ancienne.* Paris: Alcan, 1920.

Goldie, M. *John Locke: Selected Correspondence.* Oxford: Oxford University Press, 2002.

Gottschalk, H. B. "Demetrius of Phalerum: A Politician Among Philosophers and a Philosopher Among Politicians." In *Demetrius of Phalerum: Text, Translation, and Discussion*, edited by W. W. Fortenbaugh and E. Schütrumpf, 367–380. New Brunswick: Transaction, 2000.

Grant, Sir A. *The Ethics of Aristotle.* 2 vols. London: Longmans, Green, 1885.

Greenwood, L. H. G. *Aristotle Nicomachean Ethics Book Six.* Cambridge: Cambridge University Press, 1909.

Guía, M. V., and J. Gallego. "Athenian *Zeugitai* and the Solonian Census Classes: New Reflections and Perspectives." *Historia: Zeitschrift für Alte Geschichte* 59 (2010): 257–281.

Habgood, J. *The Concept of Nature.* London: Darton, Longman & Todd, 2002.

Hansen, M. H. "Aristotle's Alternative to the Sixfold Model of Constitutions." In *Aristote et Athènes*, edited by M. Piérart, 91–101. Paris: Boccard, 1993.

Hardie, W. F. R. *Aristotle's Ethical Theory.* Oxford: Clarendon Press, 1968.

Harrison, A. R. W. *The Law of Athens: Vol. 2, The Family and Property.* Oxford: Clarendon Press, 1968.

Harte, V., and M. Lane. *Politeia in Greek and Roman Philosophy.* Cambridge: Cambridge University Press, 2013.

Heath, M. "Aristotle on Natural Slavery." *Phronesis* 53 (2008): 243–270.

Heinaman, R. *Aristotle and Moral Realism.* London: UCL Press, 1995.

Hennig, B. "Aristotle on Ownership." *Phronesis* 69 (2024): 1–21.

Jackson, H. *ΠΕΡΙ ΔΙΚΑΙΟΣΥΝΗΣ: The Fifth Book of the Nicomachean Ethics of Aristotle.* Cambridge: Cambridge University Press, 1879.

Jaulin, A. "Aristote: le nécessaire et le beau dans la cité 'selon nos vœux'." *Polis* 36, no. 1 (2019): 97–116.

Joachim, H. H. *Aristotle: The Nicomachean Ethics.* Oxford: Clarendon Press. 1955.

Jones, H. S., and J. E. Powell. *Thucydidis historiae.* 2 vols. Oxford: Clarendon Press, 1942.

Jowett, B. *The Politics of Aristotle.* 2 vols. Oxford: Clarendon Press, 1885.

Kant, I. *Kritik der reinen Vernunft.* Hamburg: Felix Meiner, 1956.

Kast, F. E., and J. E. Rosenzweig. *Organization and Management: A Systems and Contingency Approach.* 4th ed. New York: McGraw-Hill, 1985.

Keaney, J. J. *The Composition of Aristotle's Athenaion Politeia: Observation and Explanation.* New York: Oxford University Press, 1992.

Kempshall, M. S. *The Common Good in Late Medieval Political Thought.* Oxford: Clarendon Press, 1999.

Kenyon, F. G. *Aristotle On the Constitution of Athens,* 2nd ed. Oxford: Clarendon Press, 1891.

Keyt, D. "Aristotle's Theory of Distributive Justice." In *A Companion to Aristotle's Politics,* edited by D. Keyt and F. D. Miller, Jr., 238–278. Oxford: Blackwell, 1991.

Keyt, D. "Supplementary Essay." In R. Robinson, *Aristotle's Politics: Books III and IV.* Oxford: Clarendon Press, 1995.

Keyt, D. *Aristotle Politics: Books V and VI.* Oxford: Clarendon Press, 1999.

Keyt, D., and F. D. Miller, Jr. *A Companion to Aristotle's Politics.* Oxford: Blackwell, 1991.

Kneale, W., and M. Kneale. *The Development of Logic.* Oxford: Clarendon Press, 1962.

Kraut, R. "Nature in Aristotle's Ethics and Politics." *Social Philosophy and Policy* 24 (2007): 199–219.

Lamb, W. R. M. *Lysias.* Cambridge: Harvard University Press, 1930.

Lattimore, R. *The Iliad of Homer.* Chicago: University of Chicago Press, 1951.

Legrand, Ph.-E. *Hérodote, Histoires.* 10 vols. Paris: Les Belles Lettres, 1932–1954.

Lindblom, C. E. *The Policy-Making Process.* 2nd ed. Englewood Cliffs: Prentice-Hall, 1980.

Loomis, W. T. *Wages, Welfare Costs, and Inflation in Classical Athens.* Ann Arbor: University of Michigan Press, 1998.

Lord, C. *Aristotle's Politics.* 2nd ed. Chicago: University of Chicago Press, 2013. https://archive.org/stream/AristotlesPoliticsLord2nd.num/Aristotle%27s%20 Politics%20%5BLord%202nd.num%5D_djvu.txt.

Maloy, J. S. "The Aristotelianism of Locke's Politics." *Journal of the History of Ideas* 70 (2009): 235–257.

McIlwain, C. H. *Constitutionalism, Ancient and Modern.* Ithaca: Cornell University Press, 1940.

McKeon, R. *The Basic Works of Aristotle.* New York: Random House, 1941.

Miller, F. D., Jr. *Nature, Justice, and Rights in Aristotle's Politics.* Oxford: Clarendon Press, 1995.

Moore, J. M. *Aristotle and Xenophon on Democracy and Oligarchy.* Berkeley: University of California Press, 1975. Reprinted in S. Everson, ed., *Aristotle: The Politics and The Constitution of Athens.* Cambridge: Cambridge University Press, 1996.

Morrow, G. R. *Plato's Cretan City: A Historical Interpretation of the Laws.* Princeton: Princeton University Press, 1960.

Muirhead, R. *The Promise of Party in a Polarized Age.* Cambridge: Harvard University Press, 2014.

Mulhern, J. J. "ΜΙΑ ΜΟΝΟΝ ΠΑΝΤΑΧΟΥ ΚΑΤΑ ΦΥΣΙΝ Η ΑΡΙΣΤΗ (*EN* 1135a5)." *Phronesis* 17 (1972): 260–268.

Mulhern, J. J. " 'Universally', 'Universal', 'The Universal'." *Teorema* 5 (1975): 277–284.

Mulhern, J. J. "ΤΑ ΚΑΘ' ΕΚΑΣΤΑ ΓΝΩΡΙΖΕΙΝ (*EN* 1141b14–21)." *Classical Philology* 70 (1975): 124–125.

Mulhern, J. J. "ΠΑΡΡΗΣΙΑ in Aristotle." In *Free Speech in Classical Antiquity*, edited by I. Sluiter and R. M. Rosen, 313–339. Leiden: Brill, 2004.

Mulhern, J. J. "The *Aristē Politeia* and Aristotle's Intended Audience in the *Politica*." *Polis* 24 (2007): 284–297.

Mulhern, J. J. "*Politeia* as Citizenship in Aristotle." *Society for Ancient Greek Philosophy Newsletter* 12, no. 2 (2012): 41–47. http://orb.binghamton.edu/sagp/458.

Mulhern, J. J. "*Politeia* in Aristotle's *Politica*: An Annotated Catalogue." University of Pennsylvania Library Scholarly Commons: Departmental Papers (Classical Studies), 2014. http://repository.upenn.edu/classics_papers/31/.

Mulhern, J. J. "*Politeia* in Greek Literature and Inscriptions and in Aristotle's *Politics*: Reflections on Translation and Interpretation." In *Aristotle's Politics: A Critical Guide*, edited by T. Lockwood and T. Samaras, 84–102. Cambridge: Cambridge University Press, 2015.

Mulhern, J. J. "*Politeia* in Aristotle's *Nicomachean Ethics*." In *Studies in Ancient Greek Philosophy in Honor of Professor Anthony Preus*, edited by D. M. Spitzer, 230–241. London: Routledge, 2023.

Mulhern, J. J. "ΠΟΝΟΣ and ΠΟΝΕΩ in Aristotle." In *Valuing Labour in Greco-Roman Antiquity*, edited by M. Flohr and K. Bowes, 41–61. Mnemosyne Supplements 481. Leiden: Brill, 2024.

Mulhern, J. J. "Φύσις as *Natura* in St. Thomas Aquinas's Commentary on the *Politics* and in *STh* I–II Question 94." *The Thomist* 88 (2024): 599–626.

Myres, J. L. *The Political Ideas of the Greeks.* New York: Abingdon Press, 1927.

Naddaf, G. *The Greek Concept of Nature.* Albany: State University of New York Press, 2009.

Nagle, D. B. *The Household as the Foundation of Aristotle's Polis.* New York: Cambridge University Press, 2006.

Newman, W. L. *The Politics of Aristotle.* 4 vols. Oxford: Clarendon Press, 1887–1902.

Nichols, M. P. *Citizens and Statesmen: A Study of Aristotle's Politics*. Lanham: Rowman & Littlefield, 1992.

Nussbaum, M. 1995. "Aristotle on Human Nature and the Foundations of Ethics." In *World, Mind, and Ethics: Essays on the Philosophy of Bernard Williams*, edited by J. E. J. Altham and R. Harrison, 86–131. Cambridge: Cambridge University Press, 1995.

Osborne, M. J. *Naturalization in Athens, Vol. III: The Testimonia for Grants of Citizenship*. Brussels: Palais des Acadamiën, 1983.

Ostwald, M. *Aristotle, Nicomachean Ethics*. Indianapolis: Bobbs-Merrill, 1962.

Ostwald, M. "Shares and Rights: 'Citizenship' Greek Style and American Style." In *Demokratia: A Conversation on Democracies, Ancient and Modern*, edited by J. Ober and C. Hedrick, 49–61. Princeton: Princeton University Press, 1996.

Ostwald, M. *Oligarchia: The Development of a Constitutional Form in Ancient Greece*. Stuttgart: Franz Steiner Verlag, 2000.

Ostwald, M. *Language and History in Ancient Greek Culture*. Philadelphia: University of Pennsylvania Press, 2009.

Owen, G. E. L. *Aristotle on Dialectic: The Topics*. Proceedings of the Third Symposium Aristotelicum. Oxford: Clarendon Press, 1968.

Pellegrin, P. *Les Politiques*. Paris: Flammarion, 1990.

Pellegrin, P. *L'Excellence menacée: Sur la philosophie politique d'Aristote*. Paris: Classiques Garnier, 2017; Translation: *Endangered Excellence: On the Political Philosophy of Aristotle*. Translated by A. Preus. Albany: State University of New York Press, 2020.

Perrin, B. *Plutarch: Lives*. Vol. 1. Cambridge: Harvard University Press, 1914.

Quandt, K. "Some Puns in Aristotle." *Transactions of the American Philological Association* 111 (1981): 179–196.

Rackham, H. *Aristotle: Politics*. Cambridge: Harvard University Press, 1932.

Reeve, C. D. C. *Aristotle Politics: A New Translation*. Indianapolis: Hackett, 2017.

Rhodes, P. J. "Athenian Democracy After 403 B.C." *Classical Journal* 75 (1980): 305–323.

Rhodes, P. J. *A Commentary on the Aristotelian Athenaion Politeia*. Oxford: Clarendon Press, 1981.

Rhodes, P. J. *Aristotle: The Athenian Constitution*. Harmondsworth: Penguin, 1984.

Rhodes, P. J. Review of *Democracy and Knowledge: Innovation and Learning in Classical Athens*, by J. Ober. *Polis* 26 (2009): 167.

Robinson, R. *Definition*. Oxford: Clarendon Press, 1954; repr. 1995.

Robinson, R. *Aristotle's Politics: Books III and IV*. Oxford: Clarendon Press, 1962.

Roller, L. E. "The Legend of Midas." *Classical Antiquity* 2, no. 2 (1983): 299–313.

Rosivach, V. J. "The Requirements of the Solonic Classes in *AP* 7.4." *Hermes* 130 (2002): 36–47.

Ross, W. D. *Aristotle's Physics*. Oxford: Clarendon Press, 1936.

Ross, W. D. *Aristotle's Metaphysics*. Corr. ed., 2 vols. Oxford: Clarendon Press, 1953.

Ross, W. D. *Aristotelis Politica*. Oxford: Clarendon Press, 1957.

Ryffel, H. *Metabolē Politeiōn: Der Wandel der Staatsverfassungen*. Bern: P. Haubt, 1949.

Samaras, A. "Aristotle's Politics: The City of Book Seven and the Question of Ideology." *Classical Quarterly* 57 (2007): 77–89.

Saunders, T. J. *Notes on the Laws of Plato*. London: Institute of Classical Studies, 1972.

Saunders, T. J. *Aristotle: Politics, Books I and II*. Oxford: Clarendon Press, 1995.

Schofield, M. "Ideology and Philosophy in Aristotle's Theory of Slavery." In *Aristoteles' "Politik": Akten des Xi. Symposium Aristotelicum*, edited by G. Patzig, 1–27. Göttingen: Vandenhoeck & Ruprecht, 1990.

Schofield, M. "Sharing in the Constitution." *Review of Metaphysics* 49 (1996): 831–839.

Schofield, M. *Plato: Political Philosophy*. Oxford: Oxford University Press, 2006.

Schütrumpf, E. "Platonic Methodology in the Program of Aristotle's Political Philosophy: *Politics* VI.1." *Transactions of the American Philological Association* 119 (1989): 209–218.

Schütrumpf, E. *Aristoteles Werke: in Deutscher Übersetzung. Politik*. 4 vols. Berlin: Akademie Verlag, 2009.

Schütrumpf, E. *The Earliest Translations of Aristotle's Politics and the Creation of Political Terminology*. Paderborn: Wilhelm Fink, 2004.

Seymour, T. D. *The First Six Books of Homer's Iliad: Introduction, Commentary, and Vocabulary*. Rev. ed. Boston: Ginn, 1903.

Shorey, P. *Plato: The Republic*. 2 vols. London: William Heinemann, 1937.

Simpson, P. L. P. *The Politics of Aristotle*. Chapel Hill: University of North Carolina Press, 1997.

Simpson, P. L. P. *A Philosophical Commentary on the Politics of Aristotle*. Chapel Hill: University of North Carolina Press, 1998.

Simpson, P. L. P. "Aristotle's City of God." Annual Meeting, New York State Political Science Association, New York, April 25, 2009.

Sinclair, T. A., and T. J. Saunders. *Aristotle: The Politics*. London: Penguin, 1992.

Smith, C. F. *Thucydides*. 4 vols. Cambridge: Harvard University Press, 1919–1923.

Smith, T. W. "Aristotle on the Conditions for and Limits of the Common Good." *American Political Science Review* 93 (1999): 625–636.

Smyth, H. W. *Greek Grammar*. Rev. G. M. Messing. Cambridge: Harvard University Press, 1956.

Spiazzi, R. M. *Sancti Thomae Aquinatis In Decem Libros Ethicorum Aristotelis ad Nicomachum Expositio*. 3rd ed. Turin: Marietti, 1964.

Spiazzi, R. M. *Sancti Thomae Aquinatis In Octo Libros Politicorum Aristotelis Expositio*. Turin: Marietti, 1966.

Stark, S. "Executive Foresight: Definitions, Illustrations, Importance." *Journal of Business* 34 (1961): 31–44.

Stevenson, C. L. *Ethics and Language*. New Haven: Yale University Press, 1944.

Strauss, L. *What Is Political Philosophy and Other Studies*. Glencoe: Free Press, 1959.

Stroud, R. S. *The Athenian Grain-Tax Law of 374/3 B.C.* Princeton: American School of Classical Studies at Athens, 1998.

Supplementum Epigraphicum Graecum. Leiden: Brill, various dates.

Susemihl, F. *Aristotelis Politicorum Libri Octo cum Vetusta Translatione Guilelmi de Moerbeke*. Leipzig: Teubner, 1872.

Terrel, J. "En quel sens la cité décrite au livre VII est-elle κατ᾽εὐχὴν, conforme au vœu de la science politique?" *Polis* 36, no. 1 (2019): 117–138.

Thomsen, R. *Eisphora*. Copenhagen: Glydendalske Boghandel, 1965.

Todd, S. C. *The Shape of Athenian* Law. Oxford: Clarendon Press, 1993.

Todd, S. C., and P. C. Millett. "Law, Society and Athens." In *Nomos: Essays in Athenian Law, Politics and Society*, ed. P. A. Cartledge, P. C. Millett, and S. C. Todd, 1–18. Cambridge: Cambridge University Press, 1990.

von Fritz, K., and E. Kapp. "The Development of Aristotle's Political Philosophy and the Concept of Nature." In *Essays on Aristotle*, edited by J. Barnes, M. Schofield, and R. Sorabji, 113–134. London: Duckworth, 1977.

West, M. L. "Phocylides." *Journal of Hellenic Studies* 98 (1978): 164–167.

Whitehead, A. N. *The Concept of Nature*. Cambridge: Cambridge University Press, 1920.

Wycherley, R. E. *The Athenian Agora, Vol. III: Literary and Epigraphical Testimonia*. Princeton: American School of Classical Studies at Athens, 1957.

Zetzel, J. E. G. *Cicero: On the Commonwealth and On the Laws*. Cambridge: Cambridge University Press, 1999.

Ziegler, K. *Plutarchi Vitae Parallelae*. 4th ed. Leipzig: Teubner, 1969.

Index

Grant, A., 162n8
Greenwood, L. H. G., 31n5
Guía, M. V., 55n1, 60n14

Habgood, J., 11
haplōs, chapter 7; 7, 38, 44
Hardie, W. F. R., 161n5, 162
Harrison, A. R. W., 56nn2, 3
Harrison, R., 6n15, 200
Heath, M., 6n14, 29n1, 30, 34, 35,
    36, 37
Hennig, B., 6n17
Herodotus, 30n3, 107, 122, 136, 191
Hesiod, 58
Hippodamus, 130
Homer, 11, 24, 128, 149n22, 160, 175,
    177, 178n7
homonoia, 102–3

idios, chapter 3; 190
Isocrates, 30n3

Jackson, H., 15n17, 161n6, 162n7,
    192n1
Joachim, H. H., 32n6, 89–90nn13,14,
    187n30
Jowett, B., 3n9, 9, 13n10, 17, 20,
    31n4, 39, 57, 65n24, 95, 99, 132,
    143n9, 144, 146n15, 154, 162,
    176

Kant, I., 176n3
Kapp, E., 32, 33n8
Kearney, J. J., 118n4
Kenyon, F. G., 119n6
Keyt, D., 7n19, 8, 64n21, 107, 108n3,
    140n4, 167n15, 168n16, 169,
    171–72
koinōnia, 152
Kraut, R., 14n14, 16n20
ktaomai, *ktēma*, chapter 3; 6, 7, 41,
    42, 47, 48, 56, 67n26, 190

Lattimore, R., 178n7
Lindblom, C. E., 36n17
Locke, J., 1n1, 189
Loomis, W. T., 59n9
Lord, C., 139n2
Lysias, 7, 76, 79–84, 88–89

Miller, F. D., Jr., 4, 75, 78n5, 83, 90,
    91n15, 108n3, 140
Moore, J. M., 122, 123n11
Morrow, G. R., 142–43n7
Muirhead, R., 93n2
Myres, J., 13n12

Naddaf, G., 12n5
natura, chapter1; 169n20
Newman, W. L., 13n11, 18n26, 19,
    20n33, 30n3, 39, 95, 97, 98n7,
    99, 104n21, 109n6, 131nn17-19,
    132, 139n2, 150n28, 179, 181n15,
    186n26, 187n28
nomos, 12, 127
Nussbaum, M., 6n15, 34

Ostwald, M., 4n13, 15, 60n14, 75n1,
    92, 101n15, 102, 117n1, 121n10,
    127, 128n13, 159n2, 165
ousia, chapter 3

pantachou, chapter 10; 8.
Peisistratus, 120, 124
Pellegrin, P., 6n16, 8, 18n28, 25n37,
    112n11, 166, 167n14, 172n28,
    173
penēs, 4
Phaleas, 46
phuō, *phusis*, chapter 1
phusei doulos, chapter 2; 5–6
plousios, 4
Plutarch, 104
polis, 17, 24, 107, 110, 180, 185,
    188

Index Locorum

Aristotle

Topics (Top.)
102a18–19, 43
115b29-35, 109
148b9, 31
155b13, 31
156a18, 31

Sophistici Elenchi (SE)
177a6–8, 31

Physics (Ph.)
193b12–13, 12

De Anima (de An.)
432b21–23, 25

De Somno et Vigilia (Somn.Vig.)
453b21, 32

De Divinatione per Somnia (Div.Somn.)
464a18–19, 32

History of Animals (HA)
524a14, 31
614b26, 31, 32

Parts of Animals (PA)
656b31, 31

Problems (Pr.)
892b7, 31

Metaphysics (Metaph.)
1014b16–17, 12, 33
1024a29–31, 140

Nicomachean Ethics (EN)
1098a16, 113
1103b6, 127, 160
1105a17–b18, 89–90
1111a3–5, 86, 111n10, 177n5
1113a8, 128, 160
1123b13–15, 84
1124a26–28, 84
1130b31–32, 85
1130b32, 126, 160
1131a13, 85
[1131]a18–19, 85
[1131]a20–21, 85
[1131]a29, 85, 89
1131a31–32, 86
1131b4, 86
1134b19, 163–64, 166, 171
1134b25, 165
1134b35–1135a1, 101
1135a1–3, 59n8, 163, 164
1135a3, 161
1135a3–5, 162
1135a4, 127, 164